CHURCHILL
AND
MALTA'S WAR
1939–1943

About the author

DOUGLAS AUSTIN was born in Malta in 1934 when his father was serving in the Royal Navy. He has studied at Oxford and Harvard Universities, and in 2002 received his PhD in Military History from University College London. This is his third study of the military history of Malta in the early twentieth century. *Malta and British Strategic Policy 1925–1943* was published in 2004, and *Churchill and Malta: A Special Relationship* was published in 2006.

By the same author

Malta and British Strategic Policy 1925–1943
Foreword by Professor David French

Churchill and Malta: A Special Relationship
Foreword by Sir Martin Gilbert

CHURCHILL
AND
MALTA'S WAR
1939–1943

DOUGLAS AUSTIN

AMBERLEY

To my good friends

Father George Aquilina, OFM

Michael A. Refalo

Antoine Attard

First published 2010
This edition first published 2015

Amberley Publishing
The Hill, Merrywalks
Stroud, Gloucestershire, GL5 4EP
www.amberley-books.com

British Library Cataloguing in Publication Data.
A catalogue record for this book is available from the British Library.

ISBN 978 1 4456 5328 0 (paperback)
ISBN 978 1 4456 2039 8 (ebook)

Typeset in 10pt on 12pt Sabon.
Typesetting and Origination by Amberley Publishing.
Printed in the UK.

CONTENTS

LIST OF ILLUSTRATIONS

Maps

PREFACE

On 10 November 1954, shortly before Churchill's eightieth birthday on 30 November, an eminent member of the Maltese Judiciary, Mr Justice Montanaro-Gauci, wrote to Churchill. The opening paragraphs of his letter read as follows:

> Dear Prime Minister,
>
> The Council of the Malta Society of Arts, Manufactures and Commerce – of which I have the honour to be President – has taken the initiative and has organised the raising of a fund among all sections of the Maltese people to arrange for Malta's present to you on the occasion of your 80th birthday.
>
> May I begin by saying that we, the people of Malta, recognise the great debt we owe to you personally in the steps which you took in the war to ensure the protection of Malta and its ultimate relief at a time when the risk of invasion seemed very real.
>
> We would like our present to take a personal form and a form which we hope will give you personal pleasure. It happens that we have in Malta one of the world's leading sculptors, Mr. Vincent Apap. He has had the good fortune to sculpt many of the world's notable people including no less a person than Her Majesty Queen Elizabeth II. He is now in England doing a bust of His Royal Highness The Duke of Edinburgh. We have arranged, subject to your permission, that he shall make a bust of you which we will have cast in bronze for presentation to you from the people of Malta.

After suggesting several possible arrangements for a sitting with Mr Apap, Justice Montanaro-Gauci concluded his letter by writing: 'May I finally say that your acceptance of this offer from the people of Malta will give unbounded pleasure to your many admirers and friends throughout the islands of Malta and Gozo.'[1]

John Colville, Churchill's Private Secretary, replied to Justice Montanaro-Gauci on 14 November, conveying the Prime Minister's pleasure at the proposed gift, and he added that it was the Prime Minister's hope that, after its presentation, the bust be kept in Malta. Arrangements were then made for Mr Apap to call on the Prime Minister, and in the event, despite his busy schedule, Churchill made time between other meetings for two sittings at 10 Downing Street on 9 and 10 December. Mr Apap later recorded that Churchill, after the second sitting, was so pleased with the initial clay model that he invited some of his Cabinet colleagues to inspect it.

It took some time to complete the final bronze bust, and it was not until the summer of 1955 that Justice Montanaro-Gauci was able to bring the bust to London. Before then Churchill had resigned as Prime Minister and it was accordingly arranged that the presentation be made at Churchill's London home at 28 Hyde Park Gate. The presentation took place on Wednesday 3 August 1955, and, in addition to the bust, Justice Montanaro-Gauci presented to Churchill an illuminated address bearing the names of all those who had contributed to the gift.[2] The text of the address read:

To the Right Honourable Sir Winston Churchill, K.G. On the initiative of the Council of the Malta Society of Arts, Manufactures and Commerce, the people of Malta and Gozo offer you a bronze portrait sculpted by a Maltese artist, as a token of their deep appreciation of your inestimable services to the British Commonwealth and Empire and to Western Civilisation. It will be a lasting pledge of their affection and gratitude for your personal interest to relieve and save Malta during her siege in the last war. To you half the world owes its freedom, democracy its survival, and justice its triumph. In war you have led us to victory, in peace you have guided us to security. May Divine Providence spare you in good health and happiness for many years to come, that you may see the fruits of your wisdom in a lasting peace among nations and a glorious revival of Christian Ideals.

After Justice Montanaro-Gauci had returned to Malta, Churchill wrote to thank him:

My dear Judge

Your visit on August 3, and the gracious and complimentary remarks you made, gave me the greatest pleasure. Would you please express my warm thanks to all the donors of the bust? I am indeed moved by this gift from the people of Malta, who suffered the strokes of war so long and with such admirable tenacity. Would you please also convey my compliments on their work to the sculptor, Mr. Apap, and to those who executed the beautiful presentation book?

I am happy to know that the bust will overlook the Grand Harbour at Malta, the scene of so many pages of history.

Yours very sincerely,
Winston Churchill

The bust was returned to Malta and formally unveiled on 5 May 1956 by the Governor, Sir Robert Laycock. Justice Montanaro-Gauci wrote to Churchill on 17 August to describe the ceremony, and enclosed two photographs. He concluded his letter by writing:

The buglers of the Salesian Boys Brigade saluted the unveiling with a fanfare and the band played Elgar's Land of Hope and Glory in your honour. The bust stands proudly in a very conspicuous place overlooking the Grand Harbour, and people and tourists stop to look at it.

It was a very kind gesture on your part to ask that your bust be kept in Malta, where you rightly enjoy the admiration, gratitude and affection of her people.

Kindly accept the photographs as a souvenir of Malta's manifestation of her profound esteem for you.

With kindest regards
Yours very sincerely,
A. Montanaro-Gauci

The bust, surrounded by trees and flowers, stands in the Upper Barrakka Gardens in Valletta overlooking the Grand Harbour. It looks down over Fort St Angelo from where Churchill's illustrious predecessor, Grand Master Jean de la Valette, led the people of Malta in the Great Siege of 1565.

ACKNOWLEDGEMENTS

Any author writing about Sir Winston Churchill must have constant recourse to the volumes of the official biography, begun by Randolph Churchill and completed by Sir Martin Gilbert. The three volumes of associated documents, comprising the Churchill War Papers, which cover the period from September 1939 to the end of 1941, were of particular value, and the author wishes to thank Sir Martin for allowing him to read through the documents assembled for the next volume.

Many of the documents quoted in this study are official British government records held at the National Archives at Kew. These documents are Crown Copyright, and permission to quote from them is hereby acknowledged. The three maps reproduced in this volume are taken from the Official History of the Second World War, *The Mediterranean and Middle East*. These, too, are Crown Copyright and permission to reproduce them is hereby acknowledged.

Numerous quotations have also been included from books, letters and memoranda written by Sir Winston Churchill. These are reproduced with permission of Curtis Brown Ltd, London, on behalf of The Estate of Sir Winston Churchill. Text Copyright © The Estate of Sir Winston Churchill.

Most of the illustrations included in this volume are reproduced, with permission, from the collection held by the Imperial War Museum, London. These are Nos. 1–11, 13–14, 16–19, 21–27. The copyright holders of the other illustrations are as follows: Times of Malta, Nos. 12, 15; Crown, No. 20; National Trust, No. 28; author, Nos. 29, 30. Permission to reproduce these is hereby acknowledged.

INTRODUCTION

After Winston Churchill became Prime Minister on 10 May 1940, and especially after Mussolini declared war on Britain and France on 10 June, he saw the Mediterranean as a theatre of war in which British naval and military forces could be deployed with advantage. In the eye of this rising Mediterranean hurricane lay the historic island fortress of Malta, well known to Churchill from four earlier visits to the island.[1] Subjected to fierce Italian air attack from 11 June, Malta's first need was for strengthened air and gun defences and the establishment of the means to resupply the island's garrison and people with food and other essentials, without which the island must surrender. But Churchill looked beyond these initial tasks. Always impatient with purely defensive operations, as his military advisers and commanders were soon to discover, he saw Malta as a unique base from which the operation of the enemy forces in North Africa might be made difficult, and perhaps impossible.

The unfolding of this conception and its ultimate realisation, after three years of hard fighting and much suffering and hardship, is narrated in this volume by drawing upon the 1,000 pages of Churchill's Malta War Papers and other official British government records held at the British National Archives at Kew. The reader, as it were, can thus look over Churchill's shoulder as he read through the telegrams and reports in his black boxes relating to Malta. He can then listen as the Prime Minister dictated and sent out minutes and directives, and examine the replies he received. In his own memoirs of the war, Churchill printed some of these documents, but these only deal with the most important events, and, as has often been observed, he rarely printed the replies. As often as not in the war's early years the news that Churchill read was of defeats, setbacks and losses, but his papers also show that he responded to events, however discouraging, by directives and minutes designed to 'stiffen the sinews and summon up the blood'.

It is possible to tell Malta's wartime story in this way because Churchill insisted that official business be transacted in writing. On 19 July 1940, 'to make sure that my name was not used loosely', as he later wrote, he sent the following minute:

Prime Minister to General Ismay, C.I.G.S., and Sir Edward Bridges   19.VII.40

Let it be clearly understood that all directions emanating from me are made in writing, or should be immediately afterwards confirmed in writing, and that I do not accept any responsibility for matters relating to national defence on which I am alleged to have given decisions unless they are recorded in writing.[2]

As a result of this directive it is not surprising that the volume of the Prime Minister's papers held at Kew, under the designation PREM 3, is immense. These many thousands of documents are divided into many different subject groups, and among these is a series of files in which Churchill's papers relating to Malta are collected. These are designated PREM 3/266/1–10A, and are more fully described in the bibliography. These files, of varying length, contain the papers relating to Churchill's involvement with Malta during the war. The contents of each are filed in chronological order, as they arose, and only occasionally is a paper out of order, or placed in the wrong file. By and large, therefore, the reader can turn the pages and follow events as they claimed Churchill's attention.

It will be necessary to describe, briefly, the system that was established to enable the Prime Minister to deal effectively with such an enormous quantity of papers, which inevitably grew in number and variety as the European war turned into a World War when, first, Russia and then the United States of America were drawn in.[3] From the outset of his premiership, Churchill saw it as his prime duty to direct the British war effort. To do this he needed to know in detail what was happening, and then to decide, with the War Cabinet and the Chiefs of Staff, how to respond to events and, where possible, seize the initiative. The first task, therefore, was to gather together each day the most important telegrams and reports, and this was undertaken by his small group of Private Secretaries. These were selected from various departments of the Civil Service and they were fully conversant with the working practices and personnel of Whitehall. One of them was on duty wherever Churchill might be.

One of their main daily duties was the preparation each morning of the Prime Minister's black dispatch box, which went with him at all times. Briefly, given the need to bring to Churchill's attention the most important papers in some logical order, the box contained about a dozen separate cardboard folders. The first was entitled 'Top of the box', and a number of papers we shall be examining bear this handwritten notation at the top. These were judged by the Secretary on duty to require Churchill's most urgent attention. Others were entitled, 'Foreign Office Telegrams', 'Service Telegrams', 'Periodical Returns', 'General Ismay', 'For signature', 'Parliamentary questions', and so forth. It was this system, placing on the Private Secretaries a heavy responsibility for reading all the incoming papers and selecting those of most importance, and categorising the others, that generated most of the documents quoted in this volume.[4] To the black dispatch box there was soon added another, in a buff colour. This bore the instruction, 'Only to be opened by the Prime Minister in person'. Only the sender and Churchill had keys to this box, and the latter kept his fastened to his watch chain. This box was prepared, and often delivered to 10 Downing Street, by 'C', the Head of the Secret Service, otherwise Colonel Stewart Menzies. This box contained the most important of the growing number of deciphered 'Enigma' signals and extreme precautions were taken to preserve the vital secret of British success in deciphering these signals. For Churchill these were his 'golden eggs', and the information they provided guided and influenced many of Churchill's minutes and directives. Some of these, too, will appear in these pages.

Churchill himself has described his typical working day.[5] When he awoke at about 8.00 a.m. he took breakfast in bed, and then, still in bed, read through all the papers he found in his black or buff dispatch boxes. As he made his way through these papers, red ink pen in hand, he dictated to a staff of typists a stream of minutes, directives and enquiries. These, once typed and corrected in pen as necessary, were handed to General Ismay, who in turn delivered them to the addressees and collected the relevant replies. Many went to the Chiefs of Staff of the three services, who met at 10.30 a.m. each day. By late afternoon, after any contentious matters had been resolved, or deferred for further study, a whole series of orders and telegrams were ready for dispatch. Churchill ordered a series of coloured stickers, which he liked to attach to important minutes. The most urgent was ACTION THIS DAY, but there were others such as, REPORT IN THREE DAYS. Later, however, Ismay recorded that all were treated as being of the greatest urgency, whatever sticker might be attached.

When Churchill became Prime Minister, General Hastings Ismay was already the experienced Deputy Secretary (Military) to the War Cabinet, whose Secretary was Sir Edward Bridges. Ismay was Churchill's representative on the Chiefs of Staff Committee, and his two principal assistants, Colonel Leslie Hollis and Colonel Ian Jacob, headed a small staff of officers from the three services. This secretariat acted as the staff of the office of the Minister of Defence, a title that Churchill assumed when he became Prime Minister. Ismay was in effect Churchill's own Chief of Staff. After the war each of these officers published his personal account of working with Churchill and these are listed in the bibliography at the end of this volume.

Throughout the war, Churchill's most frequent military contacts were with the three Chiefs of Staff (COS), either in committee, or individually where appropriate. Ismay was a fourth member of the COS Committee, but he attended as Churchill's representative and did not sign their reports. Churchill at times took the chair at the COS meetings, but, even when not present, he always received the minutes of their meetings. Moreover, telegrams that they wished to send were first forwarded to him in draft form for his approval or amendment. A number of writers have subsequently stated that Churchill, at times, overruled the COS. General Ismay, who was best able to judge, roundly rejected this allegation, writing that not once during the whole war did he overrule his military advisers on a purely military question. Nevertheless, Churchill had a powerful and persuasive personality and Ismay went on to write that if the Prime Minister and his advisers disagreed on a particular matter the discussion might become heated, and hard words might be exchanged. But if the Chiefs of Staff stuck to their guns, Churchill would concede.[6] In a speech to the House of Commons about the War Situation on 11 November 1942, Churchill made his position clear. 'I am certainly not,' he told the House, 'one of those who need to be prodded. In fact, in anything, I am a prod. My difficulties rather lie in finding the patience and self-restraint to wait through many anxious weeks for the results to be achieved.'[7] Readers should bear this confession in mind when considering various disputes that are narrated in the following pages.

Churchill's Malta papers naturally assume much that would be unknown to most of today's readers. In order, therefore, to place them in an understandable context the author has drawn on other official papers, including, in particular, those held in the records of the War Cabinet, Defence Committee, Chiefs of Staff Committee, Admiralty, War Office, Air Ministry, and Colonial Office. Although the plight of Malta at times engaged the world's attention, events concerning the island form, of course, only a small part of the Second World War and brief references to developments elsewhere have been inserted, where necessary. These are designed to enable the reader to see how the decisions affecting Malta were often dependent on the demands of other theatres. At the end of the book, references are given to the principal documents quoted in each chapter. In addition, throughout the narrative the author has quoted extracts from personal diaries, letters and post-war memoirs, including Churchill's, where these help to explain or illuminate the matters they describe. These extracts often throw a revealing light on the tensions and emotions that lie under the surface of the documents. We may cite here just one example, which is quoted in Chapter XII. When Churchill in Cairo received details from Lord Gort of the 'Pedestal' convoy to Malta, Lord Moran, his doctor, noted in his diary: 'The PM's relief is a joyful sight. The plight of the island – short of food and ammunition – had been distracting to him … The PM dabbed his eyes with a handkerchief as he listened to Malta's story.'[8]

So we must now begin our story. On 3 September 1939, as Britain once more found herself at war with Germany, Churchill again took his place at the Cabinet table as First Lord of the Admiralty. None of his colleagues was better prepared by experience or by temperament for what lay ahead.

I

AT THE ADMIRALTY
SEPTEMBER 1939 – MAY 1940

*Once again we must fight for life and honour against all the might and
fury of the valiant, disciplined and ruthless German race. Once again!
So be it.*

Winston S. Churchill, *The Second World War*, Vol. I

At 11.00 a.m. on 3 September 1939 the British ultimatum to Germany
expired unanswered and Britain was once again at war with Germany.
Neville Chamberlain then invited Churchill to become First Lord of the
Admiralty. Churchill has related how, at 6.00 p.m. that day, he went
to the Admiralty to 'lay his hands on the naval affair'. Behind the First
Lord's chair was the map box installed when he was there in 1911, and
still containing the charts showing the disposition of the German High
Seas Fleet.[1] As a stream of Admiralty signals put into effect the naval war
plans against Germany, a question of vital importance, not least to the
people of Malta, at once arose. What would Mussolini do? Churchill must
have been struck by the similarity to the position he faced in early August
1914. Then, too, Italy was allied to Germany and Austria in the Triple
Alliance, and her potential hostility threatened Malta and British interests
in the Mediterranean. However, on 4 August 1914, Italy had declared her
neutrality and, a year later, in May 1915, had entered the war on the Allied
side. But were Mussolini on this occasion to fight with Hitler against Britain
and France, it seemed inevitable that the bombing of Malta, perhaps even
invasion, would be among the first of the dictator's actions.

During the early months of 1939 there had been much discussion at the
Admiralty and among the Chiefs of Staff about Italy. In some quarters it was
argued that, in the event of war, it would be best to 'knock out Italy first'.
Churchill contributed to this debate with a paper addressed to the Prime
Minister on 27 March 1939.[2] In this paper, bearing the title 'Memorandum
on Sea Power 1939', Churchill urged an all-out attack on the Italian fleet
in order to gain early control of the Mediterranean. But what if, despite
her alliance with Germany, Italy remained neutral? Should Britain and

France force the issue by declaring war on Italy? Further consideration of this matter led to the conclusion, shared by Churchill, that Italian neutrality was preferable if Britain and France were at war with Germany. This strategic conclusion mirrored the overall policy of appeasing Italy that had been pursued by Chamberlain since Anthony Eden's resignation as Foreign Secretary in February 1938. To further this policy, Chamberlain and his new Foreign Secretary, Lord Halifax, had visited Mussolini in Rome in January 1939. However, in the words of Count Ciano, the Italian Foreign Minister and Mussolini's son-in-law, their meeting had been a 'fiasco'. He recorded in his diary Mussolini's contemptuous verdict that his visitors were 'not made of the same stuff as the Francis Drakes and the other magnificent adventurers who created the empire. These, after all, are the tired sons of a long line of rich men, and they will lose their empire.'[3]

Nevertheless, the British preference for a neutral Italy left open the possibility that Mussolini would honour his commitment to Hitler – most recently reaffirmed in May 1939 in the 'Pact of Steel' – and at once enter the war on Germany's side. Fortunately, Italy was in no position in 1939 to engage in war with Britain and France. Mussolini's ambitions in the Mediterranean had put a severe strain on Italy's always limited resources. The invasion and occupation of Abyssinia in 1935–6 was followed almost immediately by Mussolini's heavy commitment to General Franco in the Spanish Civil War. As if this were not enough, the dictator in April 1939 had invaded Albania, suggesting that he had further aggressive intentions in the Balkans. Consequently, when it became clear to him in late August 1939 that a German attack on Poland was imminent, he was forced to tell Hitler that, for the present at least, Italy must remain neutral. He then declared that Italy would adopt a position of 'non-belligerence'. This deliberately enigmatic phrase, while easing Churchill's immediate anxieties, left considerable doubt about Mussolini's future intentions. That Mussolini would wait and see how the fighting developed, while accelerating his own war preparations, seemed the safest assumption.

On the evening of 4 September, Churchill conferred with his naval advisers, headed by Admiral Sir Dudley Pound, the First Sea Lord. Subsequently, Churchill circulated a note of their discussions 'for criticism and correction'. Among other matters, it was decided to maintain the diversion of Mediterranean merchant shipping, other than protected troop convoys, around the Cape of Good Hope. His note then continued:

This unpleasant situation would be eased by ... the determination of the attitude of Italy. We cannot be sure that the Italian uncertainty will be cleared up in the next six weeks, though we should press HMG [His Majesty's Government] to bring it to a head in a favourable sense as soon as possible. Meanwhile the heavy ships in the Mediterranean will be on the defensive, and can therefore spare some of the destroyer protection they would need if they were required to approach Italian waters.[4]

A week later Chamberlain and his French counterpart, Edouard Daladier, met at Abbeville in northern France. Among other matters, they discussed their joint policy towards Italy. Daladier 'felt that from the military point of view it was very desirable that Italy should remain neutral, and advocated the policy of treating her very carefully'. Chamberlain agreed. 'The British Government,' he noted, 'were certainly taking pains to make it as easy as possible for Italy, but favours and bribes should not be proffered. It was not inconceivable that she might one day be on the Allied side.'[5] One result of this policy decision not to provoke Italy was an instruction to Admiral Sir Andrew Cunningham, who was then Commander-in-Chief of the Mediterranean Fleet, that the fleet should observe a six-mile limit around Italian waters, rather than the internationally recognised three-mile limit. Steps were also taken to warn Italy of the risk to any of their submarines that were submerged outside well-known training areas.

After a short visit in mid-September to the Home Fleet at Scapa Flow in the Orkney Islands, Churchill circulated to the War Cabinet a full report about naval preparations and early operations. This included the following comment:

> In the event of Italy becoming an enemy she would have grave need of reinforcing and supplying Libya, and opportunities for action might therefore be offered to the superior French and British Fleets. It is recognised that the securing of the command of the Mediterranean would in the circumstances apprehended become the main objective of the Royal Navy and their French allies.[6]

The Navy's Mediterranean War Plan was also discussed at the Admiralty on 18 September, Admiral Pound explaining the intention of sealing the Mediterranean at both ends in order to put economic pressure on Italy.[7]

By this time the main units of the Mediterranean Fleet had left Malta to concentrate, as planned, at its war station at Alexandria. Admiral Cunningham had, however, left at Malta seven submarines and twelve motor torpedo boats for the local defence of the island against possible naval attack. Nevertheless, it had long been recognised that the principal threat to Malta was heavy and sustained air attack from bases in Sicily no more than sixty miles away. The defence of Malta against air attack had been the subject of searching enquiry since the Abyssinian crisis in 1935 had revealed Mussolini's hostility. The author has considered this complex problem in an earlier study, and only the principal conclusions are reviewed here.[8]

After much discussion and planning, but very little action, the Committee of Imperial Defence (CID) had in July 1939 ruled that Malta should be protected by 112 heavy and 60 light AA guns, and by four squadrons of fighters. This was referred to as Scale B, the Committee having rejected Scale A, which proposed only 48 heavy and 16 light AA guns, with one fighter squadron. It was, nevertheless, appreciated that it would take some time to achieve this objective for the stark reality was that Britain's production of modern AA guns and eight-gun Hurricane and Spitfire fighters was woefully inadequate. Nor was Malta the only vital naval base without adequate air defence. Churchill's recent visit to Scapa Flow had revealed that this base, too, lacked proper defences, while Alexandria was even more vulnerable to possible Italian air attack. The allocation of new AA guns was the subject of anxious study by the Chiefs of Staff in the early years of the war, as we shall see later. Churchill also intervened. When the Naval Staff recommended in September the installation of as many as eighty new 3.7-inch AA guns at Scapa Flow, he approved only the first sixteen of these and then continued: 'The second 20 equipments should be considered in relation to the needs of Malta, as well as to the aircraft factories in England.'[9] He then called for a report about Malta which revealed that only twenty-four AA guns had been installed and that there were no fighters of any kind. The only useful improvements were the steady progress in the construction of a new all-weather airfield at Luqa, and the installation of the first early warning radar station.

In these early months of the war, Churchill was mainly preoccupied by naval operations against German U-boats and surface raiders. A naval action that was of particular significance to Churchill was the destruction in December of the German pocket-battleship *Graf Spee* after a fierce fight with two British and one New Zealand cruiser. This successful action contrasted with the disastrous mistakes that led to the escape in August 1914 of the German battle cruiser *Goeben* in the waters around Malta. Nevertheless, Churchill could not afford to ignore Italy. He supported the Anglo-French policy of cultivating Italian friendship in several ways. Among these was a proposal, outlined in a paper to the War Cabinet in October, designed to seek agreement with France and Italy to 'keep the U-boat warfare out of the Mediterranean'.[10] In the following month, in a wide-ranging BBC broadcast, Churchill noted with satisfaction that 'Italy has adopted a wise policy of peace.'[11] Again, on 28 December, he advised Admiral Pound that, although it was intended to reinstate the three-mile limit around Italian coastal waters, the Mediterranean Fleet should continue 'to treat Italian shipping with special leniency, and to avoid causes of friction or complaint with that favoured country'.[12] Churchill was not alone in hoping that Italy might eventually, as in 1915, join the Allies.

One aspect of Churchill's many-faceted character was his interest in the application of science to the problems of war, an early illustration of which was his involvement in the development of the tank. In his memoirs of the Second World War he explained: 'I knew nothing about science, but I knew something of scientists, and had had much practice as a Minister in handling things I did not understand.' He also pointed out that Professor Lindemann's greatest value to him was his ability to explain complex scientific matters in terms that Churchill could understand.[13] Much thought had been given to the use of novel methods to destroy bombers. Rockets, then referred to as 'Unrotated Projectiles', or U.P. for short, offered interesting possibilities, not least because they and their launchers could be manufactured more cheaply than AA guns and by non-specialist firms. They might also be engineered to carry aloft what were known as 'aerial mines'. With all this in mind, Churchill wrote on 14 November to Sir Kingsley Wood, the Secretary of State for Air.[14]

> We see very clearly a multiple projector which could send 20 rockets carrying aerial mines, suspended on thousand-foot wires from parachutes, thus laying a curtain in front of a dive-bombing attack, which would seem to be effectual. The importance of this to our ships and to the whole strategy of the naval war cannot be overestimated ... With regard to the discharge of aerial mines from aircraft, I am not at all convinced that this is not useful in certain circumstances, and Tizard* used to hold the opinion that it would be particularly valuable in regard to a place like Malta.

Churchill returned to the use of these devices at Malta later.

By November, since Italy showed no sign of wishing to participate in what Churchill called 'the Twilight War', the Mediterranean Fleet was slowly reduced in size to reinforce other areas. Accordingly, on 1 November, Admiral Cunningham returned to Malta to re-establish his command of a much-reduced fleet of light cruisers and destroyers. Churchill advised the War Cabinet of these developments, adding, 'Now that Italy is neutral and may even become a friend, the British Fleet has again become entirely mobile.'[15]

In early December, the Chiefs of Staff presented to the War Cabinet a review of strategic policy in the Middle East.[16] The report did little more than recommend 'the necessary administrative development' in the area. However, rather ominously, it warned that as regards air reinforcement:

---

* Sir Henry Tizard had been, since 1933, Chairman of the Air Defence Research Committee, which Churchill had joined in 1935.

We cannot at present afford to reinforce Egypt at the expense of Home Defence and the Western Front, even to the extent of providing adequate forces to meet Italian attack, let alone build up reserves against the further contingencies we are considering. Some time must elapse before the situation changes.

The War Cabinet minutes record that 'the attitude of Italy must remain a very uncertain factor'.[17]

A matter of more immediate relevance to Malta came before the Military Co-ordination Committee (MCC) in early 1940. The CID, as noted earlier, had in August 1939 approved Scale B rearmament at Malta. However, the provision of so many AA guns for Malta when they were still in short supply was questioned by the War Office in November. The Treasury also pointed out that the manufacture of additional AA guns for Malta would delay the production of equally vital 25-pounder guns for the Army. The Chiefs of Staff, weighing the 'Air Defence of Malta' on 25 January, were quite clear that 'nothing had yet occurred to modify the decision arrived at before the war on the vital necessity of securing for use by the Navy the essential facilities of Malta'. Furthermore, they added, 'it was most desirable that fighter defences should be provided as soon as they can be made available'.[18] The MCC debated the problem on 8 February 1940.[19] Churchill's views were recorded in the minutes as follows:

(2) Air Defence of Malta
Mr. Churchill ... thought that Scale A should be completed as the immediate aim, and Scale B accepted, with a very low priority, as the ultimate objective. It might prove from experience, before Scale B was provided, that some different form of defence would be more effective. It would be unwise, therefore, to order additional anti-aircraft guns for eventual provision at Malta if by so doing the provision of 25-pounders was delayed.

The Committee accepted Churchill's recommendation.

Doubts about Italian intentions began to grow in the early part of 1940. In the latter months of 1939, Britain, in an attempt to maintain friendly relations, had placed orders for military equipment with various Italian firms. These included motor launches, anti-tank guns, and 400 Caproni aircraft. However, on 8 February Mussolini, who had previously sanctioned these contracts, ordered them to be cancelled. Shortly after this the British government, as a way of tightening the economic blockade of Germany, decided not to allow the passage of any more Italian vessels carrying German coal from the port of Rotterdam.

In this less friendly atmosphere, Churchill thought it right to take precautions. On 1 March he minuted Admiral Pound: 'A plan should be prepared for a battleship concentration in the Mediterranean (with other craft), supposing trouble should arise in March. I do not expect trouble; but it would be well to have all the combinations surveyed in advance.' A week later he wrote again: 'I think it would be only prudent for you to concert with the French the necessary regroupings of the Allied Fleets, which would be appropriate to a hostile or menacing Italian attitude.'[20] Churchill's instincts were sound. Mussolini was veering towards Germany, and on 18 March he met Hitler at the Brenner Pass on the Italian-Austrian border. German records show that, at that meeting, Mussolini undertook to enter the war on Germany's side 'within a few months'.[21]

Reference was made earlier to Churchill's keen interest in the development of aerial mines as a form of anti-aircraft defence. He now addressed a minute to Admiral Bruce Fraser, the Third Sea Lord:

> We must now immediately drive ahead with the aerial mines from aircraft. To avoid confusion, this can be called the Egg-layer. We have, I am afraid, rather lost sight of it while pressing on with the UP ... The Fleet Air Arm may be helpful in this form of defence. Above all, it is suited to places like Scapa or Malta, where the enemy come for a particular point and probably return home by the shortest route. It is of particular use at night.[22]

At Malta, however, the most pressing need was for further deliveries of heavy and light AA guns, together with a squadron of fighter aircraft. Some thought had been given by the Air Ministry to the formation of the first squadron towards the end of 1939, but this had then been postponed until the spring of the following year. As regards AA guns, demand still far outstripped supply. Of the 112 heavy AA guns authorised for Malta only 34 had been installed, and Alexandria had received only 12 out of an authorised scale of 48. The difficult task of allocating new guns was delegated to the Deputy Chiefs of Staff (DCOS) and on 3 April 1940 they met to decide the allocation of AA guns for April and May. Their decision was recorded in the minutes:

<u>Allocation of Anti-Aircraft Guns for April and May</u>
Discussion focused on increasing Anti-Aircraft defence in the Mediterranean in the light of the possibility of the deterioration in our relations with Italy. It was pointed out that if all, or at any rate a very high percentage, of the Anti-Aircraft defences which had been approved before the war as adequate to defend Malta, could be provided, the Fleet would be based at Malta and consequently, in the event of war with Italy, we should not have to keep a Fleet at each end of the Mediterranean. The provision of an adequate scale of Anti-Aircraft defence at Malta, however, was out of the question in the near future and it would, therefore, be

necessary to base the Fleet at Alexandria. In consequence, any immediate increases in the Anti-Aircraft defences in the Mediterranean should be provided at Alexandria.[23]

This harsh, but in the circumstances unavoidable, decision was clearly a setback for the defenders of Malta, but it was difficult to challenge the verdict that the main fleet base at Alexandria deserved priority. It was simply another consequence of what Churchill, in the House of Commons on 12 November 1936, had described as 'the years that the locust hath eaten'.[24]

Four days later, the British and French governments faced a new crisis. At dawn on 7 April 1940, in a well-planned and executed operation, German forces landed at several places in Norway. One force was carried on a flotilla of destroyers to the northern port of Narvik. The French Prime Minister, Paul Reynaud, who had succeeded Daladier on 21 March, at once flew to London for a meeting of the Supreme War Council. Although most of their discussions related to Norway, the two Prime Ministers wondered whether Mussolini would now choose this moment to enter the war. Reynaud asked 'whether the British Government had any information regarding the possibility of an Italian attack; and whether, if any such attack were made or if the Italian Government ordered a general mobilisation, any plans had been prepared for Allied action'. Churchill replied to this:

> The British Admiralty had been in close touch with the French Ministry of Marine on the subject, and had arranged for the concentration in the Mediterranean of naval forces which the two Admiralties believed would give the Allies the command of that sea, in the sense that, while it would not be possible for commerce to pass freely through the Mediterranean, the two outlets would be securely held. At the same time, communications between Italy and her possessions in Libya and Abyssinia would immediately be severed, and would remain cut. British shipping to the East would for the time being be diverted by the Cape route. Admittedly the present was not a convenient time for such an operation, in view of the situation in the North Sea; but that situation would clear itself in a short time.[25]

Even before the end of March, the Admiralty was making plans to reinforce the Mediterranean Fleet. The battleship HMS *Warspite* was under orders to proceed to Alexandria, but she was then diverted to Norwegian waters where she led the assault that resulted in the destruction of eight German destroyers at Narvik. More seriously, the aircraft carrier HMS *Glorious*, which had been recalled from the Mediterranean, was sunk in the North Sea. Two other battleships, HMS *Malaya* and *Royal Sovereign*, were ordered to the Mediterranean, while *Warspite*, after her action in Narvik fjord, was also ordered to Gibraltar. The proposed passage of these valuable ships through the Sicilian Narrows to join the Mediterranean Fleet at Alexandria prompted Churchill, on 27 April, to send the following minute to Admiral Pound:

> In my opinion the battleships should not sail for the Eastern Mediterranean in present circumstances unless all three are together, unless three French battleships are with them, and unless there is an ample flotilla escort. If these conditions can be established I am willing to authorise the movement.
>
> The most dangerous disposition would appear to be to send two ships through now and let *Warspite* follow four days later – thus dividing the flotilla escort.[26]

Meanwhile, the Chiefs of Staff had been considering what action might deter Mussolini from entering the war. The Foreign Office had warned that 'an attempt to gain a spectacular success against Malta or Gibraltar is a possible move by Italy'. The Chiefs, therefore, recommended to the War Cabinet that an additional battalion of infantry be sent to Gibraltar, despite its distance from any Italian threat. With regard to Malta, however, they concluded that 'there is nothing practicable we can do to increase the power of resistance of Malta'.[27] This was not, however, their last word on this question, as we shall see later. On 30 April, the War Cabinet approved the manning of defences at Alexandria, Haifa, Malta and Gibraltar.[28]

Churchill's observant eye, sweeping over the Mediterranean, fell, on 3 May, on the Malta dockyard. He had already complained about the delay to the repair of HMS *Hood* in Malta dockyard and he now sent another minute to Admiral Pound:

> It seems that a good deal of valuable repair work is being done at Malta which we cannot dispense with; but, on the assumption that we are getting ready to resist an Italian attack, surely everything that can quit Malta should proceed to one end of the Mediterranean or the other ... I am not quite sure that C-in-C, Med, is in fact preparing himself for a possible Italian attack. He may be convinced there may be none, and he may well be right, but our position is that precaution should be taken ... What are his orders in the event of war with Italy?[29]

On 9 May, Churchill was able to advise the War Cabinet that *Malaya*, *Royal Sovereign* and *Warspite* had all passed the Sicilian Narrows safely. On 3 May, Admiral Cunningham returned to Alexandria, and on 14 May hoisted his flag on *Warspite*.

On 10 May 1940, overwhelming German army and air forces struck at France and the Low Countries. Neville Chamberlain, after some initial hesitation, resigned as Prime Minister, and at 6.00 p.m. that day King George VI invited Churchill to form a coalition government. Churchill's personal bodyguard, Detective-Inspector W. H. Thompson, later recalled the scene as Churchill returned from Buckingham Palace to the Admiralty. Thompson congratulated the new Prime Minister as he got out of the car, and added that he had assumed an enormous task. Churchill replied: 'God alone knows how great it is. All I hope is that it is not too late. I am very much afraid it is. We can only do our best.' Thompson then remembered: 'As he turned away, he muttered something to himself. Then he set his jaw, and with a look of determination, mastering all emotion, he began to climb the stairs.'[30]

Churchill himself later wrote in one of the most striking passages of his history of the war: 'I was conscious of a profound sense of relief. At last I had the authority to give directions over the whole scene. I felt as if I were walking with destiny, and that all my past life had been but a preparation for this hour and this trial … I thought I knew a good deal about it all, and I was sure I would not fail. Therefore, although impatient for the morning, I slept soundly and had no need for cheering dreams. Facts are better than dreams.'[31]

1. Churchill on 10 May 1940, the day of his appointment as Prime Minister.

THE THREAT FROM ITALY

Is it too late to stop a river of blood from flowing between the British and Italian peoples?

Churchill letter to Mussolini, 16 May 1940

Churchill became Prime Minister on the day when the 'Twilight War' came to an end. At dawn on 10 May 1940, as German army and air forces struck at the Netherlands, Belgium and France, French and British divisions advanced into Belgium to engage them. Far to the south, Mussolini, already morally committed to Hitler, watched events carefully, seeking to judge the best moment for ending Italian 'non-belligerency'. During the next three weeks the German blitzkrieg swept through France and the Low Countries to the Channel ports, driving a corridor between the BEF and the French First Army to the north and the bulk of the French Army to the south. On 16 and 22 May, Churchill flew to Paris in an attempt to co-ordinate Allied operations and to stiffen French resolution to continue the fight against Germany.

Amid all the pressures of these calamitous events in France, it may seem surprising that Churchill and his advisers found any time to consider possible repercussions in the Mediterranean. But the growing threat of Italian attack could not be ignored, and it is with the steps that were taken to meet this additional danger that this chapter is mostly concerned. These decisions, however, must be seen in the context of the struggle in France to which the attention of Churchill and his advisers was mainly directed. Consequently, the principal events that led to the growing crisis in France are also briefly recounted. When considering these discussions and decisions, the reader should also bear in mind the stress and the desperate conditions in which these matters were considered. The pace of events, as one disaster followed closely on another, allowed no time for rest and calm reflection. As Churchill later recalled: 'It was a severe experience for me, bearing so heavy an overall responsibility, to watch during these days in flickering glimpses this drama in which control was impossible, and intervention more likely to do harm than good.'[1] Decisions were as essential as they were difficult to make. Perhaps most difficult of all, and one that caused Churchill much anxiety and grief, was the judgement about continued military aid to a faltering ally that had borne the brunt of the German attack. How far should Britain's limited military and air resources be committed to France when those very resources might soon be critical for Britain's own survival? All of these pressures ultimately fell upon Churchill and many contemporaries have recorded their belief that it was only his courage, resolution and unflagging energy that carried Britain through those dark days in the summer of 1940.

With the Mediterranean Fleet assembled at Alexandria, and all British and French forces in the Mediterranean at a high state of readiness, Churchill, at Lord Halifax's suggestion, wrote to Mussolini, whom he had visited in Rome in January 1927:

Prime Minister to Signor Mussolini,   16 May 1940

Now that I have taken up my office as Prime Minister and Minister of Defence I look back to our meetings in Rome and feel a desire to speak words of goodwill to you as Chief of the Italian nation across what seems to be a swiftly-widening gulf. Is it too late to stop a river of blood from flowing between the British and Italian peoples? We can no doubt inflict grievous injuries on one another and maul each other cruelly, and darken the Mediterranean with our strife. If you so decree it must be so; but I declare that I have never been the enemy of Italian greatness, nor ever at heart the foe of the Italian lawgiver. It is idle to predict the course of the great battles now raging in Europe, but I am sure that whatever may happen on the Continent England will go on to the end, even quite alone, as we have done before, and I believe with some assurance that we shall be aided in increasing measure by the United States, and, indeed, by all the Americas.

I beg you to believe that it is in no spirit of weakness or of fear that I make this solemn appeal, which will remain on record. Down the ages above all other calls comes the cry that the joint heirs of Latin and Christian civilisation must not be ranged against one another in mortal strife. Hearken to it, I beseech you in all honour and respect, before the dread signal is given. It will never be given by us.

At the time, Ciano described this as 'a message of good will, couched in vague terms, but none the less dignified and noble. Even Mussolini appreciates the tone of it.'[2] Two days later Mussolini replied:

Signor Mussolini to Prime Minister,   18 May 1940

I reply to the message which you have sent me in order to tell you that you are certainly aware of grave reasons of an historical and contingent character which have ranged our two countries in opposite camps. Without going back very far in time I remind you of the initiative taken in 1935 by your Government to organise at Geneva sanctions against Italy, engaged in securing for herself a small space in the African sun without causing the slightest injury to your interests and territories or those of others. I remind you also of the real and actual state of servitude in which Italy finds herself in her own sea. If it was to honour your signature that your Government declared war on Germany, you will understand that the same sense of honour and respect for engagements assumed in the Italian-German Treaty guides Italian policy today and to-morrow in the face of any event whatsoever.

On this response Churchill later commented: 'The response was hard. It had at least the merit of candour.'[3] He went on to write: 'From this moment we could have no doubt of Mussolini's intention to enter the war at his most favourable moment. His resolve had in fact been made as soon as the defeat of the French armies was obvious.' Although this was written many years later, there can be little doubt that it reflected his views at the time, and this should be borne in mind when the question of a possible approach to Mussolini was raised two weeks later.

On 14 May, the COS considered a paper that outlined possible Allied military action in the Mediterranean should Italy declare war.[4] The initial strategy, it was recommended, should be a defensive one designed to secure Allied interests in the area, and only limited offensive operations would be possible. With regard to Malta the report was not reassuring:

6. In the case of Malta no direct relief can be afforded in the initial stages of war with Italy, and we should hope that the garrison would be able to hold out until relieved. While the island should be reasonably secure against seaborne attack, provided that periodical food convoys can be passed through, the absence of fighter aircraft will expose it to a very heavy scale of attack.

The COS approved a telegram to the Middle East C-in-Cs on those lines.

Two days later, the Defence Committee, composed of the three service Ministers and the COS, had before them an urgent request for reinforcements from General Sir William Dobbie, the Acting Governor of Malta. The Governor, General Sir Charles Bonham-Carter, had returned to London for medical treatment and General Dobbie had arrived in Malta as his replacement on 28 April 1940. This was intended to be a temporary appointment since it was expected that General Bonham-Carter would in due course be able to resume his duties. This, however, proved impossible and General Dobbie became the effective Governor as soon as he arrived, although his appointment was not formally confirmed until May 1941. General Dobbie was then sixty years old, a Royal Engineer, whose most recent appointment had been as General Officer Commanding (GOC) in Malaya.[5]

On 15 May, General Dobbie signalled the War Office to warn that, with a garrison of only four regular British battalions, supported by a battalion of the King's Own Malta Regiment (KOMR), Malta was vulnerable to an airborne assault such as the German army had successfully employed in the opening hours of the attack on France and the Low Countries. The Chief of the Imperial General Staff (CIGS), General Sir Edmund Ironside, accepted that the existing garrison required strengthening, and General Dewing, the Director of Military Operations (DMO), pointed out that an additional battalion could be sent from Gibraltar within a few days. The Defence Committee agreed to these proposals,[6] and a fifth battalion arrived at Malta several days later. It will be noticed that this decision reversed the judgement that the COS had reached on 30 April when they had said that 'there is nothing practicable we can do to increase the power of resistance of Malta'. To supplement these trained troops, Dobbie had had considerable success in recruiting substantial numbers of Maltese civilians, many of them well used to handling sporting and hunting rifles, to Home Guard and Civil Defence units. Such men, familiar with the close-walled countryside, were likely to be of great value against dispersed parachutists.

This meeting of the Defence Committee was chaired by Neville Chamberlain since on the afternoon of 16 May Churchill had made his first flying visit to Paris. We must now deal briefly with the fast-moving events in France and Belgium that overshadowed all other considerations during these desperate weeks. Early on 15 May, Churchill had been woken to receive a despondent telephone call from Paul Reynaud, the French Prime Minister, who told him that German armoured forces had broken through the French line on the Meuse. 'We are beaten: we have lost the battle,' he repeated to Churchill's consternation. On the following day Churchill flew to Paris and in discussions later that day he learned that General Gamelin, the French C-in-C, had no strategic reserve to seal off the German penetration. 'I was dumbfounded,' Churchill later wrote. 'I admit this was one of the greatest surprises I have had in my life.'[7] Gamelin was at once replaced by General Weygand, but the latter's plan to cut off the panzer spearhead proved impossible to implement. Despite attempts by Churchill on a second visit to Paris on 22 May to stiffen French morale, General Lord Gort, the Commander of the BEF, anxious about the German advance towards Boulogne and Calais and an impending Belgian collapse on his northern flank, ordered a withdrawal to the coast on 25 May. Operation 'Dynamo', the evacuation of the BEF from Dunkirk, began on the evening of 26 May, in the expectation that only a small proportion of the British force could be rescued.

Churchill was so alarmed by the despondency he encountered in Paris that, upon his return to London, he instructed the COS to consider the effects of a French surrender. Their paper, entitled 'British Strategy in a Certain Eventuality',[8] was circulated to the War Cabinet on 25 May and, although largely concerned with the threat of an invasion of Britain, also considered the consequences in the Mediterranean. In their view, Italy would, after the surrender of the French fleet, be free to concentrate her forces against Malta, Gibraltar and Egypt. The paper went on:

> Malta has six months' food reserve for the population and garrison, but AA guns and ammunition are short, and the island is not likely to withstand more than one serious seaborne assault, nor could it be used as a naval base.

While this was being circulated, the Defence Committee met on 25 May to review, among other matters, naval strategy in the Mediterranean.[9] Included in the papers before them was a telegram of 23 May from Admiral Cunningham, the C-in-C Mediterranean, in which he warned of the difficulties of operating even light forces from Malta without effective long-range air reconnaissance. He added, however, that 'the above does not mean that central Mediterranean will be neglected. It is intended to carry out a prime sweep in this area.' Admiral Pound stressed the need for stronger fighter protection for the Fleet at sea, but Air Chief Marshal Newall replied that all modern fighter aircraft would, for the immediate future, be needed for home defence. At the end of this discussion, Churchill said that he 'hoped that the Fleet would adopt a vigorously offensive attitude against the Italians if they came into the war'.

While the COS and the Defence Committee were studying all these developments and deciding on the appropriate response, the Joint Intelligence Committee (JIC) was steadily collecting and assessing a growing volume of information about Italian preparations.[10] As Sir Harry Hinsley has made clear in his history of British wartime intelligence, the British authorities had by September 1939 mastered all the important Italian military and diplomatic ciphers. Numerous decrypts confirmed that in April the Italian armed forces were being mobilised for war, or, at least, the threat of war. As Hinsley wrote: 'Sigint in fact gave good notice of Italy's entry [into the war], if only for a month before the event.'[11] On 24 May, the JIC felt confident enough to circulate their assessment of 'The Italian Situation'.[12] This began by asserting that 'during recent weeks Italy has been engaged busily in preparing for war. In Italy the army has been mobilised for the last fortnight ... The air force will be ready by the end of the month.' The report acknowledged the difficulties still facing the Italian forces but concluded: 'We consider that all the indications point to the fact that Signor Mussolini has made up his mind to enter the war on the side of Germany.'

We must now consider in some detail the discussions in the War Cabinet in late May about a possible approach to Mussolini.[13] The French government, under Paul Reynaud, urged that such an approach be made. This was in part designed to seek Italy's continued neutrality, but more importantly to explore the possibility that Mussolini might intercede with Hitler to obtain acceptable terms for ending the war. The significance of these discussions for Maltese history is their bearing on the question whether, as has been alleged, Churchill and the War Cabinet planned, or were prepared, to offer Malta to Italy as a bribe to secure Mussolini's co-operation.

The urgency of an approach to Mussolini grew as German forces pushed deeper and deeper into France. The British government, therefore, agreed to a French proposal to invite President Roosevelt to send a message to Mussolini, and they suggested what might be expressed in such a message. The President was authorised to state that 'the Allies are aware that the Italian Government entertains certain grievances in regard to the Italian position in the Mediterranean', and to invite 'Signor Mussolini to state what claims would ensure the establishment in the Mediterranean of a new order guaranteeing to Italy satisfaction of Italian legitimate aspirations in that area'. The President accepted this proposal and his message was telegraphed to Rome on 26 May.

On the previous day, Lord Halifax, the Foreign Secretary, took another initiative. After gaining the consent of the War Cabinet, he invited Signor Bastianini, the Italian Ambassador in London, to meet him to discuss what might be done to ensure continued Italian neutrality. Halifax later circulated his own note of these discussions to his colleagues. During a long discussion Bastianini, according to Halifax, suggested that any matters of dispute between Italy and the Allies should be examined 'within the larger framework of a European settlement'. Halifax said that he agreed with this, and added that the British government 'would never be unwilling to consider any proposal made with authority that gave promise of the establishment of a secure and peaceful Europe'. In this carefully worded note it is clear that Halifax had moved on from the narrow issue of Italian neutrality to the broader question of possible discussions with Hitler, through Mussolini, aimed at bringing the war to an end.

Sunday, 26 May, was an unusual day in a highly unusual month. Reynaud flew over from Paris to have lunch with the Prime Minister at Admiralty House, and then met the other members of the War Cabinet. Before that, at 10.00 a.m., Churchill and his colleagues attended a short service of intercession and prayer at Westminster Abbey, and an hour earlier Churchill had summoned a meeting of the War Cabinet. In preparation for the discussions with Reynaud, he passed on the latest news from France. Having listened to this, Halifax then remarked, in a rather gloomy way, that 'it was not so much now a question of imposing a complete defeat on Germany, but of safeguarding the independence of our own Empire'. He then described his meeting with Bastianini and added that the Italian Ambassador had asked to see him again to put forward 'fresh proposals' for a peace conference. To this Churchill replied that 'peace and security might be achieved under a German domination of Europe. That we could never accept.' He went on to say that he 'was opposed to any negotiations which might lead to a derogation of our rights and power'. This interchange was an early indication of a rift between the Prime Minister and his Foreign Secretary.

After lunching with Reynaud, Churchill met his War Cabinet colleagues again at 2.00 p.m. At the time, the other War Cabinet members were Neville Chamberlain (Lord President of the Council), Lord Halifax (Foreign Secretary), and the two Labour Party members, Clement Attlee (Lord Privy Seal), and Arthur Greenwood (Minister without Portfolio). The youngest of these was Greenwood, who was at the time sixty years old. When considering the following account of the War Cabinet discussions, the reader should bear in mind two factors over and above the heavy strain that events placed on all the participants. Firstly, since Churchill's political position as Prime Minister was not at that time as secure as it later became, he could not afford to provoke the resignation of Chamberlain or Halifax. This consideration led him at times to moderate his own strong views. Secondly, the measured prose of the War Cabinet minutes is not a verbatim record but rather records the gist of what each person said. Moreover, the minutes do not reveal the heated words that, according to other accounts, were sometimes exchanged.

At this second War Cabinet meeting of the day, Churchill told his colleagues that Reynaud had been pessimistic about France's ability to continue to resist a German force which had, he claimed, a three to one superiority. Reynaud had pressed again the need for an approach to Mussolini. In his view, Mussolini would probably require 'the neutralisation of Gibraltar and the Suez Canal, the demilitarisation of Malta, and the limitation of naval forces in the Mediterranean'. Churchill then reported to his colleagues that he had urged Reynaud to continue the fight, and told him: 'we were not prepared to give in on any account. We would rather go down fighting than be enslaved to Germany.' However, Halifax spoke in favour of Reynaud's suggested approach to Mussolini, and Churchill, while expressing his doubts whether anything would come of this, concluded by saying that the War Cabinet would have to consider the matter.

Halifax then returned to Admiralty House to draft with Reynaud the outline of a possible approach to Mussolini, and the other War Cabinet members joined them soon afterwards. After Reynaud's departure there followed what the minutes describe as 'An Informal Meeting of War Cabinet Members'. The minutes also state that the Secretary, Sir Edward Bridges, was not present during the first fifteen minutes of this meeting. For the third time that day, therefore, the War Cabinet wrestled with the question of whether to seek Mussolini's help. By then it was evident that it was not so much the continued Italian neutrality that was under consideration, but rather the possibility of seeking, through Mussolini's good offices, an acceptable peace offer from Germany.

Churchill began by saying that he hoped that France would hang on, and then continued:

> At the same time we must take care not to be forced into a weak position in which we went to Signor Mussolini and invited him to go to Herr Hitler and ask him to treat us nicely. We must not get entangled in a position of that kind before we had been involved in any serious fighting.

Halifax disagreed, and the minutes put his case in the following terms:

> The Foreign Secretary thought that we might say to Signor Mussolini that if there was any suggestion of terms which affected our independence, we should not look at them for a moment. If, however, Signor Mussolini was as alarmed as we felt that he must be in regard to Herr Hitler's power, and was prepared to look at matters from the point of view of the balance of power, then we might consider Italian claims. At any rate he could see no harm in trying this line of approach.

Greenwood interjected to say that he doubted whether 'it was in Signor Mussolini's power to take a line independent of Herr Hitler', but then went on to say that 'he saw no objection to this line of approach being tried'. Chamberlain then gave his views, after saying that 'the problem was a very difficult one, and it was right to talk it out from every point of view'. He rejected Reynaud's wish to 'do a deal with [Mussolini] in regard to certain named places', but suggested that 'if Signor Mussolini was prepared to collaborate with us in getting tolerable terms, then we might be prepared to discuss Italian demands with him'.

At this point Halifax read out the text of the telegram sent to President Roosevelt as a suggested basis for his message to Mussolini, and also his note about his discussion with Bastianini. The minutes then recorded:

The Prime Minister said that his general comment on the suggested approach to Signor Mussolini was that it implied that if we were prepared to give Germany back her colonies and to make certain concessions in the Mediterranean it was possible for us to get out of our present difficulties. He thought that no such option was open to us. For example, the terms offered would certainly prevent us from completing our re-armament.

Despite this uncompromising statement from Churchill, the minutes record that 'at the same time he did not raise objection to some approach being made to Signor Mussolini'. This can only be explained by his overriding wish not to drive Halifax, and perhaps more importantly, Chamberlain, to resignation. He may also have been concerned that a blunt rejection of the French proposal to approach Mussolini would undermine Reynaud's position with his colleagues.

It should be added that when Chamberlain later that day briefly summarised Churchill's position in his diary, he wrote:

> The PM disliked any move towards Musso. It was incredible that Hitler would consent to any terms that we could accept, though if we could get out of this jam by giving up Malta and Gibraltar and some African colonies he would jump at it. But the only safe way was to convince Hitler that that he couldn't beat us.[14]

Some writers have quoted this brief note to support an allegation that Churchill was willing to surrender Malta and other British Mediterranean possessions to buy Mussolini's goodwill. But both Chamberlain's note and the official record make clear Churchill's view that negotiation with Hitler or Mussolini was not a realistic possibility. The question, therefore, of surrendering territory simply did not arise because Churchill did not expect that Hitler, with French resistance crumbling, could be induced to offer acceptable terms.

Halifax continued by reading the draft of a possible approach to Mussolini that he and Reynaud had prepared after lunch. He explained that Reynaud had wished to name specific places but had been persuaded to omit these. Greenwood again intervened to say that 'Mussolini would be out to get Malta, Gibraltar and Suez', while Chamberlain added that Somaliland, Kenya and Uganda might also be demanded. Halifax then made the clearest statement of his position.

> The Foreign Secretary thought that if we got to the point of discussing the terms of a general settlement and found that we could obtain terms which did not postulate the destruction of our independence, we should be foolish if we did not accept them.

It is not clear from the minutes whether Churchill heard this statement since they record that: 'During the latter part of this discussion the Prime Minister was called out of the room to speak to Sir Roger Keyes.' Admiral Keyes was Churchill's special representative with the Belgian king, Leopold III. The meeting ended with a request that Halifax circulate copies of the draft approach to Mussolini for discussion on the following day.

An invaluable witness of this and later War Cabinet discussions was Sir Alexander Cadogan, the Permanent Secretary at the Foreign Office. He was one of many who kept a detailed diary, despite the enormous pressures, and he wrote of the above meeting:

> Summoned to Admiralty at 5. Found W.S.C., H.[alifax], Neville, Greenwood and Attlee. Discussed situation. W.S.C. seemed to think we might almost be better off if France did pull out and we could concentrate on defence here. Not sure he's right there. He against final appeal, which Reynaud wanted, to Muss. He may be right there. Settled nothing much. W.S.C. much too rambling and romantic and sentimental and temperamental. Old Neville still the best of the lot.[15]

It was now 6.00 p.m. but Churchill's day was far from finished. An hour later the signal to begin Operation 'Dynamo', the Dunkirk evacuation, was sent, and Churchill dined at Admiralty House with Eden and Generals Ironside and Ismay. They then took the painful decision to instruct the British force holding Calais to fight on to the end, without hope of evacuation. Churchill later wrote of this order: 'It involved Eden's own regiment, in which he had long served and fought in the previous struggle. One has to eat and drink in war, but I could not help feeling physically sick as we afterwards sat silent at the table.'[16] The day's final blow came with news from Belgium that King Leopold seemed on the verge of surrender. Towards midnight, Churchill sent a message to him, through Admiral Keyes, urging continued resistance.

At their first meeting on the morning of 27 May, the War Cabinet discussed and approved the paper prepared by the COS about future British strategy should France surrender.[17] This paper, after weighing the possible effects of large-scale German air attack on Great Britain as a prelude to invasion, concluded: 'The real test is whether the morale of our fighting personnel and civil population will counter-balance the numerical and material advantages which Germany enjoys. We believe it will.' The War Cabinet met again at 4.30 p.m. They were joined on this occasion by Sir Archibald Sinclair, the Secretary of State for Air. Churchill had invited him to the meeting since he was the Leader of the Liberal Party. However, he had long been a close friend of Churchill and, during the First World War, Sinclair had been his second in command when Churchill commanded the 6th Battalion of the Royal Scots Fusiliers in France. The War Cabinet ministers had before them Halifax's draft of a 'Suggested Approach to Signor Mussolini'.[18] Although presented as being Reynaud's proposal, most historians regard this paper as indicative of Halifax's views as well. The heart of the draft read as follows:

> If Signor Mussolini will co-operate with us in securing a settlement of all European questions which safeguard the independence and security of the Allies, and could be the basis of a just and durable peace for Europe, we will undertake at once to discuss, with the desire to find solutions, the matters in which Signor Mussolini is primarily interested. We understand that he desires the solution of certain Mediterranean questions; and if he will state in secrecy what these are, France and Great Britain will at once do their best to meet his wishes, on the basis of the co-operation set out above.

Halifax commented that 'it holds out only a very slender chance of success'.

A postscript to the memorandum added two important pieces of information. First, it had been reported from Rome by the British Ambassador, Sir Percy Loraine, that an earlier message from Roosevelt 'had been bitterly resented by Signor Mussolini as unwarrantable interference with Italy's private affairs'. Secondly, and in view of this, Loraine expressed the opinion that 'any further approach to Signor Mussolini would only be interpreted as a sign of weakness and would do no good'. This information considerably undermined the draft proposal but could not have surprised Churchill who, since Mussolini's letter of 18 May, had become convinced that Italy would in due course enter the war on the German side. Halifax also told his colleagues that, since the memorandum had been written, he had received a request from the French Ambassador in London, M. Corbin, that any proposal should have 'geographical precision'. Halifax had told Corbin that the War Cabinet was unlikely to agree to this.

The discussion that afternoon was long and, at times, heated, as other accounts make clear, and the Cabinet Secretary must have had some difficulty in constructing the minutes. Chamberlain began by saying that 'the proposed French approach to Signor Mussolini would serve no useful purpose'. Attlee then commented that the 'suggested approach would be of no practical effect and would be very damaging to us', and this was echoed by Sinclair who added that 'the suggestion that we were prepared to barter away pieces of British territory would have a deplorable effect'. Greenwood, too, was now opposed to the proposal. 'If it got out,' he argued, 'that we had sued for terms at the cost of ceding British territory the consequences would be terrible ... It would be heading for disaster to go any further with these approaches.' Fortified by these statements Churchill then spoke at length, repeating and reinforcing the arguments he had voiced at the earlier meetings. As the minutes recorded:

> The Prime Minister said that he was increasingly oppressed with the futility of the suggested approach to Signor Mussolini which the latter would certainly regard with contempt ... Further, the approach would ruin the integrity of our fighting position in this country. Even if we did not include geographical precision and mentioned no names, everybody would know what we had in mind. The best help we could give to M. Reynaud was to let him feel that, whatever happened to France, we were going to fight it out to the end ... Let us therefore avoid being dragged down the slippery slope with France.

With opposition to his plans clearly mounting, Halifax made a vigorous attempt to defend himself. 'He was,' the minutes recorded, 'conscious of certain rather profound differences of points of view which he would like to make clear ... He could not recognise any resemblance between the action which he proposed, and the suggestion that we were suing for terms and following a line which would lead us to disaster.' Halifax then protested that Churchill had changed his position.

> In the discussion on the previous day he had asked the Prime Minister whether, if he was satisfied that matters vital to the independence of this country were unaffected, he would be prepared to discuss terms. The Prime Minister had said that he would be thankful to get out of our present difficulties on such terms, provided we retain the essentials and elements of our vital strength, even at the cost of some cession of territory. On the present occasion, however, the Prime Minister seemed to suggest that under no conditions would he contemplate any course except fighting to a finish. The issue was probably academic, since we were unlikely to receive any offer which would not come up against the fundamental conditions which were essential to us. If, however, it was possible to obtain a settlement which did not impair these conditions he, for his part, doubted if he would be able to accept the view now put forward by the Prime Minister.

To this unequivocal statement the minutes record Churchill as having responded in the following way:

> The Prime Minister said that he thought that the issue which the War Cabinet was called upon to settle was difficult enough without getting involved in the discussion of an issue which was quite unreal and most

unlikely to arise. If Herr Hitler was prepared to make peace on the terms of the restoration of German colonies and the overlordship of central Europe, that was one thing. But it was quite unlikely that that he would make any such offer.

Halifax then asked Churchill whether, if Hitler offered terms to France and Britain, he would be prepared to consider them. To this Churchill replied that he would not join France in seeking terms, but, if told what they were, would be prepared to consider them. But what if, Chamberlain enquired, Hitler were to say, 'I am here. Let them send a delegate to Paris'? The Secretary then wrote: 'The War Cabinet thought that the answer to such an offer could only be "No".'

At the end of this meeting, Churchill and Halifax had a further conversation in the garden of No. 10. There is no record of what was said, but that evening Halifax noted in his diary:

> Winston talked the most frightful rot, also Greenwood, and after bearing it for some time I said exactly what I thought of them, adding that if that was really their view, and if it came to the point, our ways must separate. Winston, surprised and mellowed, and when I repeated the same thing in the garden, was full of apologies and affection. But it does drive me to despair when he works himself up into a passion of emotion when he ought to make his brain think and reason.[19]

That same evening John Colville, one of Churchill's Private Secretaries, wrote in his diary: 'The Cabinet are feverishly considering our ability to carry on the war alone in such circumstances, and there are signs that Halifax is being defeatist. He says that our aim can no longer be to crush Germany but rather to preserve our own integrity and independence.'[20] Cadogan's diary also recorded these events:

> After the afternoon Cabinet H. asked W.S.C. to come out into the garden with him. H. said to me 'I can't work with Winston any longer.' I said, 'Nonsense: his rhodomontades probably bore you as much as they do me, but don't do anything silly under the stress of that.' H. came to have tea in my room after. Said he had spoken to W., who of course had been v. affectionate! I said I hoped he really wouldn't give way to an annoyance to which we were all subject and that, before he did anything, he would consult Neville. He said that of course he would and that, as I knew, he wasn't one to take hasty decisions.[21]

The rush of events allowed no respite. At 10.00 p.m. that day, the War Cabinet met once more to hear from the Prime Minister that King Leopold had decided to surrender the Belgian Army. At their next meeting on the following morning Churchill confirmed that Belgian resistance had ceased at dawn. By then the Dunkirk evacuation had only just begun and no more than about 15,000 troops had reached England. The Belgian surrender made further evacuation more hazardous and it seemed inevitable that the greater part of the BEF would be lost. After lunch Churchill went down to the House to tell Members about the Belgian capitulation and the position of the BEF. 'The House,' he warned, 'should prepare itself for hard and heavy tidings.' But he went on to say: 'I have only to add that nothing which may happen in this battle can in any way relieve us of our duty to defend the world cause to which we have vowed ourselves.'[22]

While at the House of Commons, Churchill convened a further meeting of the War Cabinet at 4.00 p.m. to consider a renewed French request for a joint approach to Mussolini. It will not be necessary to deal with this further discussion in detail since by this time all of the Ministers had made up their minds on this matter. However, the minutes record one further mention of Malta. Chamberlain said that 'there could be no question of our making concessions to Italy while the war continued. The concessions which it was contemplated we might have to make, e.g. in regard to Malta and Gibraltar, would have to be part of a general settlement with Germany.' Halifax alone continued to argue in favour of an approach to Mussolini, saying that he 'still did not see what there was in the French suggestion of trying out the possibilities of mediation which the Prime Minister felt so wrong'. Chamberlain argued that the French proposal was unlikely to produce an offer from Mussolini or Hitler worth considering, but urged that a moderate reply should be sent to Reynaud 'so that France did not give up the struggle'. For their part, Churchill and the other members were now convinced that even the suggestion of negotiations would fatally undermine British morale.

The meeting adjourned at 6.00 p.m. so that Churchill could address twenty-five other Ministers of Cabinet rank whom he had scarcely seen since they took office. In his memoirs, Churchill later recalled what happened after he had, 'quite casually', said to Ministers, 'Of course, whatever happens at Dunkirk, we shall fight on':

> There occurred a demonstration which, considering the character of the gathering – twenty-five experienced politicians and Parliament men, who represented all the different points of view, whether right or wrong, before the war – surprised me. Quite a number seemed to jump up from the table and come running to my chair, shouting and patting me on the back. There is no doubt that had I at this juncture faltered at all in the leading of the nation I should have been hurled out of office.[23]

Churchill repeated this to his colleagues when the War Cabinet meeting reconvened at 7.00 p.m. after which Halifax finally gave up his stubborn advocacy of an approach to Mussolini. It only remained to agree a reply to Reynaud which would not appear too harsh at a time when the French Premier faced growing opposition in his own Cabinet. The final text of the lengthy message, based on a draft by Churchill amended by Chamberlain and Halifax, was telephoned to Paris shortly before midnight on 28 May and Churchill reprinted the whole of this in his memoirs.[24] In view of the German victories, Churchill doubted whether Mussolini would have any influence with Hitler and he also drew attention to Mussolini's angry rejection of President Roosevelt's telegram. He then went on:

> Therefore, without excluding the possibility of an approach to Signor Mussolini at some time, we cannot feel that this would be the right moment, and I am bound to add that in my opinion the effect on the morale of our people, which is now firm and resolute, would be extremely dangerous. You yourself can best judge what would be the effect in France.

With this message, the long drawn-out discussion about whether to join France in an approach to Mussolini finally came to an end. When, several days later, the French government made a unilateral offer of territorial concessions to Mussolini, the offer was rejected. As Ciano explained to the French Ambassador: 'Mussolini was not interested in recovering any French territories by peaceful negotiation. He had decided to make war on France.'[25]

From this extended account of these four War Cabinet debates in late May 1940, several conclusions can be drawn. In the first place, once the War Cabinet felt that it must consider the French request for an approach to Mussolini, involving some kind of territorial concessions in the Mediterranean, the status of Malta was bound to come up. By themselves the French had little with which to tempt the dictator. Concessions on the Italian-French border or in Tunisia would not be sufficient. Mussolini's eyes had long been fixed on Malta, Gibraltar and Suez, and this explains why the French government so insistently sought British participation in an approach to Mussolini. In these circumstances, some offer about the status of Malta was, in their view, essential. Hence, during the War Cabinet discussions, Malta was mentioned on several occasions and was always at the back of Ministers' minds. Nevertheless, it is clear that the fundamental issue that was debated at such length in the War Cabinet was not which territories might be offered to Mussolini as an inducement to initiate peace negotiations, but whether it was sensible to make any approach to him.

In the second place, the minutes of these tense meetings make quite it clear that it was only Halifax who steadily pressed for a joint Anglo-French approach to Mussolini, although he resisted the French request to name specific territories. The underlying purpose of such an approach was, in Halifax's mind, to explore the possibility of a negotiated settlement with Hitler. In his biography of Churchill, Roy Jenkins characterised Halifax's position as 'the equivalent of a second Munich twenty months after the first'.[26] When, after his discussions in London on 26 May, Reynaud returned to Paris he told his colleagues that only Halifax understood the situation. Chamberlain's at times ambivalent comments are best understood in the light of his statement that it was 'right to talk out [the problem] from every point of view'. At times he spoke in support of Halifax, worried about the effect on Reynaud's position of an outright rejection of the French request. Later, however, he accepted the force of Churchill's argument that any suggestion of seeking to negotiate would be fatal to British morale. Attlee, Greenwood and Sinclair, although they spoke less often, fully supported Churchill almost from the beginning.

Churchill's position was undeniably difficult, quite apart from the strain imposed by the mounting catastrophe in France. Only fifteen days earlier he had replaced Chamberlain at a time when the latter had clearly preferred that Halifax, his Foreign Secretary since Eden's resignation in February 1938, succeed him as Prime Minister. Although Churchill had served Chamberlain loyally as First Lord of the Admiralty since September 1939, he had prior to that been Chamberlain's fiercest critic. If, therefore, Churchill's wishes were to prevail, it was essential to gain Chamberlain's agreement. As Roy Jenkins expressed it, Churchill 'had little option but to play for time – and for Chamberlain'.[27] An additional complication was the need to support Reynaud up to the point where Britain's own safety and survival were imperilled. Hence the dispatch of RAF fighter squadrons to France over the protests of Air Chief Marshal Sir Hugh Dowding, C-in-C Fighter Command. But were Reynaud to feel let down by Britain and lose heart, Pétain and French surrender lay ahead.

On both counts Churchill was initially bound to allow Halifax to develop the arguments for his preferred policy. Churchill could and did express his doubts and fears about such a policy, but could not forbid discussion of it. Whether his allowing the debate on this policy to continue so long suggests that Churchill might have had some initial sympathy for Halifax's position is difficult to judge. Halifax certainly thought so since on 27 May he accused the Prime Minister of having changed his position. But had he done so? Churchill was already convinced by Mussolini's blunt letter of 18 May – and the growing evidence of Italian military preparations examined earlier in this chapter – that Italy would soon join the war on Germany's side. It is much more likely that, as he sensed that his opposition to any approach to Mussolini was gaining Chamberlain's support, Churchill need no longer go along, however reluctantly, with a policy in which he had never believed. For Chamberlain and, if possible, Halifax must be convinced by logical argument that an approach to Mussolini and Hitler was not merely futile but dangerous, and this is what Churchill achieved in the course of these tense discussions. As Kershaw has concluded: 'The other members of the War Cabinet, most notably Chamberlain, were ultimately brought behind the Prime Minister's position, rather than that of Halifax, because Churchill had the better arguments.'[28]

As the crisis deepened, Churchill seemed to gain strength, and his determination to fight on is evident not only in these secret discussions but also in his statements to Parliament and to Cabinet Ministers. His subsequent speeches and broadcasts made this known to the wider world. There would be no negotiations, no concessions involving Malta or other British territories, no surrender. As he had told his ministerial colleagues: 'Whatever happens at Dunkirk, we shall fight on.'

ITALY DECLARES WAR

The Cabinet watch with constant attention the resolute defence which your garrison and the people of Malta are making of that famous fortress and Island.

Churchill to General Dobbie, 23 June 1940

On 28 May 1940, the day on which Churchill brought to a conclusion the debates about Halifax's proposal to seek negotiations with Mussolini and Hitler, Churchill sent a minute to General Ismay for consideration by the Chiefs of Staff. This was entitled, 'Policy in the Mediterranean'.[1] In the midst of all his other concerns he had reflected on Admiral Cunningham's telegram of 23 May, which has been noted in the previous chapter, about his plans in the Mediterranean should Italy become an enemy. Churchill thought that a more aggressive policy should be adopted. After urging early action to test the quality of the Italian naval and air forces, he went on:

> The purely defensive strategy proposed by the C-in-C Mediterranean ought not to be accepted, unless it is found that the fighting qualities of the Italians are high. It will be much better that the Fleet at Alexandria should sally forth and run some risks than that it should remain in a posture so markedly defensive. Risks must be run at this juncture in all theatres.
>
> I presume the Admiralty have a plan in the event of France becoming neutral.

Before we examine the response of the COS and the Admiralty to this minute, we should briefly recount events in France in order to place the Mediterranean discussions in their proper context. Wednesday 29 May was the turning point in the Dunkirk evacuation. Despite Gort's anxiety that further escape might prove impossible, 47,000 troops were lifted on that day and night from Dunkirk and the surrounding beaches, 53,800 on 30 May, 68,000 on 31 May, and 64,000 on 1 June. By the end of

Operation 'Dynamo' on 4 June, 338,226 troops had crossed to England, including 125,000 French troops. This totally unexpected achievement was naturally greeted with a feeling of enormous relief, although, as Churchill warned the House, 'wars are not won by evacuations'.[2] Understandable relief was soon tempered by the realisation that, as the German panzer divisions refitted and regrouped, the final battles in France could not long be delayed. On 31 May, Churchill, for the third time, flew to France in an attempt to instil some of his courage and determination into the French leadership. The final German assault began on 5 June.

On 29 May, the COS discussed the Prime Minister's minute, 'Policy in the Mediterranean'.[3] Their view was that Italian air superiority in the area would compel the British forces to adopt an essentially defensive strategy while being alert to opportunities for attack. They referred the matter to the Joint Planning Committee (JPC) for further study, and the JPC came to a similar conclusion. 'The C-in-C Mediterranean,' they reported, 'appreciates the advantages of vigorous offensive action but as a result of war experience up to date it is considered inadvisable to expose important units of the Fleet to a heavy scale of air attack unless escorted by fighters.'[4] The Chiefs approved this and authorised the dispatch of signals to the Middle East C-in-Cs.

Accordingly, Admiral Pound sent a signal to Admiral Cunningham at Alexandria asking for additional information about 'his exact dispositions and intended movements'. However, he supplemented this signal with another private one which stated:

> You will be surprised, I think, to receive the telegram I sent to you, it having been suggested that the policy you outlined was defensive. I told the Prime Minister he need have no fears that you would act on the defensive, but he insisted that some telegrams should be sent to all Cs-in-C. I hope you find my telegram inoffensive.[5]

Cunningham responded by saying that he had indeed 'been rather taken aback by your signal about the defensive object'. He also expressed some concern about Malta: 'I don't know how Malta would react to aerial bombardment coupled with parachute troops and other aerial visitors.' However, in his formal reply to Pound's request for additional information he signalled that, upon the beginning of hostilities, 'it is intended that a strong force including battleships should proceed westwards at first, countering Italian action on Malta or in other directions'. His signal continued:

> Should Malta be subjected to seaborne attack it is intended to move with the whole Fleet to its relief. An attack on Port Augusta may be best

method of affording relief to Malta, but it is hoped to test out the enemy's air and submarine strength before operations so close off his coast.

If and when adequate reconnaissance has been established, working from Tunisia or Malta, it may be possible to keep a force of cruisers and destroyers in the central area almost permanently to prey on Libyan traffic. They would use Malta or a Greek island for fuelling at night.[6]

In his post-war memoirs, Cunningham, assuming correctly that Churchill had prompted Pound's signal, criticised such 'prodding' messages. He wrote: 'Such messages to those who were doing their utmost with straitened resources were not an encouragement, merely an annoyance.'[7] We shall see other interchanges between the Prime Minister and the C-in-C Mediterranean in later chapters, but it is worth noticing here a subsequent comment by John Colville, one of Churchill's Private Secretaries. He believed that Cunningham was the only senior British commander who was 'impervious to Churchill's spell'.[8] This may have been due, in part at least, to Cunningham's being based at Alexandria, which prevented any direct personal contact with the Prime Minister.

While this interchange of naval signals was taking place, the problem of the vulnerability of Malta to attack had been raised in two further reports. On 29 May, the Deputy Chiefs of Staff (DCOS) considered a paper that reported the views of General Dobbie about the deficiencies he had found in Malta's defences after his arrival. They were extensive. AA guns were still far short of requirements, the absence of fighters was 'the real danger', and the infantry available was 'very stretched'. None of this was any surprise to the DCOS, but they could only record that 'owing to the urgent commitments at home, and the threat of invasion, it would not be possible to meet any of the requests for additional defences for Malta'.[9]

The JIC had also been reviewing developments, and on 29 May presented a further paper to the COS in which they attempted an assessment of 'Possible Military Courses Open to Italy'.[10] They thought that the British and French fleets would be the principal Italian targets, but that Malta, too, would suffer attack. 'The object of an Italian attack on Malta,' they wrote, 'would be to neutralise its value as a naval base and to achieve a spectacular success; Gozo is undefended. A sudden attack by airborne troops is highly probable.' The information that lay behind these judgements was not specified and it was not until the publication in 1979 of the official history of British wartime Intelligence that light was shed on British knowledge of Italian war preparations. But before considering this it will be useful to examine what Italian plans actually were.[11]

The commitment that Mussolini gave to Hitler at their meeting at the Brenner Pass on 18 March has been mentioned in the previous chapter. On 31 March, he issued an initial strategic directive to the Italian armed services chiefs and overruled the numerous protests they made about the state of their respective services. Mussolini expected Italy's involvement in the war to be a short one. As he told Marshal Badoglio on 26 May: 'I assure you the war will be over in September, and that I need a few thousand dead so as to be able to attend the peace conference as a belligerent.' On 30 May, Count Ciano wrote in his diary: 'The decision has been taken. The die is cast. Today Mussolini gave me the communication he has sent to Hitler about our entry into the war. The date chosen is June 5th, unless Hitler himself considers it convenient to postpone it for some days.'[12] Hitler, however, requested a short delay and the Italian declaration of war was then set for 10 June. Meanwhile, Mussolini's vague directives had caused considerable confusion. Admiral Cavagnari, the naval chief, whose two new battleships were not yet ready for sea, rejected any idea of an attack on Malta, which was, he said, 'bristling with weapons of all kinds'. General Pricolo, the air force chief, thought that Yugoslavia was to be his first objective, and it was not until 5 June that he deployed his bombers to Sicily for an attack on Malta.

Although the JIC had no knowledge of the messages sent by Mussolini and Hitler to each other, they had accumulated mounting evidence of Italian preparations.[13] Numerous military signals revealed the movement of troops, aircraft and naval ships, while fragments of diplomatic intercepts helped to build up a picture of Italian preparations. For example, Italian students in London were urged to return home, and consular officials in British colonies were instructed to destroy their cipher books. Two RAF photo-reconnaissance Spitfires were flown to Toulon and in the early weeks of June photographed much of the central Mediterranean. On 7 June, the arrival of 122 Italian bombers in Sicily became known. However, despite this threat of bombing raids on Malta, there was no evidence of a build-up of troops in Sicily or southern Italy that might have suggested an invasion attempt. Nor was there any indication that the necessary transports and landing ships were being assembled in Italian ports. Only the date of Italy's intervention in the war remained in doubt, but the Admiralty judged that this was likely to fall between 10 and 20 June and advised Cunningham accordingly.

Although in the early days of June Churchill's thoughts were principally directed towards the deepening crisis in France, he was well aware of the growing dangers in the Mediterranean. The reports of the COS and the service departments, and also of the JIC, would have been contained in his black boxes and, perhaps, some of the decrypts in his buff box. He was, therefore, well-briefed on the Mediterranean position when he visited Paris again on 31 May to attend a lengthy meeting of the Supreme War Council.[14] Most of the discussion, inevitably, concerned the Dunkirk evacuation, then only just begun, and the preparations to meet the impending German attack on the Somme. However, later in the meeting, Italian intentions received some attention. 'The British view,' Churchill declared, 'was that if Italy came in against the Allies we should strike her at once in the most effective manner.' He then asked Reynaud to authorise the basing of four heavy RAF bomber squadrons on southern French airfields in order to make an immediate counter-attack on the north Italian cities. Reynaud, conscious of the danger of retaliatory attacks on French cities, agreed, but according to General Spears, who was at the meeting, 'only after a fractional hesitation during which I imagined he was considering the effect of this policy on his Italophile colleagues'.[15] Admiral Darlan, Chief of Staff of the French Navy, added that the French Admiralty had plans to bombard Italian ports between Genoa and Naples.

After Churchill had returned to London following this critical meeting, during which, as he later admitted, the attitude of Marshal Pétain, 'detached and sombre, gave me the feeling that he would face a separate peace',[16] the British Ambassador, Sir Ronald Campbell, telegraphed to Lord Halifax. He reported that the Prime Minister 'had handled the French magnificently', and continued:

At the end of the Supreme War Council meeting he made the most magnificent peroration on the implacable will of the British people to fight on to the bitter end, and to go down fighting rather than succumb to bondage. M. Reynaud responded in the same vein but one felt that it came rather from his head than his heart.[17]

That same evening Hugh Dalton, Minister for Economic Warfare, wrote in his diary: 'The King says he has to remind Winston that he is only PM in England and not in France as well.'[18]

The expected Italian declaration of war came on the afternoon of 10 June, to be effective at midnight. Ciano described in his diary his meetings with the French Ambassador, M. François-Poncet, and then with Sir Percy Loraine. He then wrote: 'Mussolini speaks from the balcony of the Palazzo Venezia. The news of the war does not surprise anyone and does not arouse very much enthusiasm. I am sad, very sad. The adventure begins. May God help Italy.'[19] In London, Churchill was woken from his usual afternoon nap to be told the news. His only comment, as the RAF prepared to bomb Italy, was: 'People who go to Italy to look at ruins won't have to go as far as Naples and Pompeii in future.'[20] Later that night, Churchill listened to President Roosevelt's radio broadcast in which he said, with anger and contempt: 'On this 10th day of June 1940 the hand that held the dagger has struck it into the back of its neighbour.'[21] On the afternoon of 11 June, as the first bombs fell on Malta, Churchill made his fourth visit to France, on this occasion to Briare, following the withdrawal of the

French government to Tours. Mention was made earlier of the intention to bomb north Italian targets if Italy declared war on the Allies, and for this purpose four RAF bomber squadrons had been flown to the south of France. However, while he was at Briare, Churchill learned that the local French authorities, fearful of Italian reprisals, had ignored orders issued by Reynaud and had placed vehicles on the runways to prevent take-off.

In the middle of June, a tide of defeat, military, political and moral, swept over and finally engulfed the government of Paul Reynaud. A fifth flight by Churchill to Tours on 13 June, a desperate appeal to President Roosevelt, and a final offer of an Anglo-French Union were all to no avail against the defeatism of Marshal Pétain and General Weygand. Churchill had planned to make a further visit to France on 16 June and had already boarded a train at Waterloo when word was received that Reynaud had cancelled the meeting. That evening Reynaud resigned and Pétain at once sought armistice terms from Hitler. Only General De Gaulle escaped from the wreckage of the Third Republic, unexpectedly boarding an RAF aircraft at Bordeaux on the morning of 17 June. In Churchill's words, 'De Gaulle carried with him, in this small aeroplane, the honour of France.'[22] Churchill was later to speculate on what might have happened had he been able to meet the French ministers on 17 June. The margin by which Reynaud

2. One of the many heavy air raids carried out on Valletta. It would become one of the most heavily bombed cities in the Second World War.

was defeated was so narrow that Churchill thought that he and his British colleagues might have tipped the balance. 'It seems to me probable,' he wrote, 'that we should have uplifted and converted the defeatists round the table, or left them in a minority or even under arrest.'[23] This seems unlikely; the cancer of defeat had spread too far.

During these desperate days, Churchill had little time to think of events in Malta, nor, indeed, was there anything he could then do to alleviate the suffering caused by the Italian bombing attacks on the island. However, as Pétain sought negotiations with Hitler, a vital question arose which had profound implications for the security of Malta. The British government had only released the French government from its obligation not to seek a separate peace on condition that the French fleet was sailed to French overseas, British or American ports. Churchill repeated this vital condition to Pétain after Reynaud's resignation. However, Admiral Darlan, who had become Minister of Marine in Pétain's government, while assuring Churchill that he would never allow his fleet to fall into German hands, refused to order the French ships to leave French waters. Since all of the Admiralty's plans for the security of the Mediterranean and the defeat of the Italian fleet were founded upon collaboration between British and French fleets, the removal of the French force, and the possibility of its falling into German hands, required a new Mediterranean strategy. The Admiralty at once began the assembly of a naval force at Gibraltar under the command of Admiral Sir James Somerville, and this was later designated as Force H. However, the position of the Mediterranean Fleet at Alexandria then gave rise to an unexpected controversy.

In his post-war memoirs Churchill wrote: 'The Admiralty's first thoughts contemplated the abandonment of the Eastern Mediterranean and concentration at Gibraltar.' He added that he resisted this policy which 'seemed to spell the doom of Malta', and concluded: 'It was resolved to fight it out at both ends.'[24] Behind these brief comments lay a debate that deserves closer examination. On 16 June, on the eve of Reynaud's resignation, Admiral Pound sent a lengthy warning signal to Admiral Cunningham at Alexandria. He pointed out that, if the French fleet surrendered, the protection of British Atlantic convoys might require the withdrawal of the Mediterranean Fleet to Gibraltar. The case for such a move would be even stronger if Spain were to enter the war on Germany's side. Pound acknowledged the 'strong political and military objections to moving the Fleet from the Eastern Mediterranean', and told Cunningham that the government had not reached a decision on the matter.[25]

On the following morning, Pound circulated to the COS a draft memorandum which had been prepared by the Admiralty's Director of Plans. This argued that, while based at Alexandria, the Mediterranean Fleet could not prevent the Italian fleet attacking the Atlantic trade route.

Moreover, since repair facilities at Alexandria were limited, the Fleet would become a 'wasting asset'. The report concluded:

> It is, therefore, considered that since the recent deterioration in the general situation has rendered our position in the Near and Middle East such that the presence of a fleet in the Eastern Mediterranean can do little to buttress it, we must now take more fully into account the requirements of naval strategy and, therefore, recommend the withdrawal of the Eastern Mediterranean Fleet to Gibraltar as soon as it is apparent that French control of the Western Mediterranean is about to be lost to us.[26]

After some unrecorded discussion the COS referred the question to the JPC with instructions to 'report, as a matter of urgency, on the military implications of the proposed Fleet movement'.[27]

By then, however, Churchill had been made aware of this proposal, and he at once sent a minute to the First Lord, A. V. Alexander. After approving certain proposed ship movements, including the sailing of HMS *Hood* and *Ark Royal* to Gibraltar, the minute continued:

> It is of the utmost importance that the fleet at Alexandria should remain to cover Egypt from an Italian invasion, which would otherwise destroy prematurely all our position in the East. The fleet is well placed to sustain our interests in Turkey, to guard Egypt and the Canal, and can, if the situation changes, either fight its way westward or go through the Canal to guard the Empire or come round the Cape on to our trade routes.
>
> The position of the Eastern fleet must be constantly watched, and can be reviewed when we know what happens to the French Fleet and whether Spain declares war or not.
>
> Even if Spain declares war it does not follow that we should quit the eastern Mediterranean. If we have to quit Gibraltar we must immediately take the Canaries, which will serve as a good base to control the western entrance to the Mediterranean.[28]

Meanwhile, in Alexandria, Cunningham had been considering Pound's signal and he gave his initial response in a cable of 17 June.[29] After explaining how such a decision could be implemented, he sounded two reservations. First, he warned that, should the fleet leave eastern waters, Egypt could not, in the opinion of the C-in-C Middle East, be held for long. His second concern was for Malta. 'If this move,' he signalled, 'is to take place the question of Malta requires urgent consideration and decision. In my opinion if the Fleet has to leave the Mediterranean the morale of the Maltese will collapse and it is only a question of time before the island falls.' Further analysis and reflection prompted Cunningham to send a second signal on the following day.[30] This more considered reply deserves quoting at greater length. After explaining that he felt that his first reply may have sounded 'somewhat acquiescent', he continued:

2. Although in my opinion it would be practicable to move the faster part of the Fleet westward from Alexandria and the rest through the Suez Canal I feel that the effects of this withdrawal would involve such a landslide in territory and prestige that I earnestly hope that such a decision will never have to be taken.

3. As already pointed out the C-in-C Middle East considers Egypt would be untenable soon after the Fleet's departure, Malta, Cyprus and Palestine could no longer be held, the Moslems would regard it as surrender, prospects of Turkey's loyalty would be discounted and even the Italians would be stirred to activity.

4. I am well aware of the paramount importance of our Atlantic trade and of home defence but I feel that with our present forces we should be able to safeguard these as well as maintaining the Eastern Mediterranean.

5. The Italian Battlefleet has so far shown no signs of life and from all the signs available here it does not appear that the Italians are yet considering serious fighting. I consider the battleships now here are sufficient to contain the Italian heavy ships with something in hand and when required the route to Malta could be opened.

However, by the time this signal had been received and deciphered at the Admiralty early on 18 June, Admiral Pound had left for Bordeaux together with A. V. Alexander, First Lord of the Admiralty, and Lord Lloyd, the Colonial Secretary. The purpose of this visit was a final attempt to persuade Admiral Darlan to remove the French fleet to British ports or at least to French overseas ports out of Hitler's reach. The Admiralty was, therefore, represented by Admiral Phillips, the Deputy Chief of Naval Staff (DCNS), when the JPC presented to the COS on 18 June their report on the implications of the withdrawal to Gibraltar of the Mediterranean Fleet.[31] The JPC accepted the force of the purely naval arguments for withdrawal, but offset against these the consequent dangers to Egypt, and emphasised that 'withdrawal would be a sign of weakness. It would give rise to serious internal security problems in Egypt and Iraq.' They concluded, therefore: 'We feel that, at the present moment, the political, economic and military reasons for retaining the Fleet in the eastern Mediterranean outweigh the purely naval reasons for its withdrawal.'

When the COS met on the morning of 18 June to consider this report, they were in some difficulty. In the first place, the advocate of withdrawal, Admiral Pound, was away in Bordeaux and it seemed unwise to decide a major naval policy in the absence of the Chief of the Naval Staff. In the second place, the success or failure of Pound's mission to secure the removal of the French fleet from Hitler's grasp would clearly have a major bearing on the Royal Navy's dispositions. The COS consequently deferred a decision and instructed the JPC to reconsider their recommendations 'when the situation regarding the French Fleet had become more clear'.[32] However, as it became clear that Admiral Darlan would not give the orders that the British government required, events moved rapidly to a tragic climax. The War Cabinet decided that, if the new Pétain government did not accept any of several options presented to them with regard to the powerful French squadron at Oran, the Royal Navy would be ordered to sink those ships. The French government rejected these proposals and, at dusk on 3 July, Force H, commanded by Admiral Somerville, opened fire. All of the French heavy units, except one, were sunk or disabled, and 1,250 French officers and ratings lost their lives. At Alexandria, where a smaller French squadron was based, the French ships were neutralised after difficult but ultimately successful negotiations between Admiral Cunningham and Admiral Godfroy.

While these decisions were being made and implemented, the JPC were instructed to consider and recommend the overall policy to be adopted in Egypt and the Middle East. Their report set out detailed recommendations for the reinforcement of the area, subject only to the overriding necessity to retain forces in the UK to meet a possible invasion attempt. The security of Egypt, they pointed out, depended on naval support, and the draft telegram they submitted stated: 'It is intended to retain the fleet in the Eastern Mediterranean as long as possible.' The COS accepted these recommendations and the policy was signalled to the Middle East C-in-Cs on 3 July, even before the result of the action at Oran had become known.[33]

During the month of June, the face of the war had changed beyond all recognition. The collapse of French military resistance and the fall of the Reynaud government had brought the victorious German forces to the English Channel coast from which the BEF had escaped after the loss of all of its heavy equipment. Churchill's refusal to permit any negotiations with Hitler raised higher the prospect of heavy air attacks upon Great Britain and the likelihood of an invasion attempt. Nevertheless, despite his inevitable preoccupation with events in France, Churchill was not oblivious to the threat posed by Mussolini and the implications of Italian hostility for Britain's position in the Mediterranean and the Middle East. The dictator's long-threatened entry into the war came as no surprise. It was no doubt some relief to the British government and to the Acting-Governor of Malta to learn through intelligence that an invasion of Malta was not being prepared, but this did not alter the fact that the island was poorly equipped to meet the bombing attacks that began on 11 June. But when on 17 June, as Pétain sought armistice terms from Hitler, Admiral Pound proposed the withdrawal of the Mediterranean fleet to Gibraltar, Churchill would not countenance a move which implied the loss of Malta and perhaps Britain's entire position in the Middle East. Supported by the other Chiefs of Staff and by Cunningham at Alexandria, Churchill established the policy of standing firm in the Mediterranean.

What this meant for Malta is the subject of the ensuing chapters. It may, however, be appropriate to end this chapter by quoting the first of many signals that Churchill sent to General Dobbie on 23 June. Churchill had not met Dobbie before he left for Malta in mid-April but he had no doubt read some of the early signals that Dobbie sent to the War Office in May and June. Dobbie's Order of the Day to his command, issued when France fell, may also have been drawn to his attention. This read:

> The decision of H.M.G. to fight on until our enemies are defeated will be heard with the greatest of satisfaction by all ranks of the garrison of Malta. It may be that hard times lie ahead of us, but I know that, however hard they may be, the courage and determination of all ranks will not falter and that, with God's help, we will maintain the security of this fortress. I call on all officers and other ranks humbly to seek God's help, and then, in reliance on Him, to do their duty unflinchingly.[34]

On 23 June, therefore, conscious of the suffering and the many hardships that were bound to fall upon the people and garrison of Malta after Mussolini's declaration of war, Churchill signalled to Dobbie:

> The Cabinet watch with constant attention the resolute defence which your garrison and the people of Malta are making of that famous fortress and Island. I have the conviction that you will make that defence glorious in British military history, and also in the history of Malta itself. You are well fitted to rouse and sustain the spirit of all in enduring severe and prolonged ordeals for a righteous cause.[35]

MALTA REARMED

First in urgency is the reinforcement of Malta.
Churchill to the Chiefs of Staff, 13 October 1940

'In July 1940,' Churchill later recalled, 'I began, as the telegrams and minutes show, to concern myself increasingly about the Middle East,' and added: 'The War Cabinet were determined to defend Egypt against all comers with whatever resources could be spared from the decisive struggle at home.'[1] The 'struggle at home' was indeed approaching a decisive climax in the summer of 1940 and, in order to establish the context for the debates and decisions that affected Malta, a brief account of the German threat to Great Britain must be given.

After the French armistice, German army and air force units were refitted and transferred to bases facing the Channel coast. On 16 July, Hitler issued a directive for the invasion of England, Operation 'Sea Lion', preparations for which were to be completed by mid-August. Churchill's expectation of such an attempt, to be preceded by heavy air attack, governed his thoughts and actions during July and August. During those two months, travelling in a specially equipped train, he spent as many as two days a week inspecting coastal defences, the divisions placed to repel an invasion, and the fighter airfields. The first large-scale bombing raids were launched on 10 July, and they gathered momentum until reaching a climax on 15 September. Churchill spent that day at the underground Operations Room of 11 Group, Fighter Command, where AVM Park, later to become AOC Malta, was controlling the air battle. There he watched quietly while the RAF was stretched almost to breaking point before the enemy aircraft were seen to be returning to France.[2] But the *Luftwaffe*'s losses on that day, and the damage caused by heavy RAF bombing attacks on the invasion fleet assembled in the Channel ports, persuaded Hitler, two days later, to postpone Operation 'Sea Lion' indefinitely. Goering then switched to massive night-time bombing raids on London and, later, on industrial centres and ports.

We have noted in the previous chapter the signal sent out by the COS to their Middle East commanders on 3 July 1940. This began: 'Retention of our position in the Middle East remains of the utmost importance to successful prosecution of the war.' The signal also confirmed, at the Prime Minister's insistence, the intention to retain the Mediterranean Fleet at Alexandria to protect the sea approach to Egypt. Vindication of this decision and confirmation, if any were needed, of Admiral Cunningham's offensive intentions, came seven days later, on 10 July. Cunningham had advanced to the west of Crete with his full force to protect a convoy sailing from Malta to Alexandria when he became aware, from intercepted signals and D/F bearings, that the Italian fleet was also at sea. He at once steered to intercept the enemy fleet off the Calabrian coast of Italy, and his flagship, HMS *Warspite*, hit the Italian battleship *Giulio Cesare* with a 15-inch shell at a range of thirteen miles. The Italian fleet then withdrew under a smoke screen and contact was lost. This indecisive encounter nevertheless established a precedent for naval operations in the Mediterranean, and was soon to lead, as we shall see, to a significant reinforcement of Cunningham's fleet.

While this action was being fought, the COS in London were considering three lengthy documents sent from Malta, each assessing the situation on the island and recommending reinforcement. The first was a letter of 4 July from the Governor, General Dobbie, to the CIGS, General Dill. Attached to this was a copy of a memorandum addressed to the Governor by his Air Force Commander, Air Commodore Maynard. The third document was a telegram from Admiral Ford, the Vice-Admiral Malta, which was a précis of another memorandum sent to General Dobbie. The COS thus had before them the considered views and recommendations of Malta's three senior commanders.[3]

Dobbie's immediate concern was to maintain the morale of the Maltese civilian population, who provided, he reminded London, 44 per cent of the garrison. 'It is,' he wrote, 'the most important factor at the present time, and the subject is never out of my thoughts.' He advised the COS that the bombing had so far caused 230 civilian casualties, including 78 deaths. Sixty of the casualties had been children. He was convinced that the only way to keep up morale was to improve air defences, but he had remaining only three Hurricanes of the handful sent to the island in late June to reinforce the original flight of Gladiators. He went on: 'If we could get a minimum of 50 good fighters, I believe we could ensure that air attack could be kept down to reasonable dimensions, whatever effort Italy would make.' However, airfield defence would require additional AA guns, and he expressed the hope that it might prove possible to send this equipment to Malta on one or two fast merchant ships before Italian air attack intensified.

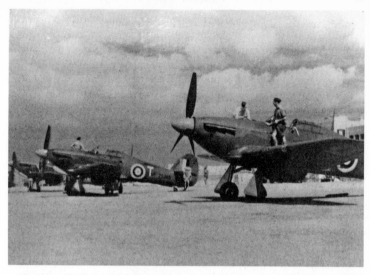

3. Hurricanes being serviced. These fighters were the mainstay of Malta's air defence until the arrival of the first Spitfires in March 1942.

Maynard's memorandum pointed out that Malta's largely defenceless condition offered the Italian air force an easy target, especially after the loss of the French air bases in Tunisia from which attacks on Sicilian airfields had been assumed in pre-war planning. Maynard urged that the four fighter squadrons, which formed part of the Scale B level of rearmament approved in principle in July 1939, would be required to provide effective air defence. In addition, 'to avoid severe aircraft casualties', strong AA reinforcements were also essential. Admiral Ford's views were similar. He, too, laid stress on the dangers to civilian morale and the continued viability of the naval base if the Italian air force could bomb with impunity. Nevertheless, he rejected any idea of abandoning Malta and concluded: 'If Malta is to be held active measures in improving AA defences are imperative. If no action is taken our defences will be imperilled and we shall be courting disaster.'

Churchill soon became aware of these three messages from Malta and, encouraged by Admiral Cunningham's attack on the Italian fleet, he dictated two minutes on 12 July. The first was addressed to the three COS, and the other to the Admiralty since this was largely a naval matter. The ensuing discussions provoked by these minutes overlapped, but it will be convenient to deal with them separately. The minute addressed to the COS had affixed to it a red label, REPORT IN THREE DAYS, and it read in part:

1. The contacts we have had with the Italians encourage the development of a more aggressive campaign against the Italian homeland by bombardment from both air and sea. It also seems most desirable that the Fleet should be able to use Malta more freely. A plan should be prepared to reinforce the air defences of Malta in the strongest manner with A.A. guns of various types and with aeroplanes ... If we could get a stronger air force there we might obtain considerable immunity from annoyance by retaliation.

2. Let a plan for the speediest anti-aircraft reinforcement of Malta be prepared forthwith, and let me have it in three days, with estimates in time. It should be possible to inform Malta to prepare emplacements for the guns before they are sent out.[4]

Even before they received this minute the COS had begun consideration of Dobbie's letter, and the defence of Malta was to appear on the agenda of most of their meetings in the following six months.[5]

ACM Newall, the CAS, told his colleagues that he could make available twelve more Hurricane fighters, and Admiral Pound proposed that these aircraft be flown to Malta from the aircraft carrier HMS *Argus* from a point in the western Mediterranean. The necessary ground crews and stores would be sent to Malta from Gibraltar on two submarines. It was then agreed that twelve more heavy and ten light AA guns were essential as a reinforcement. However, the provision of these guns caused some concern since, as noted earlier, the heavy German air raids on England had just begun and the number of AA guns installed at home was more than 2,500 below the authorised level. The Chiefs were particularly reluctant to make these guns available if they were to be sent on a seven-week voyage around the Cape of Good Hope. The question, therefore, was whether Admiral Pound was prepared to load these guns on a fifteen-knot merchantman and escort it through the western Mediterranean. After much anxious deliberation and consultation with Admiral Cunningham, he decided against such an operation. His view was that 'the chances of the ship getting through were very slight and the heavy forces escorting the vessel would also be dangerously exposed to air bombardment'. The guns, consequently, would need to go around the Cape. Until they arrived, the existing AA guns in Malta were to be redistributed to provide more protection for the airfields. The Secretary was instructed to advise Churchill accordingly. Attached to this report of 16 July from General Ismay in Churchill's Malta files is a handwritten note, which reads: 'PM saw this, & subsequently discussed it with First Sea Lord & Gen. Ismay.'[6] The meaning of this becomes clear when we turn to Churchill's second minute of 12 July addressed to the Admiralty. This carried an ACTION THIS DAY label:

I thought that *Illustrious* might well go to the Mediterranean and exchange with *Ark Royal*. In this case *Illustrious* could take perhaps a good lot of Hurricanes to Malta. As we have a number of Hurricanes surplus at the moment, could not the Malta Gladiator pilots fly the Hurricanes themselves? This would not diminish our flying strength in this country.[7]

As requested, Pound replied later that day. He explained the difficult conditions under which the Mediterranean Fleet and Force H operated when without fighter protection, and then continued:

At the moment we are faced with the immediate problem of getting aircraft and A.A. guns to Malta and aircraft to Alexandria. I am not at all certain that the risk of passing a ship with all these available stores through the Mediterranean is not too great, and that it might not be better to accept the delay of sending her round the Cape.

As we have already seen, Pound, several days later, made up his mind that the western passage was too dangerous for a merchant ship and its naval escort. However, this response, coupled with a suggestion that the Mediterranean situation might need reconsideration, prompted a further severe minute from Churchill on 15 July.[8] This began: 'I do not understand what is meant by "reviewing the whole Mediterranean situation". It is now three weeks since I vetoed the proposal to evacuate the Eastern Mediterranean and bring Admiral Cunningham's fleet to Gibraltar. I hope there will be no return to that project.' He then dwelt at some length upon the dangers to warships of air attack, which, although played down by the Admiralty before the war, he now thought to be exaggerated. 'From time to time and for sufficient objects,' he argued, 'this risk will have to be faced.' He then continued:

It becomes of high and immediate importance to build up a very strong anti-aircraft defence at Malta, and to base several squadrons of our best fighter aircraft there. This will have to be done under the fire of the enemy ... The urgent first consignment should reach Malta at the earliest moment ... The immense delay involved in passing these ships round the Cape cannot be accepted.

In writing of the dangers of air attack, Churchill touched upon one of the major uncertainties of the early war years. Fears of a widespread collapse in civilian morale under bombing had already proved misplaced. Dobbie was not alone in reporting from Malta: 'So far the morale of the people has been surprisingly good.' The people of London and other cities were soon to provide similar surprises. As regards air attack on warships at sea, the Admiralty was in two minds. Despite the improvement of naval AA defences, and the construction of specialised AA cruisers, there remained great uncertainty about the threat posed by the Italian air force to the Mediterranean Fleet. Pound's decision in July not to risk merchantmen with naval escort in the central Mediterranean was undoubtedly influenced by Cunningham's experience after the battle off the Calabrian coast. He wrote to Pound at length about the heavy bombing to which the fleet had been subjected when returning to Alexandria without fighter protection. He told him that he had been attacked all the way back by Italian bombers based in Cyrenaica and the Dodecanese Islands: 'Literally we have had to fight our way back to Alexandria against air attack.' He continued: 'We are well able to look after the Italian Fleet, but I doubt if we can tackle the Air Force as well.'[9] It was clearly with Cunningham's experience in mind that Pound resolutely resisted the full force of Churchill's pressure for the reinforcement of Malta through the Mediterranean.

These protracted and difficult discussions, prompted by Dobbie's letter and Churchill's minutes, had led to critical decisions that marked the beginning of the rearmament of Malta. The additional twelve Hurricanes promised by ACM Newall were flown to Malta from HMS *Argus* on 2 August, and this set a pattern for further flights to the island, as we shall see. The urgent need for more AA guns had been accepted, although the first batch of twenty-two was sent round the Cape. Moreover, on 23 July, General Dill was able to tell the COS that a further twenty-two guns had been earmarked for Malta. In the wider Middle East context, Admiral Pound, putting aside his earlier doubts, signalled to Cunningham on 15 July confirming the government's policy of maintaining the Mediterranean Fleet at Alexandria, and asking what reinforcements he required. Cunningham replied at length on the following day, requesting an additional modernised and radar-equipped battleship, HMS *Valiant*, an additional aircraft carrier, HMS *Illustrious*, and two more cruisers.[10] Asked how these ships should be sent out to join him, he replied: 'By carrying out a concerted movement it should be possible to pass reinforcements through the Mediterranean.'

With this reply the Admiralty staff began the planning of Operation 'Hats', and this was successfully carried out between 30 August and 5 September. Pound refused to sail, together with the warships, any merchantmen carrying AA equipment for Malta and tank reinforcements for Egypt. However, he did agree that *Valiant* and the cruisers should call in at Malta to deliver eight heavy, and ten light AA guns and related ammunition and supplies. In addition, Cunningham, when sailing from Alexandria to meet the reinforcements, escorted to Malta a small convoy of a tanker and two merchant ships loaded with ammunition, fuel and other supplies. In the House of Commons on 5 September, Churchill, in a speech on the war situation, told Members all about Operation 'Hats'. 'Some of our great ships,' he said, 'touched at Malta on the way, and carried a few things that were needed by those valiant islanders and their garrison, who, under a remarkably resolute Governor, General Dobbie, are maintaining themselves with the utmost constancy.'[11]

It will be necessary now to retrace our steps in order to examine the consequences for Malta of another decision Churchill took in July. On the tenth day of that month he suggested to the Cabinet Secretary, Sir Edward Bridges, that 'it would be well to set up a small standing Ministerial Committee to consult together upon the conduct of the war in the Middle East, and to advise me, as Minister of Defence, upon the recommendations I should make to the Cabinet.'[12] The committee was duly established with Anthony Eden, then Secretary of State of War, as Chairman. The other members were L. S. Amery, Secretary of State for India, and Lord Lloyd, the Colonial Secretary. This committee held ten meetings between 15 July and 8 October before changing circumstances brought its meetings to an end.[13]

At the committee's meeting on 25 July, the COS briefed Ministers on the steps that had been approved to strengthen the defences of Malta, and stress was laid on the importance attached to the use of the island as a fleet base. Malta was also the focus of the committee's attention at a subsequent meeting on 12 August. After Group Captain Wigglesworth for the Air Staff had explained that a number of US-built Glen Martin Maryland long-range reconnaissance aircraft would shortly be based at Malta, Lord Lloyd enquired 'if it was contemplated that Malta would be developed as a base for offensive operations'. The committee favoured this idea although Wigglesworth at once pointed out that retaliatory Italian air attacks might soon put Malta's four airfields out of action. Nevertheless, the committee thought that the Prime Minister should be invited to instruct the COS to look further into the matter, and when General Ismay put this to him, he minuted, 'Yes it is most important.'[14]

The Air Staff undertook the study of this matter since the first thought was that Malta might be used as a base for bombing raids on the Italian mainland. However, the Air Staff were strongly opposed to this. Not only, they argued, were the necessary bombers lacking, given the priority attached to raids on Germany and the reinforcement of Egypt, but they feared that raids on Italian targets would bring down heavy retaliation. This might put out of action the all-weather airfield at Luqa, which was vital to the staging of bomber reinforcements to the Middle East. When this paper was considered by the COS on 23 August, Vice-Admiral Phillips, the VCNS, added that the Navy also wished to use Malta for offensive operations but could not consider doing so while the island's defences were still so weak.

This discussion provoked a flurry of memoranda and consultations, to which Churchill contributed with a minute of 27 August in which he stated that 'we must regard the air defence of Malta as of the very first priority'.[15] The upshot of all this was a decision to establish at Malta by April 1941 the full Scale B of 112 heavy and 60 light AA guns. Until then offensive operations from the island would be restricted. A decision to base four fighter squadrons there was also taken, but only 'as soon as circumstances permit', a condition imposed by the losses being suffered in the Battle of Britain, which was then at its peak. In a lengthy signal, Admiral Cunningham agreed that, under such protection, he should be able to base at Valletta a force of cruisers and destroyers, and also provide a flotilla of submarines.[16]

A further complication stemming from the weak defences of Malta arose in mid-September. On 13 September, Marshal Graziani, after being threatened by Mussolini with dismissal, began the invasion of Egypt advancing slowly with a force of six divisions. This had long been anticipated, and General Wavell's considerably smaller force, still without the armoured reinforcements from England that Churchill had unsuccessfully urged be sent through the Mediterranean, withdrew slowly towards Mersa Matruh. The Italian advance, and his concern that further Italian offensive action might be imminent, prompted the Prime Minister at a COS meeting on the following day to suggest that the CIGS consider the dispatch of two additional infantry battalions to strengthen the Malta garrison. A fifth British battalion, as we have seen, had been sent to the island in May but a further request from General Dobbie in June had been refused. General Dill, therefore, cabled Dobbie on 14 September and received a reply five days later. The Governor pointed out that his infantry was wholly deployed around the coast of Malta, with a battalion front averaging fifteen miles, and that he had only a very small reserve. He requested at least two additional battalions, one of which would be held in reserve and the other employed to strengthen the coastal defences.

When Dill reported this to the COS, Churchill, who had seen Dobbie's cable, at once minuted:

> This telegram confirms my apprehensions about Malta. Beaches defended on an average battalion front of fifteen miles, and no reserves for counter-attack worth speaking of, leave the island at the mercy of a landing force. You must remember that we do not possess the command of the sea around Malta. The danger therefore appears to be extreme. I should have thought four battalions were needed, but owing to the difficulty of moving transports from the West we must be content with two for the moment. We must find two good ones. Apparently there is no insuperable difficulty in accommodation.[17]

Dill promptly discussed the matter again with Dobbie who decided to accept the offer of one battalion, accompanied by a battery of 25-pounder field guns. The whole problem was discussed at a meeting of the Defence Committee on 24 September when the provision of the battalion and the field guns from the UK was approved.[18] It was also agreed that Malta should receive from Alexandria drafts for the existing battalions on the island amounting to about 750 officers and men. General Wavell thought this preferable to releasing another complete battalion from his numerically inferior forces in Egypt. These troops were conveyed to Malta on two cruisers and disembarked there on 1 October.

Not for the first time Churchill was impatient about the pace at which decisions were made and executed. On 24 September, after the Defence Committee had agreed to reinforce Malta, he wrote to Eden at the War Office. 'I am much disquieted,' he wrote, 'about the position at Malta. It is now agreed that two battalions shall be sent as reinforcement; but after how much haggling and boggling, and excuses that they could not be accommodated on the island!' He went on to warn that Malta might at any time be invaded by up to 30,000 Italian troops.[19] It was in this disgruntled mood that he sent a further minute to the COS on 6 October:

Whenever the Fleet is moving from Alexandria to the Central Mediterranean reinforcements should be carried in to Malta, which I consider to be in grievous danger at the present time ... Pray let me have proposals on these lines, and make sure that at least one battalion goes to Malta on the next occasion.[20]

Two days later, the Governor cabled again to warn of Malta's high vulnerability to invasion. In his view, although his existing battalions had been strengthened by the drafts from Egypt, a further three battalions were needed, supported by additional field artillery. Once more the COS wrestled with these insistent demands from the Prime Minister and the Governor. After more discussion it was agreed at a Defence Committee meeting on 15 October that an additional battalion would be sent from Egypt, and two more 'at the earliest opportunity'. From England, Malta would receive two more field batteries, as many as forty heavy and light AA guns, and a troop of six tanks. The Air Staff agreed to send another flight of Hurricanes by aircraft carrier and six more Maryland reconnaissance aircraft. They could not undertake to provide another complete fighter squadron while the German air threat to England persisted, but the ground crews required to support a future fighter force of four squadrons would be sent to Malta in advance.

These plans had a significant bearing on the naval view about Malta. As noted earlier, Pound and Cunningham had proposed that if, by April

1941, the full Scale B defences of Malta had been established it would be possible to base a force of cruisers and destroyers at Valletta. The urgency of this was, however, underlined by the Italian invasion of Egypt in mid-September. The Italian forces in North Africa were wholly dependent on supplies shipped from Italy, and the interruption of this vulnerable supply route was the obvious prime task of the Royal Navy in the Mediterranean. Before the war, the Italian navy had come to the conclusion that it would be extremely difficult to maintain this supply line against the French and British fleets.[21] To their surprise and relief, however, the Italian convoys to North Africa traversed the Mediterranean in the last six months of 1940 with very little loss. Only a handful of merchant ships were sunk on the African routes, and 98 per cent of the supplies dispatched arrived safely.

There were several reasons for this. In the first six months of the war in the Mediterranean, the Royal Navy suffered heavy submarine losses. No fewer than ten of the twenty large ocean-going submarines sent there from home waters and from the Far East were sunk, and the remaining boats were then withdrawn from the dangerous waters around the Italian ports. As Cunningham signalled to Pound, 'it is not a question of sending them where they will be useful, but where they will be safe'.[22] The C-in-C's second difficulty was lack of intelligence. On 17 July, the Italian navy changed all of its principal operating ciphers and these were never broken by British intelligence. As a result the previously plentiful supply of Italian shipping information was abruptly cut off. Moreover, this gap could not be filled by aerial reconnaissance. The few Sunderland flying boats and the handful of Swordfish torpedo-bombers at Malta were too slow and vulnerable to operate safely around the Italian embarkation ports, and it was not until 6 September that the first three Maryland long-range reconnaissance aircraft arrived at Malta. Admiral Pound was, therefore, forced to admit to his fellow COS that very few Italian convoys had been spotted and that the Admiralty was not even sure of the routes they were following. The Admiralty's final difficulty was that of basing warships and submarines at Valletta when defence in the harbour against air attack was so limited. It was felt, too, that such attacks would become heavier if offensive operations from Malta proved successful.

But, as Field Marshal Kitchener once observed, 'we have to make war as we must and not as we would like to'. Thus, the invasion of Egypt and the urgent need to reduce the flow of Italian supplies to Libya forced the Admiralty to alter its plans. Pound signalled to Cunningham on 2 October to ask what additional reinforcements might enable him to establish a surface force at Valletta. Cunningham in reply requested five more cruisers, four fleet destroyers, more reconnaissance aircraft, and as many fighters and AA guns at Malta as could be provided. Reporting all this to a meeting of the Defence Committee on 15 October, Pound declared that a force of surface ships could be sent to Malta as soon as the fighter and reconnaissance aircraft already authorised had arrived, and the AA gun strength had risen to seventy heavy and thirty-four light guns, a level expected to be reached in November, although still well short of the Scale B defences.

After this long series of discussions about the rearmament of Malta and the part that the island's forces might play in the defeat of Italy, Churchill sent the COS a lengthy memorandum about the whole military situation.[23] The first two paragraphs of this, which deal with Malta, deserve quoting at length since they demonstrate how strongly Churchill had insisted that, whatever the difficulties, Malta must be properly defended, not merely for the safety of the population and garrison, but so that the island could contribute to the defeat of the King's enemies.

1. First in urgency is the reinforcement of Malta:
   a) by further Hurricane aircraft flown there as best can be managed;
   b) by the convoy now being prepared, which should carry the largest anti-aircraft outfit possible, as well as the battalions and the battery – I understand another M.T. ship can be made available;
   c) by one, or better still, two more battalions released from police duty on the Canal or in Palestine, and carried to Malta when next the Fleet moves thither from Alexandria. General Dobbie's latest appreciation bears out the grievous need of strengthening the garrison. Every effort should be made to meet his needs, observing that once Malta becomes a thorn in the Italian side the enemy's forces may be turned upon it. The movement of these forces should therefore precede any marked activity from Malta.
   d) Even three Infantry tanks at Malta would be important, not only in actual defence, but as a deterrent if it were known that they were there. Some mock-up tanks also might be exhibited where they would be detected from the air.
2. The movement of the Fleet to Malta must await this strengthening of the air defences. It is however a most needful and profoundly advantageous step. I welcome the possibility of basing even light forces upon Malta, as they immediately increase its security. I understand that it is intended that they shall sally forth by day and only lie in harbour as a rule at night. It must be observed that a strong ship like the Valiant can far better withstand a hit from a bomb than light craft, and in addition she carries a battery of twenty very high class A.A guns. Apart from the stake being higher, it is not seen why, if light forces can be exposed in Malta harbour, well-armoured and well-armed ships cannot use it too.

   I should be glad to be more fully informed by the Admiralty about this.

Occasional visits by the whole Battle Fleet would be an immense deterrent on hostile attack, and also a threat to the Libyan communications while they last.

Let me have the number of A.A. guns now in position, and the whole maximum content [of them in] the new convoy, together with estimated dates for their being mounted.

By early October the situation in the Middle East had become so complex that Churchill suggested to Eden that he make an extended visit to the area. Eden welcomed this proposal and left London on 11 October. After a brief stop at Gibraltar he spent a day in Malta on 13 October. There he visited the island's defences and airfields, and then held lengthy discussions with the Governor and his senior naval and air force commanders. Before leaving he cabled back to London his view that one additional battalion with supporting artillery might be enough to secure the island against invasion. The Governor, however, disagreed. Supported by his commanders, he persisted in his request for three more battalions, and repeated his opposition to the use of Malta as an offensive base before the full Scale B defences had been attained in April 1941.

However, all these plans being made in London, Valletta and Cairo were suddenly overtaken on the morning of 28 October when Mussolini launched an invasion of Greece. The Greek government at once invoked the guarantee that Neville Chamberlain had extended to Greece in April 1939, and Churchill and his advisers considered how best to respond. We are concerned here largely with the effects on Malta of this Italian move, and they were considerable. Churchill's first thought was for the immediate establishment in Crete of an air base and a naval anchorage at Suda Bay on the north coast of the island. For this purpose the infantry battalion that Wavell was preparing to send to Malta was diverted to Crete together with AA guns and other supplies. Although Malta was, therefore, deprived of these reinforcements it was, nevertheless, clear that the Italian invasion of Greece had, for the moment at least, substantially reduced the threat of an attack on Malta. With his already substantial commitments in North Africa, and another war now begun in Greece, Mussolini could hardly be expected to launch a third military adventure against Malta. Moreover, as Churchill noted to the COS, the British presence at Suda Bay gave Malta much greater naval protection against invasion.

The second decision taken in London was to begin the bombing of Italian targets from Malta. For this purpose the newly-appointed CAS, ACM Sir Charles Portal, presented plans to establish at Luqa a new Wellington squadron formed from the aircraft that had been flying through Malta to Egypt. 148 Squadron was, therefore, established in mid-December and later comprised as many as sixteen aircraft. The necessary bombs, supplies and maintenance crews were sent out by warship and the squadron bombed port facilities at Naples, Brindisi, and Bari. It also attacked targets in North Africa, including a damaging raid on the Italian air base at Castel Benito near Tripoli.

The measures required to support Greece diverted Churchill's attention from Malta, but during November more of the reinforcements he had been urging for several months reached the island. First to arrive from England on 10 November were the men of one infantry battalion, two 25-pounder field batteries, three AA batteries and one tank troop, a total of 2,150 men. These were all carried to Malta, as part of Operation 'Coat', crowded into the battleship *Barham*, the cruisers *Berwick* and *Glasgow*, and in six destroyers. A week later, the cruiser *Newcastle* brought 200 airmen and equipment to service the new Wellington squadron at Luqa. Finally, on 28 November, in Operation 'Collar', the guns, tanks, vehicles and equipment for all these reinforcements were brought in on two fast merchant ships. As the 'Coat' reinforcements arrived, Admiral Cunningham wrote in his report:

> The entry of HM Ships, *Barham, Berwick* and *Glasgow* into the Grand Harbour with troops fallen in and bands playing, was reported by the VA Malta to have had a most excellent effect on the Maltese.[24]

4. A flight of Wellington medium bombers in January 1941. They could carry a bomb load of 4,500 lbs over 1,500 miles. Other versions were equipped to carry torpedoes and ship-detection radar.

No doubt the Governor was equally impressed, and relieved.

There was, unfortunately, a serious setback with regard to the fighter reinforcements. Once again the aircraft carrier *Argus* carried twelve Hurricanes and two Fleet Air Arm Skuas into the Mediterranean before they were flown off on 17 November. However, for a variety of reasons, nine out of the fourteen aircraft ran out of fuel before reaching Malta and were lost. Only four Hurricanes and one Skua arrived to provide a very limited reinforcement for the hard-pressed fighter squadron.

Tragic as these losses were, Malta's security was soon further assured. On 13 November, Churchill rose in the House of Commons to make a statement. 'I have some news for the House,' he said. 'It is good news.' He went on to tell Members of Admiral Cunningham's attack on the Italian fleet at anchor in Taranto harbour on the night of 11/12 November. In this attack twenty Swordfish aircraft from HMS *Illustrious* sank or seriously damaged three of Italy's six battleships. On the following night, a Wellington raid from Malta caused further damage in the docks. The accuracy of this devastating attack was made possible by aerial photographs taken by the Maryland aircraft of 431 Flight operating from Malta. For several days before the raid, photographs were taken of Taranto harbour, and the latest, flown to *Illustrious* on the afternoon of 11 November, told the Swordfish crews where each battleship was moored. Subsequent photographs revealed the damage inflicted, and the departure of the remaining heavy units for safer ports further north. In his after-action report Cunningham paid tribute to the reconnaissance aircraft:

> In the event the success of the FAA attack was due in no small part to the excellent reconnaissances carried out by the Glen Martin Flight (No. 431) from Malta, under very difficult conditions and often in the face of fighter opposition.[25]

To *Illustrious*, as she rejoined the Fleet, Cunningham simply signalled: '*Illustrious* manoeuvre well executed.'

The Italian losses at Taranto and the establishment of the base at Suda Bay considerably strengthened the Royal Navy's grip on the central Mediterranean. On 23 November, Churchill minuted to Alexander and Pound: 'Now that we have Suda as well as Malta, a couple of cruisers might possibly be withdrawn for necessary convoy duties as proposed, and the occupation of Malta by light forces, on which you were so recently set, postponed.'[26] He also minuted General Ismay on 1 December to say that, in view of Malta's increased defences, he thought it no longer necessary to send there another two infantry battalions from Egypt.[27] There was another reason for this decision. When Eden returned to London from Cairo on 8 November, Churchill learned for the first time of Wavell's plan, despite

his numerically inferior force, to take the offensive in Egypt. Operation
'Compass' was launched at dawn on 9 December. By 15 December, the
Italian army had been driven out of Egypt, and 35,000 prisoners had
already been taken.

On 1 December Churchill enquired of Ismay:

> I should be glad to have a return on one sheet of paper showing:
> a) what actually we have put into Malta in the last couple of months or
>   so, both in guns and men.[28]

In reply he was told that Malta, since 15 September, had received twenty-
four 25-pounder guns, twenty-eight heavy and sixteen light AA guns, one
tank troop of six tanks, a battalion of infantry, drafts of 1,000 men for the
other battalions, making an overall total of 126 officers and 2,795 men. In
addition, the island had received fourteen Hurricanes and one Glen Martin
Maryland reconnaissance aircraft. RAF Malta had been strengthened by
ten officers and 430 men.[29]

Several years after the war had ended, Churchill began writing his
account of what had happened. Reflecting then, in the quiet of his study
at Chartwell, on all the difficulties and setbacks which marked the war's
early years, he wrote: 'The only thing that really frightened me during the
war was the U-boat peril.'[30] If Britain's Atlantic supply route could not be
sustained, she could not continue the fight. On a far smaller scale, Malta
presented a similar problem, although there the dangers were to be found
in the air and on the surface rather than underwater. A civilian population
of, then, about 270,000 people and an expanding military garrison
were largely dependent upon imports of foodstuffs and other essential
supplies. Added to this was a growing volume of military equipment and
stores required for the defence of the island. We have already traced the
slow build-up of the military garrison and air force, and we must now
consider how Churchill and his advisers responded to Malta's supply
requirements.

The problem was hardly new. Isolated in the central Mediterranean and
not self sufficient in food and other essentials, Malta's value as a naval and
military base rested upon external supplies which, if Malta were at war
with a Mediterranean power, might need to be fought through. Plans to
meet this difficulty had long been made in London by the Oversea Defence
Committee (ODC), a Cabinet committee charged with the defence of
Britain's colonies. In February 1939, the ODC reconsidered Malta's
predicament. They then decided that the uncertainty of holding open
the sea routes to the island necessitated the establishment of a reserve
of essential stocks equal to six months' consumption. By June 1940, at
the outbreak of war in the Mediterranean, the stocks of wheat, flour and

edible oils had reached an eight-month level; coal and coffee stocks stood at a six-month level, while reserves of kerosene (essential for domestic cooking), sugar, soap and fats had risen to a five months' supply.

In the two months after Italy declared war, no supplies reached Malta, and on 23 August the COS considered a telegram sent to the Admiralty by Admiral Ford from Malta.[31] Ford pointed out how much stocks had fallen since June, and recommended that an overall target of an eight-month reserve level be aimed at by April 1941. By that time, it had been agreed, Malta would be sufficiently well-defended to allow the basing of a naval force at Valletta. The maintenance of such a target would require a substantial convoy every two months, and this would allow the stock level to vary between a six- and eight-month level. The COS accepted this recommendation and authorised the establishment of an organisation in London and Cairo to co-ordinate the collection and dispatch of the necessary goods.

The whole problem was drawn to Churchill's attention by a memorandum from Lord Lloyd on 11 September. Lloyd was the Colonial Secretary and it was to the Colonial Office that the Governor reported on Maltese civil matters. Lloyd first reported that some supplies, excluding wheat and coal, might be exhausted as early as the end of October. More seriously, the agreed intention to raise stocks to an eight-month consumption level would require more frequent and larger convoys. Instead of shipments of 40,000 tons every two months on 2–3 ships, 80,000 tons would now be needed every month, and this would mean convoys of 5–6 ships. He told Churchill that Dobbie's figures were being very carefully examined but the increased scale deserved War Cabinet attention. On his copy of this memorandum, Churchill wrote: 'General Ismay: For your observations', and Ismay replied on 17 September:

Prime Minister

With reference to your note on the attached minute from Lord Lloyd, the Departments concerned have already been in consultation on the subject of supplies for Malta. In order to meet the immediate situation, the Ministry of Shipping have arranged for five fast ships to leave Egypt early in October with such supplies for Malta as are available locally. The Commander-in-Chief, Mediterranean, has been asked to provide the necessary escort.[32]

The War Cabinet reviewed the matter on 19 September.[33] The Minister of Shipping, Mr R. H. Cross, advised that 'we were very short of the fast ships which would be necessary to carry the stores through the Mediterranean, but that he would do his best to meet these new demands'. The War Cabinet endorsed the proposed programme. In response to a further enquiry from the Colonial Office, the Governor sent a lengthy three-part telegram on 24/25 September explaining in considerable detail the measures that he had taken or planned to reduce the volume of imports. Petrol consumption, for example, had already been reduced by more than one half by taking off the roads 3,259 private cars out of a total of 3,600. Overall, the Governor estimated that total imports, civil and government, for the following fourteen months would amount to 182,000 tons compared with 312,000 tons in the 1939 year. Churchill's Malta files contain a copy of this telegram with a simple tick at the top.[34]

After the earlier doubts expressed by Pound and Cunningham about the safety of merchant ships in the Mediterranean, the results of the autumn convoys to Malta came as a welcome surprise. In the last six and a half months of 1940, 160,000 tons of cargo were discharged at Valletta without any loss, and reserve stocks had risen to a seven-month consumption level. The success of these operations owed much, as noted in the previous chapter, to the Royal Navy's recovery of control of the central Mediterranean, helped by the diversion of Italian air forces to support their land offensives in Egypt and Greece. However, this significant and encouraging strengthening of Malta's supply position was, in January 1941, put in jeopardy by the German arrival in the Mediterranean.

Between mid-June, when Mussolini declared war, and December 1940 the situation in the Mediterranean had been transformed. Despite the surrender of France and the threat of a German invasion of England, resources had been scraped together to fight Italy. Initial uncertainty about the fighting quality of the numerically superior and well-armed Italian land, air, and sea forces was soon shown to be without substance. Moreover, after Mussolini had blundered into Greece in October, British forces at Taranto and in the Egyptian desert seized the initiative and the outwardly impressive Italian façade began to crumble. At Malta, firmly in the eye of the storm, and with limited defences, the early anxieties eased somewhat. A handful of Hurricanes, and the arrival of additional AA guns and infantry began to make a difference. There were 104 Italian air raids in June and July, but only 50 in November and December as Malta's defences grew stronger. No invasion had been attempted and Admiral Cunningham was able to make more frequent use of Malta's invaluable dockyard repair facilities. On 20 December his flagship, HMS *Warspite*, steamed into the Grand Harbour with band playing and guard paraded and received a warm welcome.

The impetus for the strengthening of the British position in the Mediterranean came from the Prime Minister. His determination to defend British territory in the area is illustrated in the signals and minutes quoted in this chapter, while his ruthlessness was demonstrated in the bombardment of the French fleet at Oran. He was prepared to take greater risks than some of his advisers thought acceptable, and he was at times impatient at what he saw as unwarranted tardiness in getting to grips with the enemy. When, for example, Portal explained to him the difficulties of reinforcing the Middle East air forces, Churchill minuted:

> Perhaps you will say that all I propose is impossible. If so, I shall be very sorry, because a great opportunity will have been missed, and we shall have to pay heavily hereafter for it. Please try your best.[35]

From the very beginning, Churchill refused to contemplate the surrender or neglect of Malta, and repeatedly pressed the COS to send to the island aircraft, guns and troops, notwithstanding the acute shortage of these resources and the great difficulty in getting them to Malta. Churchill was, no doubt, relieved and pleased, at least to a degree, at what had been achieved in these six months, but it was only a beginning. Moreover, the pendulum of war was about to swing back. As Churchill had for some time anticipated, the scale of Mussolini's defeats had persuaded Hitler that he must intervene in the Mediterranean war.

THE FIRST GERMAN AIR ATTACK
JANUARY – JUNE 1941

The first duty of the AOC-in-C ME is none the less to sustain the resistance of Malta by a proper flow of fighter reinforcements.
Churchill minute to Chiefs of Staff, 21 January 1941[1]

Before we consider in detail Churchill's response to matters directly affecting Malta in the first six months of 1941, we must again pause to see these decisions in the wider context of the Mediterranean war. The principal military operation around which all else revolved was the German invasion and occupation of Greece in April, and the subsequent evacuation of the British and Commonwealth force that had been sent there in March. One month later the remnants of these forces were driven out of Crete with further heavy army and naval losses. Equally damaging was the loss of Cyrenaica as Rommel, in a characteristically daring campaign, drove back the weakened force that Wavell had positioned to hold the desert flank. Only isolated Tobruk held firm against the tide of the German advance. The only British successes were the defeat of the Italian forces in East Africa and the quelling of the revolt in Iraq in May. But while these severe setbacks inevitably dominated the deliberations and decisions of the Prime Minister and his Chiefs of Staff, Malta's predicament was not by any means ignored. For it was realised, more than ever before, that the island could, if properly defended and sustained, play a vital part in weakening the Axis offensive in North Africa.[2] In this chapter, attention is focused on Churchill's concern with strengthening Malta's defences against air attack and possible invasion, while the build up of the island's offensive capabilities is examined in the following chapter.

Churchill had for some time expected that Hitler, his plans for the invasion of England thwarted by the RAF, would turn his attention to the Middle East. Such a move, he felt, was likely to be accelerated by the Italian defeats in North Africa and Greece. His instinct proved correct. On 10 December 1940, Hitler ordered *Fliegerkorps X*, a powerful force of over 350 aircraft, from Norway to southern Italy, and on 11 January

1941 in his Directive No. 22 he issued instructions for an intensive attack on British sea communications through the central Mediterranean. Nor was that all. Three weeks later, a German armoured force was ordered to Libya and on 12 February General Erwin Rommel landed at Tripoli to take command.

The arrival of *Fliegerkorps X* in Sicily coincided with the passage through the Mediterranean of the 'Excess' convoy of five fast merchantmen. One of these, the 11,000-ton cargo-liner *Essex*, was bound for Malta with a cargo of great value. For in her holds were twelve crated Hurricanes, twenty-four 3.7-inch and eighteen Bofors AA guns, 4,000 tons of ammunition and, not least important, 3,000 tons of seed potatoes. On the afternoon of 10 January, the convoy was attacked fifty miles west of Malta by a large force of German dive-bombers, and the aircraft carrier HMS *Illustrious* was severely damaged. Emergency repairs were carried out at Malta under heavy air attack and on 23 January the crippled aircraft carrier slipped away to Alexandria. *Essex* arrived at Malta safely but was then subjected to heavy air attack at her moorings in the Grand Harbour and suffered many casualties before her cargo was unloaded.

When news of these events reached London, Churchill at once sent a minute to the COS which began: 'The effective arrival of German aviation in Sicily may be the beginning of evil developments in the Central Mediterranean.'[3] The new situation was discussed at a Defence Committee meeting on 13 January when Churchill deplored the failure to provide

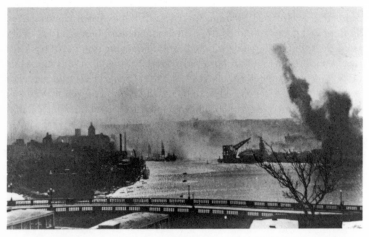

5. The aircraft carrier HMS *Illustrious* under air attack in the Malta Dockyard in January 1941. Despite repeated attacks, she was repaired and sailed for Alexandria on 23 January.

better AA defence against dive-bomber attack. He also urged again that plans be considered to seize the Italian island of Pantelleria, situated 100 miles west of Malta in the narrow waters between Sicily and Tunisia. In the event, after lengthy consideration the COS concluded that such an attempt would complicate, rather than assist, the defence of Malta, a view which the Prime Minister never wholly accepted but was unwilling to overrule.

As the German air attacks on Malta intensified, the Governor, General Dobbie, on 19 January telegraphed to the Colonial Office. 'Malta,' he signalled, 'has taken a very heavy toll of the enemy in the recent attacks from the air. The spirit of the people of Malta is as strong as ever.'[4] The Colonial Office sent a copy of this to Churchill who replied on 21 January as follows:

> Prime Minister to General Dobbie, Malta
> I send you, on behalf of the War Cabinet, our heartfelt congratulations upon the magnificent and ever-memorable defence which your heroic garrison and citizens, aided by the Navy and above all by the Royal Air Force, are making against Italian and German attacks. The eyes of all Britain, and indeed of the whole British Empire, are watching Malta in her struggle day by day, and we are sure that success as well as glory will reward your efforts.[5]

To this the Governor replied:

> Following for Prime Minister. Your telegram No. 18 of 21st January greatly appreciated by the garrison and people of Malta. By God's help Malta will not weaken. We are glad to be able to make a contribution to the victory which we know is sure and certain.

On 9 February in a radio broadcast Churchill described the attack on the *Illustrious* in the Grand Harbour and claimed the German and Italian forces had lost over ninety aircraft in the air and by bombing attacks on their Sicilian bases. He went on to say: 'I dwell upon this incident, not at all because I think it disposes of the danger in the Central Mediterranean, but in order to show that there, as elsewhere, we intend to give a good account of ourselves.'[6] Churchill's admiration for General Dobbie was expressed in his post-war memoirs when he wrote:

> In General Dobbie Malta found a Governor of outstanding character who inspired all ranks and classes, military and civil, with his own determination. He was a soldier who in fighting leadership and religious zeal recalled memories of General Gordon, and, looking further back, of the Ironsides and Covenanters of the past.[7]

Two days earlier, on the evening of 20 January, Churchill chaired a Defence Committee meeting at which a lengthy COS review of the Mediterranean theatre was discussed.[8] Most of this review related to the possibility of a German invasion of Greece and assistance to the Italian forces in Libya. However, one of the COS's conclusions was: 'In the meanwhile we must take toll of the German air forces from our air base in Malta.' During the subsequent discussion Churchill was highly critical, saying that 'he had read the Chiefs of Staff Report with considerable concern, since it seemed to lead to the minimum of aggressive action'. He then went on to say that 'he was anxious to give the war a more active scope in the Mediterranean', and urged the dispatch of more fighters to Malta 'so that it could continue the highly successful resistance which it was putting up'. He confirmed these views in a wide-ranging minute to the COS on the following day in which he directed: 'The first duty of the AOC-in-C ME is none the less to sustain the resistance of Malta by a proper flow of fighter reinforcements. To enable these tasks to be performed *Furious* will make another voyage with a third consignment of forty Hurricanes.'[9] (This was a reference to the delivery of aircraft by aircraft carrier to Takoradi in West Africa from where they were flown across Africa to Khartoum and Cairo.) In response to Churchill's directive, AM Longmore, the AOC-in-C, signalled on 23 February that he was sending to Malta that day a further six Hurricanes. In addition, he would shortly be able to send a further seven Fleet Air Arm Fulmars that Cunningham had made available from the disabled *Illustrious*. The heavy and persistent German air attacks in the latter part of January prompted a flurry of signals to London from the Governor and his Service Commanders about the course of the air battle in Malta's skies. One such from Air Vice-Marshal Maynard on 19 January reported to the CAS that in a three-day period thirty-seven enemy aircraft had been shot down by fighters and guns, for the loss of only two Hurricanes and two Fulmars, which had been landed from *Illustrious* before she left Malta for Alexandria.

Amid these mounting concerns about air attack, another potential danger to Malta emerged. Rumours and reports – some 'planted', it was thought – began to come in mentioning the massing of German troops, including armoured units, in Sicily and southern Italy. As noted earlier, these units were in fact on their way to Libya, but it seemed equally possible to observers in London and Valletta that they might be employed to invade Malta, if only to clear the sea route to North Africa.[10] On 21 January, Dobbie asked the CIGS, General Dill, 'whether there are known to be German Field Army Formations now in Sicily or en route there which render seaborne attack on Malta an immediate possibility'. He added: 'In any case we are quite ready for them.' Dill replied on the following day:

We have had many reports of presence of German troops in Sicily, including parachutists. But volume of these reports is greater than their reliability which we cannot check and we have received no identification of German formations ... At present therefore we have no grounds for believing attack on Malta immediate though possibility exists. Would be glad to know how you feel as regards garrison to meet attack.[11]

A second signal later that day passed on further rumours of German troops, including armoured and motorised divisions, 'reported to be destined for landing operations in Malta or in the rear of British Army in Libya. We have nothing to confirm or refute this information.'

To these signals Dobbie replied on 23 January. He dismissed any idea that German troops could be landed behind the British lines in Libya and continued:

As for its being intended for an attack on Malta I would point out that armoured or motorised divisions are not suited for such an operation ... If they exist in Sicily it seems likely that they are intended for use on mainland of Africa ... Although I would naturally like the full garrison mentioned [on 8 October 1940], i.e. three more battalions, yet I am confident that in the existing situation the present garrison should suffice to do the trick.

The Governor ended this signal by repeating that Malta's real need was for 'an immediate and substantial increase in the number of fighter aircraft'.

The Governor's assessment of the Sicilian rumours, no doubt deliberately spread by German Intelligence, proved correct, but within two weeks he had changed his mind about the adequacy of his garrison. On 5 February, he sent a lengthy signal to the War Office which General Dill read out to his fellow Chiefs on the following day.[12] The Governor now requested an additional infantry battalion and gave two reasons for this. Rumours, he noted, continued to circulate about a possible invasion of Malta, and this was 'a contingency which must be faced'. But he then went on:

I am anxious about the reactions of the civil population in face of a determined attack. They have undoubtedly been strained by the recent heavy air attacks, and may become difficult to control, and thus hamper military movements. The police could not be relied on to control them and the Army might have to accept this further commitment which would be a most unwelcome additional strain on our resources.

The Governor gave no reasons for arriving at this pessimistic view about civilian morale, although an attempted invasion of such a crowded island might have led to severe fighting with the possibility of heavy civilian casualties. Mercifully, this was never put to the test.

The COS agreed to dispatch an additional battalion from the Middle East as requested, but when Col. Hollis reported this to the Prime Minister the latter at once responded with one of his memorable ACTION THIS DAY minutes. This read:

> Prime Minister to General Ismay, for C.O.S. Committee
> Although of course the difficulties of [the enemy in] assaulting Malta are enormously increased by the British fuelling base in Suda Bay [Crete], nevertheless I shall be glad to see a second battalion sent there at the earliest opportunity, making seven British battalions in all. Considering that in view of the Italian rout there should be no great difficulty in sparing this seventh battalion from Egypt, and that the trouble is carrying them there by the Fleet, one must ask whether it is not as easy to carry two as it is to carry one. It seems a pity to let the baker's cart go with only one loaf, when the journey is so expensive and the load available, and it might as easily carry two. Pray consider this. But no delay.[13]

Churchill chaired the COS meeting on the following day and the dispatch of two additional battalions was agreed. When Wavell in Cairo asked the Governor whether a machine-gun battalion would be a sufficient reinforcement, the Governor replied that the need was not for firepower but manpower. The two battalions arrived by cruiser on 21 February.

Having made this further provision against the threat of invasion – an anxiety that was to recur on several occasions in the months ahead – Churchill's attention returned to the reality of increasingly heavy air attacks. Although units of *Fliegerkorps X* had been moved to North Africa to support the retreating remnants of the Italian Army, an experienced force of 250 German and Italian aircraft remained in Sicily. The intensity of the Axis air attack on Malta is revealed in the following figures taken from post-war Italian sources.[14]

Bomber and Fighter Attack Sorties on Malta, January – May 1941

January	February	March	April	May
315	296	394	455	483

On 9 February, Air Vice-Marshal Maynard reported that the Germans had begun night attacks, and in a longer signal of 16 February reported 'a systematic attempt to neutralise our small fighter effort'. 261 Squadron, he reported, had only nineteen serviceable Hurricanes. He made an urgent appeal for another complete fighter squadron equipped with Mark II

Hurricanes or Spitfires, and emphasised that the Mark I aircraft could not match the performance of the latest German fighters. It was on 12 February that the RAF in Malta first encountered a recently arrived squadron of ME109E fighters commanded by Oberleutnant Joachim Müncheberg. He and his squadron pilots had obtained considerable combat experience in the Battle of Britain, and their aircraft were equipped with two 20 mm cannon with armour plating around the cockpit. In the next three months this squadron of no more than nine aircraft claimed the destruction of forty-two RAF aircraft, twenty of which were credited to Müncheberg.

As the situation continued to deteriorate, ACM Portal received further signals in early March from both Maynard and the Governor. Maynard reported raids of as many as 100 aircraft, and the Governor supported Maynard's plea for 'a fighter force adequate in numbers and performance'. Portal read out these signals at a COS meeting on 8 March, remarking that additional aircraft could only be delivered directly to Malta by a fast merchant ship, or flown in from an aircraft carrier. Portal at once told the Governor and Maynard of what he had done and went on: 'Our plan is to give you the first priority in all you need but that its execution is limited by transportation difficulties.' After studying all these signals, Churchill intervened with a minute of 9 March, which read:

1. AM Longmore has been told that Malta is a first charge on his resources; but in view of all the other strains upon him a resolute effort should be made to put in the Fighter reinforcements from here.

2. I understand that ARGUS is now loading with the highest type Hurricanes and could arrive about the 21st or 22nd at Gibraltar. If instead of going into Gibraltar she went on to Takoradi her aeroplanes would reach Malta a fortnight later than the other way.

3. Whether she can be sent into the Mediterranean to fly off her aircraft depends on whether Force H is free from raider preoccupation around the 21st or 22nd instant. It is important to keep this option open and decide which to do about the 20th in the light of what is going on. It would be a very fine thing to reinforce Malta direct.[15]

However, when the COS discussed this minute two days later, Admiral Pound raised several difficulties, which he repeated to the Prime Minister in a memorandum of 16 March. Pound's difficulties can only be understood in the light of two other developments in early March. Firstly, on 7 March the War Cabinet, albeit with considerable misgivings, endorsed the decision to send a military force to Greece, although it did so for political rather than strictly military reasons. This decision had been urged by Eden, who had been sent to the Middle East with wide powers in February, and supported by Generals Dill and Wavell. Admiral Cunningham also endorsed this decision but warned that the dispatch of this force and its subsequent resupply from Egypt would tax his resources to the limit. Secondly, in early March, Pound had reported rising shipping losses in the Atlantic, aggravated by surface attacks from the German battlecruisers *Scharnhorst* and *Gneisenau*. These had now taken refuge in the French port of Brest. As a result Churchill had, on 6 March, declared the 'Battle of the Atlantic', issued a directive on the subject and established a weekly committee to co-ordinate the efforts of all the relevant departments to solve this critical problem.[16] It was against this background that Pound warned the COS and Churchill that the diversion of an aircraft carrier to fly fighters to Malta would not only expose the ship to the dive-bombing attacks that had crippled HMS *Illustrious*, but also reduce the protection that could be given to Atlantic convoys should the German battlecruisers sail from Brest. The Admiralty wrestled with all these interrelated demands for more than a week until Churchill finally decided to bring the matter to a decision at a meeting of the Defence Committee on 27 March.[17]

The Prime Minister was blunt. Despite the urgent appeals of the Governor and others for the strengthening of Malta's fighter defences, 'all kinds of objections had been raised', and he proceeded to enumerate them. Pound protested that the Admiralty 'had done everything in their power to find means by which [air reinforcement] could be carried out'. He had been told, he reminded the Committee, that the 'Battle of the Atlantic' was the Admiralty's main task and they could not fight this battle 'if their forces were liable at any moment to be snatched away for other operations'. A. V. Alexander, the First Lord, supported him, but the Prime Minister responded by saying that he thought the risks in the Bay of Biscay were overstated. 'Against this,' he continued, 'must be weighed the arrival of twelve aeroplanes of the highest performance to Malta.' Portal also stressed the importance to the RAF in Malta of receiving a reinforcement of Mark II Hurricanes. Attlee and Beaverbrook sided with Portal, and it was finally agreed that Operation 'Winch' should be carried out 'at the earliest opportunity'. As a result, on the morning of 3 April, twelve Mark II Hurricanes landed at Malta after a flight from HMS *Ark Royal* in the western Mediterranean. The day after these aircraft had landed, Churchill urged that the operation be repeated with twice as many aircraft – an operation he referred to as 'Double Winch'. Accordingly, four weeks later on 28 April a further twenty-three Hurricanes were flown to Malta in Operation 'Dunlop', and, at Portal's instigation, Maynard made plans to establish a second fighter squadron.

One other attempt to supply Hurricanes to Malta, although it failed, deserves special attention if only because Churchill took a special interest in it. In March, when the Admiralty were being pressed by Churchill to employ aircraft carriers to fly Hurricanes to Malta, they decided to attempt the passage to Malta of a single merchant ship, SS *Parracombe*, without escort. The vessel, after passing Gibraltar, would sail along the Spanish and French North African coast flying Spanish and French flags as a disguise. The ship, loaded with twenty-one crated Hurricanes but also carrying sixty-eight rocket launchers and ammunition in her holds, entered the Mediterranean on 28 April. However, after passing along the North African coast without incident, the *Parracombe* struck a mine and sank as she headed towards Malta from Cape Bon in Tunisia. Eighteen members of her crew, including her Captain, Lt. Com. Patterson, RN, were picked up and interned.

Churchill was concerned when he first learned of this plan, and on 19 March in a minute to the First Lord of the Admiralty, A. V. Alexander, which was unusually marked 'In a locked box. Private to First Lord alone', he wrote:

> This is surely a pretty humble role for the Admiralty to play. I should like to know the reason why Potato Jones and his merchant seamen in a poor little tramp steamer are to carry out 12 Hurricanes, vitally needed by Malta, while the Royal Navy has to be kept far from these dangers. I never thought we should come to this.

'Potato Jones' was the sobriquet given by the press to a Welsh sea captain who, during the Spanish Civil War, attempted to break the Nationalist blockade of Bilbao by sailing into the port with a cargo of potatoes.

Alexander at once replied:

> I feel sure your minute must have been written under some misapprehension. It is true that the Admiralty sent the signal with regard to the S.S. 'Parracombe', and you may have thought that this was in substitution of the plans we had discussed for passing reinforcements of Hurricanes through to Malta: this is not so.
>
> This is an additional proposal made, I understand, by the RAF for sending extra machines through, together with some equipment, by this means of evasion. The naval plan for flying off Hurricanes is not interfered with.

Churchill later enquired about the fate of this ship. On 13 May he asked, 'What happened to Potato Jones?' and was told by the Admiralty that air searches from Malta had failed to locate the ship, and she was feared lost. On this reply Churchill noted, 'I was never an enthusiast. I trust Potato Jones is saved.' The Admiralty then advised Churchill that the American Consul at Tunis had confirmed that the *Parracombe* had indeed struck a mine and sank on 2 May, and that eighteen survivors were being held at Bizerta.[18]

Despite these strenuous efforts to strengthen Malta's aircraft defences, the *Luftwaffe* attacks intensified in March and April. This placed even greater strain on the AA guns and crews of the Royal Artillery and the Royal Malta Artillery, and we must now review this vital element of Malta's defences. As described earlier, Churchill had pressed the War Office and the Admiralty to ship to Malta as quickly as possible the guns required to complete the agreed AA scale of 112 heavy, and 60 light guns, together with the necessary crews and ammunition. The safe arrival of the *Essex* with 24 heavy and 18 light guns in mid-January was a significant step forward. At the same time Colonel Sadler, who had organised the AA defence of Dover, arrived in Malta just in time to arrange a complex barrage to protect the *Illustrious* while she was undergoing emergency repairs in the Malta dockyard.[19] When Churchill enquired in April about the scale of the island's AA establishment, General Ismay told him that by mid-April 94 heavy and 52 light guns had been installed, and that a further 18 and 20, respectively, were on their way by the Cape route. It should be observed that the number of light Bofors guns continued to increase well beyond the initial target of 60, so that by mid-1942 over 130 such guns were deployed to counter dive-bomber and low-level attack.

This growing weight of anti-aircraft fire had two consequences. Firstly, ammunition expenditure rose dramatically. Between 16 January and 31 March 1941, the heavies fired 21,176 rounds, compared with 9,546 between 10 June 1940 and 15 January 1941. The light guns fired a further 18,660 rounds in early 1941 compared with only 1,078 in the earlier period. Secondly, the result of this prodigious increase in firepower, made more effective by improved radar, barrage programmes and greater war experience, was the destruction of 46 enemy aircraft in the first ten weeks of 1941.

On one aspect of AA defence, however, the Prime Minister was unable to have his own way. This was his hope for the deployment in Malta of rockets, which he always referred to as 'U.P.', i.e. Unrotated Projectiles. These were steadily developed and increasingly widely deployed in England to supplement conventional AA guns around vital targets.[20] Churchill's interest in these new weapons, and their potential use in Malta has been noted in earlier chapters. He raised the matter again after reading a signal from the Governor describing the loss on the ground of thirteen Wellington bombers on 26 February 1941. These had been destroyed by a series of dive-bombing and low level fighter attacks on Malta's airfields. Churchill at once suggested the dispatch of rocket batteries to Malta, and asked if they could be 'rushed through the Mediterranean' by warship. Admiral Pound, however, was not prepared to authorise the use of a cruiser for this purpose, but promised to send the equipment in a convoy. As noted earlier, the *Parracombe* carried a number of U.P. launchers and rockets, but after she was sunk replacement equipment only got as far as Egypt, and none was ever deployed in Malta. It seems clear that the War Office were not fully convinced that rockets would be more effective in Malta than Bofors or machine guns.

While these discussions continued, Admiral Cunningham was fully occupied with Operation 'Lustre', the transfer to Greece of the British and Anzac force of 58,000 men and their supplies. Four merchant ships with supplies for Malta had, however, reached Alexandria after the long passage around the Cape, and on 23 March these were safely escorted to Valletta. Two of the ships were hit by bombs at their moorings but nearly all the cargo was unloaded. It was shortly after this that, on 28 March, Cunningham struck a further heavy blow on the Italian navy when, off Cape Matapan, three heavy cruisers and two destroyers were sunk, and the battleship *Vittorio Veneto* damaged. This dramatic night-time encounter was aided by a sighting from a Malta-based Sunderland.

In April 1941, British Mediterranean strategy suffered a severe reverse. When in January Churchill had warned his colleagues that the arrival of the *Luftwaffe* in Sicily threatened 'evil developments' in the Mediterranean, he could hardly have anticipated the military defeats that arose in April. The British Expeditionary Force to Greece and its Greek allies were on 6 April attacked by overwhelming German land and air forces, and the decision to evacuate the British and Anzac force was taken on the 21st. By the end of April the last of 50,000 troops had been evacuated, although 12,000 men, 20 per cent of the original force, were lost. More ominously, Rommel, on 31 March, launched probing attacks on Wavell's western desert flank, quickly pushed aside a weak holding force, and by 12 April had recovered the whole of Cyrenaica apart from the port of Tobruk. To Churchill and his colleagues in London these simultaneous German offensives in the Greek peninsula and in North Africa seemed to be two pincer movements aimed at Britain's vital position in Egypt.

Far from being discouraged by these severe setbacks, Churchill and his colleagues responded with a determination to defend the British position in the Middle East. As he explained to President Roosevelt on 13 April:

> We are of course going all out to fight for the Nile Valley. No other conclusion is physically possible. We have half a million men there or on the way and mountains of stores. All questions of cutting the loss are ruled out. Tobruk must be held not as a defensive position, but as an invaluable bridgehead on the flank of any serious by-pass advance on Egypt. Our Air and Navy must cut or impede enemy communications across Central Mediterranean. Matter has to be fought out, and must in any case take some time ... I personally feel that this situation is not only manageable, but hopeful. Dill and Eden, who have just come back, concur.[21]

With his military advisers Churchill could employ more forceful, even peremptory, language. After referring to 'the gravity of the situation', he spoke of the danger of losing 'our whole army of about half a million men and all their equipment. This would not mean losing the war, but it was unthinkable that we should suffer a disaster of such magnitude without making a supreme effort to avert it.'[22] In a crisis such as this, Churchill was at his best. In May 1940 he had done his utmost, by repeated visits, to inspire and fortify the faltering French government of Paul Reynaud. These efforts had proved fruitless, not least because he lacked the power to command. A year later, in a similar crisis he had such power, and he used it with all the force of his determination and his eloquence to galvanise the British military machine to a supreme effort. Greece was lost and Crete was soon to follow, but Egypt, the linchpin of the British position in the Middle East, must be held no matter what the cost.

On 14 April, Churchill addressed to the COS a lengthy and comprehensive directive on 'The War in the Mediterranean'.[23] Much of this document related to measures designed to attack the Italian supply routes to North Africa and these will be examined in the following chapter. However, he had this to say about Malta itself:

> 5. In order to control the sea communications across the Mediterranean
> sufficient suitable naval forces must be based on Malta, and protection
> must be afforded to these naval forces by the Air Force at Malta, which
> must be kept at the highest strength in fighters of the latest and best
> quality that the Malta aerodromes can contain. The duty of affording
> fighter protection to the naval forces holding Malta should have
> priority over the use of aerodromes by bombers engaged in attacking
> Tripoli.

However, although attacks on Rommel's supply route were to be intensified the other urgent task was to strengthen Wavell's force after the losses suffered in Cyrenaica and Greece. For this purpose Churchill ordered two principal operations. The first, Operation 'Tiger', was the delivery through the Mediterranean of large tank reinforcements. The second, Operation 'Jaguar', was a plan to use four of the Royal Navy's aircraft carriers to fly fighter reinforcements to the RAF in Malta and Egypt. These overlapped but will be considered separately in order to judge their impact upon the defence of Malta.

In an earlier chapter we have noted that, in August 1940, Churchill wanted to send tank reinforcements to Egypt through the Mediterranean, but eventually bowed to Admiral Pound's judgement that this was too risky. On this occasion, however, he was, if necessary, prepared to overrule the Admiralty. On Sunday 20 April, he read signals from General Wavell, which warned of the arrival of an additional German armoured division in North Africa. He at once directed the COS to consider diverting through the Mediterranean a convoy already being loaded with 300 tanks and 50 crated Hurricanes. After much anxious discussion Pound agreed to this proposal and the 'Tiger' convoy passed Gibraltar on 6 May. To help protect its passage through the Sicilian Narrows, ACM Portal had sent to Malta thirteen long-range Beaufighters of 252 Squadron. The 'Tiger' convoy lost one ship when it struck a mine, but, aided by unusual mid-summer cloud and fog, the other four arrived at Alexandria on 12 May. More importantly for Malta, when Cunningham sailed with the Fleet to meet the 'Tiger' convoy, he escorted into Valletta a slow convoy of two tankers in addition to a fast convoy of four merchantmen and the naval supply ship HMS *Breconshire*. These vital supplies, totalling approximately 24,000 tons of oils and 40,000 tons of general supplies, all reached Malta safely, although only after mines were cleared from the entrance to the Grand Harbour by exploding depth charges.

With the plans for the tank reinforcements for the Middle East agreed, Churchill's attention next turned to the need for massive strengthening of the RAF in Malta and Egypt. On 30 April (at 1.30 a.m.) he issued another ACTION THIS DAY minute to the COS.[24] After a brief reference to the 'Tiger' convoy, the minute continued:

2. 'Winch' and 'Double Winch' [i.e. 'Dunlop'] have succeeded, and 'Triple Winch' [i.e. 'Splice'] is in preparation, but this is not enough to get us out of the accusation of 'driblets'. An operation similar to 'Tiger' must be planned for the Air.

3. Accordingly, arrangements should be made to add to 'Triple Winch' which carries 30 fighters, Furious which should carry 50, and Victorious which may carry 60. But say, in all, 130.

He then went into further detail about the complex naval arrangements required, and instructed: 'Let all this be concerted and synchronised this day, 30th April. General Ismay is charged with this task.' He concluded by reminding the COS that 'the failure to win the battle of Egypt would be a disaster of the first magnitude to Great Britain … Thus a true sense of proportion must rule, and the necessary accommodation must be made and the inevitable risks run.' This minute was discussed and agreed at a Defence Committee meeting later that day. As a result, during May and June, Operations 'Splice', 'Rocket' and 'Tracer', referred to collectively as 'Jaguar' by Churchill, delivered 140 Hurricanes to Malta by aircraft carriers. Most of the Mark I arrivals were flown on to Egypt while Malta retained the Mark II aircraft. The aircraft carriers suffered no damage.

But it was one thing to supply these new aircraft; to make them effective in the defence of the island was quite another. For in Malta a crisis was developing, the inevitable result of the devastating German and Italian air attack, much of it concentrated on the dwindling number of serviceable RAF fighters and their few airfields. Churchill makes no reference to this in his memoirs of the war, and the official history also passes over this crisis. The scale of the problem was clearly set out in a lengthy letter addressed by the Governor on 8 May to the CAS, ACM Sir Charles Portal, after consultation with the AOC Malta, AVM Maynard, who also wrote to Portal on the same day. After reminding the CAS that he, as Governor, held overall responsibility for the 'security of this place', he reported that 'the effectiveness of its Air Defence ... is causing me considerable concern'. He then listed five principal area of weakness, extracts from which can be summarised as follows:

(a) Shortage of efficient personnel on Maynard's Staff ... I can assure you that a very generous increase in the number of really first class staff officers is needed ... Real first class men, 'fizzers' should be sent.

(b) The fighter personnel must be well trained and experienced before coming here. They are up against a very tough proposition, and have to compete with very superior numbers ... The ones we have had are grand fellows, but they are mostly lacking in experience, and have had a very poor chance.

(c) The best type of machines, and only the best must be sent ... The Mark IIs we have had have only been comparatively few, but most of the fighting has fallen to their lot, and there have been heavy losses. We must have a lot more, manned by experienced men and we must keep on getting fresh supplies.

(d) A number of officers and others, have been here for a long time and are tired and jaded. They must be relieved by others from home.

(e) The ground staff of Malta is hopelessly inadequate, and this, I am told, cuts right across the effectiveness ... We cannot hope successfully to maintain and operate the many machines of varying types we are to have here, without a substantial increase. I understand some hundreds are needed.

Nevertheless, the Governor paid a warm tribute to Maynard himself. 'Maynard,' he wrote, 'has done extremely well. He has made bricks without straw, but unless he gets the sort of help I have indicated he will be unable to compete, and his command will be unable to deliver the goods.' A postscript to this letter advised: 'I hear that Sanderson [Maynard's Senior Air Staff Officer (SASO)] is sick. If he becomes unfit it will be a real calamity and throw an intolerable burden on Maynard.' Attached to the Governor's letter was a request for additional senior staff officers, which had been agreed with Maynard. The latter's own letter to Portal shed further light on the growing difficulties in Malta:

I am well aware of the difficulties over finding personnel with the endless tasks now confronting us all and had every intention of holding out as long as I could without squealing for help; perhaps, however, I was wrong in this and should have squealed already; anyway, here it is. If what we want cannot be supplied I shall naturally struggle on as long as the machine will work, but the pace is hot and we are in almost continuous battle and many personnel are shaky and very tired.

Portal immediately sent copies of these two letters to the Air Members for Personnel, and for Supply and Organisation with instructions that Malta's requirements be given urgent attention. 'I regard Malta,' he wrote, 'as the station which, above all others anywhere, should have priority in personnel and material.' There should be a regular relief of fighter pilots, and the latest version of the Mark II Hurricane, equipped with cannon, should be sent there. He asked for a report within forty-eight hours on what could be done. While this was being done, signals continued to arrive from Maynard stressing the need for more Mark II aircraft, of which he had only seven remaining. On 15 May he advised: 'Disparity in aircraft performance and lack of experienced leadership amongst our fighter pilots continues to seriously affect morale. Enemy fighters well led by old hands getting more daring every day.' Later that day he added: 'Position is such that serious consideration should be given to immediate dispatch of crack Spitfire squadron ... It is no doubt realised by now that we have lost control of the air over Malta temporarily.'

Churchill had now become aware of the growing crisis in Malta. In his dispatch box on the morning of 16 May he found a copy of a signal from Admiral Ford, the Vice-Admiral Malta (VAM), to Cunningham and Pound. This began by reporting: 'I am getting extremely perturbed with the state of our air defences.' The enemy were becoming 'bolder every day', and had gained complete air superiority. He ascribed this to inferior aircraft, inexperienced pilots, and 'reasons which I will send to C-in-C Mediterranean in writing'. Upon this signal Churchill wrote: 'CAS For immediate report.' On the same day the Governor sent a further alarming signal:

Most secret and personal for CAS from Governor, Malta.
Since I wrote my letter of 8 May situation regarding air superiority here has gravely deteriorated. It has completely passed into enemy's hands. Enemy is obviously set on eliminating our fighters and has gone a considerable way towards achieving this end by incessant attacks by forces superior in numbers and performance ... This has inevitably affected morale to the extent of almost destroying it in one squadron.

Portal replied to the Prime Minister that evening. After disputing one or two of Admiral Ford's comments he continued:

> I am sure that the real trouble is that many of [the pilots] are now tired and need relief, and that there have been certain deficiencies in the higher control which have only just come to light. We are taking urgent steps to strengthen Malta on the personnel side and we are sending all the cannon Hurricane IIs we can scrape together, but these cannot be available for 'Splice' which, however, will contain 20 eight-gun Hurricane IIs.
>
> The best pilots from 'Splice' are being retained as a unit in Malta to relieve some of the tired pilots at present there, who will go on to Egypt. Some 200 mechanics are also on their way.

Portal at once cabled instructions that, upon the arrival of the 'Splice' reinforcements, 'all pilots of 249 Squadron, which is one of the best squadrons from Fighter Command, be retained at Malta to relieve pilots of 261, who clearly need a rest'.

What is also clear, although not recorded in the official papers, is that Portal and Churchill had reached the conclusion that Maynard, too, needed, and fully deserved, a rest. Moreover, Portal had recommended that he be relieved by AVM Stevenson, who was at the time AOC, No. 2 Bomber Group in England. Thus, on 16 May, Churchill telegraphed to General Dobbie:

> Am sure Stevenson is your man. I watched his work here very closely. Since beginning of March he has revolutionized East and South coast fighting against German shipping. He embodies offensive warfare. Results have been extraordinary. Will keep on feeding you. All good wishes.

In his reply on the following day the Governor once again praised the 'magnificent work Maynard has done since war with Italy began ... The satisfactory defence of Malta up to date is largely due to him.' He concluded by writing: 'All is well here and when our fighter problem is solved hope Malta will continue to be thorn in enemy's side.' No doubt cheered by Dobbie's confident reply, Churchill cabled again. He had to report that Stevenson had become unfit but would be replaced by 'another first-class Officer'. He continued: 'Everyone here appreciates splendid work Maynard has done working up from the very beginning, but it is felt that a change would be better now. Maynard will be well looked after here.'

History has not fairly recognised AVM Maynard's contribution to the defence of Malta. He was one of those senior commanders of all services who, in the war's early years, had the misfortune to be sent into battle against a well-prepared enemy with the inadequate resources provided by a government more intent on appeasing, rather than preparing to fight, the enemy. Many young men under Maynard's command paid a higher price for such neglect. General Dobbie, however, left no doubt in his letters and signals that Maynard had given more than could be reasonably be expected of him, and in his equally generous cable Churchill gladly accepted this judgement. On his return to England, Maynard was appointed to be a Companion of the Order of the Bath (CB) and later held other senior commands in the RAF until the end of the war. This was richly deserved. It is perhaps worth concluding this story by remarking that when Maynard's successor, AVM Lloyd, set out for Malta, he was told by Portal that 'You will be on the Island for six months as a minimum and nine months as a maximum as by that time you will be worn out.'[25] Maynard had been in Malta throughout the first twelve difficult months of the Mediterranean war.

With the arrival in June 1941 of a new AOC, more and better aircraft, and fresh pilots of greater combat experience, the process of regaining air superiority began, and this will be considered in a later chapter. It will be appropriate to conclude this chapter by examining the attention that Churchill gave to the increasing dangers and hardships faced by the people of Malta. Although his main attention was inevitably focused on the military decisions required by fast-moving events, he was by no means oblivious to the sufferings of the civilian population. In Britain he frequently visited bombed towns and cities, often speaking to dazed and homeless people while the firemen and rescue teams were still at work. As a result of his four visits to Malta between 1907 and 1927,[26] Churchill, as he read the signals from Malta, was able to visualise the devastation inflicted on the noble city of the Knights of St John. Had he visited Malta in the spring of 1941 he would surely have been at General Dobbie's side as he made his way around the rubble-strewn streets of Valletta and the Three Cities.

Soon after the heavy German bombing in January, targeted at the damaged *Illustrious*, General Dobbie signalled home on 21 January describing the heavy damage to buildings in Valletta and the dockyard area. He went on to ask if he could be authorised to state that the British government would accept responsibility for the post-war repair of damaged buildings.[27] In reply the Colonial Office said that this request 'raised important questions of policy', which would require careful consideration. Upon seeing this correspondence, Churchill, on 23 January, at once sent an ACTION THIS DAY minute to the Chancellor of the Exchequer, Sir Kingsley Wood:

Chancellor of the Exchequer
Surely they should be allowed to come into our scheme on exactly the same terms as our own people, and in retrospective effect.
They are under siege. Your answer is pretty frigid.

Above: 6. A Valletta street blocked by bomb damage.

Left: 7. Another blocked street in Valletta, showing the shattered limestone blocks from which Maltese houses are constructed.

On the following day, having read a further rather vague telegram from the Colonial Office to the Governor, he minuted the Chancellor again:

Chancellor of the Exchequer

Frankly, I do not think the conventional phrases about 'urgent consideration' and 'sympathy and support' are good enough at this time for these people who have so loyally espoused our cause, and are under constant attack. A more detailed statement should be made.

These brisk interventions prompted a further signal to the Governor after the Prime Minister had approved it. Although this, too, was couched in rather general terms, it established the principle that the British government would stand behind any relevant Maltese legislation on this essential matter, if Maltese resources were found to be inadequate. We need not follow these exchanges in detail at this stage since they were later overtaken by other measures, as we shall see later. However, Churchill's minutes demonstrate his concern to avoid an injustice.

The growing intensity of the enemy air raids has been noted earlier in this chapter with a peak figure of 483 sorties in the crisis month of May. It has been estimated that as many as 650 tons of bombs fell on Malta during April and although this tonnage was exceeded by a large margin a year later, extensive damage was caused to Valletta and the surrounding communities. On 10 May the Governor told the Colonial Office that the damage from bombs and aerial mines had been greatest in Valletta and continued:

This extensive damage to their principal city which was founded immediately after the Great Siege in 1565 and has stood unchanged since the time of the Knights has been a profound shock to Maltese sentiment, and damage to several large churches including the Cathedral of St. John has given deep offence.[28]

A week later he reported that, since June 1940, the total of the civilian population who had lost their lives had risen to 274, while 204 more had been seriously injured. 55,000 people had left their homes and the population of the Three Cities had fallen to 5,000.

At the outset of the war in the Mediterranean it is now clear that insufficient attention and resources had been devoted to air raid shelters.[29] Plans had been drawn up in 1939 and the substantial sum of £250,000 allocated by the British government for shelter construction, but it was not until June 1940 that Mr Mavity, a senior dockyard engineer, was recalled from leave and put in charge of a new Shelter Construction Department in the Malta government. Shelter construction and tunnelling then accelerated. Churchill's Malta files contain a lengthy telegram from the Governor dated 14 June 1941. He advised that 5,500 men were now engaged on shelter construction, and that the whole population should have some underground cover by the end of August. The costs had naturally risen well above the sums allocated for this work, but he went on:

> I am convinced, however, that we have no choice but to press on with digging of shelters with the maximum force of miners available. Ever since the entry of Italy provision of shelters has been a question of greatest interest to the whole of the population who have allowed us no rest in their constant suggestions of ways of speeding up construction. The fact that casualties have been so exceedingly small is mainly due to the protection afforded by shelters which has also contributed to a large extent to the present admirable calm of the population.

This report was circulated to the Cabinet in London with a note to Churchill stating that no trouble with the Treasury was anticipated.

The stocks of essential supplies were the Governor's other constant problem. As noted above, despite the escalating air onslaught, a steady stream of merchant ships had been escorted into Malta and nearly all their cargoes safely unloaded. Nevertheless, the Governor had thought it necessary in April to introduce rationing of several essential commodities in an attempt to curtail hoarding and black market operations. In a signal of 6 June, the Governor advised that, with the exception of aviation spirit and animal fodder, 'present stocks, with the greatest care, can last until early January 1942'.

This chapter has concentrated on Malta's defensive problems and needs in the first five months of 1941, and the steps taken to meet those needs. But this is only one side of Malta's war experience in this period. The other was the build-up of the island's offensive capability, and it is to this that we must now turn.

BUILDING MALTA'S
OFFENSIVE CAPABILITY

Not only should destroyers and light cruisers from Malta prey on the convoys, aided by our submarines, but a strong assault should be made by capital ships.

Churchill Directive to Chiefs of Staff, 14 April 1941

In this chapter we will concentrate upon the steps taken in the first five months of 1941 to expand Malta's offensive capabilities in the face of the mounting German air attack on the island. However, it is important that the reader keep in mind that these measures were interwoven, and at times in conflict, with Malta's defensive needs. Furthermore, all decisions about Malta were necessarily affected by wider developments in the Mediterranean, particularly after the German offensives in Cyrenaica and Greece in April. Beyond that again, Churchill's attention as Prime Minister was often claimed by other aspects of the war, such as the 'Battle of the Atlantic', and also by home affairs. One example, perhaps, far distant from Malta, may serve to illustrate how many other cares and responsibilities Churchill bore in these difficult months. As we shall see below, Churchill held an important Sunday morning meeting on 13 April. But on the previous morning he had been touring the wrecked streets of Bristol, talking to the injured and dazed victims of a heavy overnight air raid. Later that day, as Chancellor of the University of Bristol, he conferred honorary degrees on Gilbert Winant, the US Ambassador, and on Sir Robert Menzies, the Australian Prime Minister. In his memoirs, Churchill recalled that 'the bright academic robes did not conceal the soaked and grimy uniforms of the night's toil.'[1] That night he returned to Chequers, the Prime Minister's official country home outside London, where, with the devastation at Bristol clear in his mind, Malta and the Mediterranean again demanded his attention.

Those of his military advisers who had not known Churchill before the war were soon to learn that an eagerness to attack the enemy was a central element of his personality. When, for example, it seemed clear in early June

1940 that Mussolini was about to declare war, Churchill demanded that an immediate air attack be made on Milan and Turin. Thus did Churchill and the RAF respond on the night of 12 June to the bombing of Malta in the dawn hours of the previous day. It came as no surprise, therefore, that he should urge that Malta be developed, as quickly as possible, as a base from which to attack Italy and her sea communications with Libya. It was with the greatest reluctance that he accepted the judgement of his military advisers in the summer of 1940 that such operations should not be launched until Malta had been more adequately defended, and that this might not be achieved until April 1941. However, Mussolini's invasion of Greece on 28 October 1940 prompted, as we have already seen, the establishment of a Wellington medium bomber squadron at Luqa to bomb Italian targets. From this beginning, Churchill continually pressed his naval and air commanders in London and Cairo to expand these offensive operations, and this chapter will consider what was achieved in the early months of 1941.

In the last weeks of 1940, the weight of Italian air attack on Malta had diminished and this respite, coupled with General Wavell's continued advance in North Africa, raised hopes that Malta's offensive operations might be developed further, although the planned AA defences were still incomplete. To an enquiry by Churchill on 2 January 1941, ACM Portal replied that there were then fifteen serviceable Wellingtons at Luqa.[2] At the same time, however, the Middle East C-in-Cs signalled that 'we are greatly concerned over the present weakness in air resources required in connection with the control of sea communications in the Central Mediterranean'. They proceeded to repeat an earlier request for the basing at Malta of a full reconnaissance squadron, a force of torpedo-bombers, 'of the Beaufort type', and a night bomber force. On his copy of this signal Churchill enquired: 'General Ismay. Please report what can be done.' He was then advised that the COS, struggling with the many claims on limited resources, had decided, 'in principle', to send to Malta as soon as possible a flight of seven Glen Martin reconnaissance aircraft, and, at a later date, a flight of Beaufort torpedo-bombers. However, they warned, no date for the latter could be promised, although the maintenance crews and the torpedoes would be sent in advance. Until then the AOC Malta must make do with the Fleet Air Arm Swordfish torpedo-bombers of 830 Squadron, although these aircraft had limited range and operated at considerable risk against even Italian fighters.

However, Hitler had already decided to come to the aid of his crumbling ally. Fearing such a development, Churchill warned, in a lengthy Appreciation sent to the COS on 6 January:

We must continually expect that Hitler will soon strike some heavy blow, and that he is now making preparations on a vast scale with customary

German thoroughness. He can of course easily come down through Italy and establish air-power in Sicily. Perhaps this is already taking place.[3]

This Appreciation, and Churchill's later account, do not mention that decrypts of the German Air Force's Enigma signals had revealed that the first aircraft of *Fliegerkorps X* has already arrived in Sicily. This closely guarded secret was known to the COS but to very few others, and these decrypts are not even contained in the Prime Minister's normal PREM files. Within days the *Luftwaffe* dive-bombers had struck a heavy blow at the aircraft carrier HMS *Illustrious*, and the bombing of Malta had intensified.

The rapid build-up of the German air force in Sicily removed any early hopes that Malta might soon be able to turn to the offensive. The RAF lost an increasing number of aircraft at its three operational airfields. The large Wellingtons of 148 Squadron, dispersed around the perimeter, were particularly vulnerable to low-level attack. On 26 February, six were destroyed and a further seven badly damaged in a single day's raids, and in early March Maynard signalled that the remaining aircraft had been flown to Egypt. The Sunderlands of 228 Squadron, easy targets at their moorings at Kalafrana, also left, further reducing Malta's limited reconnaissance capability.[4] In these worsening conditions, more fully examined in the previous chapter, successful convoy attacks were rare. Nevertheless, the attempt was made. On 28 January, a Combined Services Report from Malta described a successful Swordfish attack on a small convoy off the Tunisian coast, claiming one 5,000-ton ship sunk and a larger one damaged. Three days later, a further signal reported, a Swordfish patrol sighted another two ships in the same area 'but did not attack as M/Vs were in territorial waters'.[5] This restriction on attacking enemy ships in French territorial waters was quickly removed by the War Cabinet.[6] These brave but altogether inadequate offensive sorties were quite unable to impede the steady stream of convoys which, from early February, began the transfer to North Africa of the German armoured units, the command of which General Rommel assumed at Tripoli on 12 February.

Although more immediately concerned to strengthen Malta's defences, Churchill and the COS were well aware of these German moves. One advantage of the *Luftwaffe's* arrival in Sicily was its use of Enigma ciphers which had most easily been broken by British Intelligence. Consequently, an increasing volume of decrypts described in considerable detail the German build-up in Libya. However, eyes in London and Cairo were fixed on Greece and the Balkans. After a lengthy discussion at a Defence Committee meeting on 11 February, the Prime Minister cabled Wavell congratulating him on the capture of Benghazi, but then continued:

But this does not alter, indeed it rather confirms, our previous directive, namely, that your major effort must now be to aid Greece and/or Turkey. This rules out any serious effort against Tripoli, although minor demonstrations thitherwards would be a useful feint. You should therefore make yourself secure in Benghazi and concentrate all available forces in the Delta in preparation for movement to Europe.[7]

The decision to send a military force to the aid of Greece was taken by the War Cabinet, after considerable discussion and no little hesitation, on 7 March.

But as the signal quoted above makes clear, this decision was taken on the assumption that the position in Cyrenaica was secure. Churchill later wrote: 'The Desert Flank was the peg on which all else hung, and there was no idea in any quarter of losing or risking that for the sake of Greece or anything in the Balkans.'[8] Nevertheless, on 2 March, General Wavell met warnings from London about the growing German force in Libya with the judgement that no serious German attack could be launched for several months. Later that month, however, he signalled: 'I have to admit having taken considerable risk in Cyrenaica after capture of Benghazi in order to provide maximum support for Greece.' He added that the March removal of the Wellingtons from Malta had prevented the bombing of Tripoli 'on which I had counted.'[9]

It was not, therefore, a complete surprise when Rommel attacked the British position on 31 March. What soon caused concern and then consternation was the speed with which the Desert Flank crumbled and German armoured units routed the British and Australian forces in Cyrenaica. Some of the steps that Churchill then took, and parts of his Directive of 14 April which affected Malta, have been examined in the preceding chapter. These included the 'Winch' and 'Jaguar' Operations to strengthen the island's hard-pressed Hurricane forces. What we are concerned with in this chapter is the heavy pressure that Churchill put upon the RAF and the Navy to do more to interrupt the flow of men and supplies from Italy to North Africa, in particular by the more active use of bases in Malta.

On 3 April, the first inkling of the defeat looming on the Cyrenaican border reached Churchill when General Wavell, after a quick visit to the front, warned that the evacuation of the port of Benghazi was imminent. On the following day, Churchill presided over meetings of the COS and Defence Committee to review the position. The COS, with Wavell's telegram before them, at once declared that 'the re-establishment of a front in Cyrenaica should have priority in the resources of all three Services in the Middle East'.[10] The Prime Minister then put before the Chiefs a number of suggestions which he asked them to explore. The Admiralty should consider a repeat of Operation 'Winch' to Malta, the dispatch of tanks to Egypt through the Mediterranean, possibly by an aircraft carrier, and 'the basing of the largest possible concentration of submarines on Malta with a view to interrupting enemy sea communications with Africa'. The Air Ministry was asked to examine the concentration of resources to 'dominate the air in Cyrenaica', and 'the employment of bombers, if necessary on Malta, to interrupt the enemy lines of communication in Libya and to bombard Tripoli'. The immediate dispatch of six Beauforts to Malta was also to be considered. The need to attack Tripoli from Malta arose because, with the loss of the airfields in Cyrenaica, bombers could no longer reach the principal North African landing port from Egypt. After rapid deliberations, the COS reported back to the Prime Minister later that day.[11] Admiral Pound advised that Operation 'Winch' would be repeated, that additional submarines were being concentrated in the central Mediterranean, and that destroyers were being ordered from the Red Sea to Alexandria to enable Admiral Cunningham to release others to be sent to Malta. For the Air Staff ACM Portal reported that a force of Wellingtons would return to Malta, and that 'orders had been given for six Beauforts to fly to Malta at first opportunity'.

Further alarming news then came in. The gist of an Enigma decrypt was forwarded to Cairo on 2 April by a recently established direct link:

> Advanced elements of GERMAN fifteenth armoured division moving second April from TRAPANI to PALERMO (STOP) Probably going to TRIPOLI.[12]

Professor Hinsley, in his history of British Intelligence, has considered why this information may not have received the attention it deserved.[13] There were, he observed, administrative and procedural failings in both England and Cairo, much of it resulting from the essential need to protect the source of this information. Hinsley concluded that, at this time, 'the Enigma traffic was still invaluable for its strategic information, if not on the tactical level'. However, a second decrypt of 7 April caught the Prime Minister's eye in London. This, addressed by the Admiralty to Cunningham, with a copy to Vice-Admiral Ford in Malta, read:

> Advanced element of German fifteenth armoured division embarking at Palermo on or after 9th April probably for Tripoli.[14]

At a meeting of the COS on 7 April, Churchill drew attention to this signal and said that 'it was vitally important that we should attack the German transports by surface, submarine and air forces with the utmost vigour'. Pound responded by saying that Cunningham had been requested to send light forces to Malta as soon as possible.[15] On the next day Cunningham signalled:

> Although Red Sea destroyers will probably not reach me for six to seven days, at expense of convoy escort HMS Jervis, HMS Janus, HMS Mohawk and HMS Nubian are being sent to Malta where I hope they will arrive at daybreak 10th if weather permits, otherwise daybreak 11th. I must emphasise that these destroyers run considerable risk of damage from air attack at Malta but in view of situation I consider this risk must be accepted. The presence of a cruiser would only draw heavy attack on Malta.[16]

It was in the early months of 1941 that Malta's renowned submarine force became established at its base in Lazaretto Creek on the north side of Valletta. Soon to be designated the 10th Flotilla, this force of small, slow 'U' class submarines, under the command of Commander Simpson,[17] steadily grew in numbers under the impetus of Churchill's directive of 4 April, ordering 'the basing of the largest possible concentration of submarines at Malta'. These 'U' class submarines, reinforced at times by visiting boats of the 1st Flotilla from Alexandria, were, like the destroyers, handicapped by the inadequacy of usable intelligence and by the effects of the heavy bombing and aerial mining around Valletta's harbours. Nevertheless, as their captains gained war experience, the number of successful attacks rose. After the sinking of four merchant ships in January and February, four more were sunk in March, two in April, and five in May, bringing the total for the first five months of 1941 to fifteen with an aggregate tonnage of 64,650 tons. Among the ships sunk in May was the 18,000-ton liner *Conte Rosso*, an exploit which earned Lt-Com. Wanklyn, commanding HMS *Upholder,* the Victoria Cross. During the 1941–43 period as a whole, it was the submarines that proved the Royal Navy's most effective weapon against the enemy convoys to North Africa.

On 10 April, while the four destroyers of the 14th Flotilla under the command of Captain P. J. Mack were approaching Malta, Admiral Cunningham sent another lengthy signal, warning of the threat to Alexandria if the German advance were not halted. Then, after stating that he was doing all he could with destroyers, submarines and the Swordfish of 830 Squadron, he went on to urge that RAF bombing attacks on Tripoli be stepped up.[18] When Churchill saw a copy of this signal he at once sent an ACTION THIS DAY minute to A. V. Alexander and Admiral Pound:

> I am distressed at C-in-C's signal which begins by pointing out vital consequences of stopping German reinforcements via Tripoli, and reaches the very easy conclusion that, in spite of the numerous difficulties

about Malta, the Air Force must do it. In my view a heavy risk should be run by the Royal Navy to break up Tripoli, and cut the communications. Not only should destroyers and light cruisers from Malta prey on the convoys, aided by our submarines, but a strong assault should be made by capital ships ...

We must be prepared to face some losses at sea, instead of the Navy sitting passive and leaving it to the Air. But of course the Air should act to the full as well. It is the duty of the Navy, assisted by the Air, to cut the communications between Italy and Tripoli.

At the foot of this minute there is a further notation in Churchill's hand: 'P.S. I am most relieved to hear the tenor of First Sea Lord's personal telegram to Admiral Cunningham.' In this telegram, Admiral Pound, after saying that he was sending a further eight submarines to the Mediterranean, and that 'Beauforts should reach you shortly, if not already there', continued by signalling that the possibility of a naval attack on Tripoli was being studied at the Admiralty.

It was in the light of these dangerous developments, which were fully reviewed at a Sunday morning meeting of the Defence Committee at Chequers on 13 April after his return from Bristol, that Churchill delivered to the COS a further Directive entitled 'The War in the Mediterranean'.[19] An extract from this, which ordered that the priority task of the RAF in Malta was the protection of the newly arrived destroyer force, has been quoted in the previous chapter. The greater part, however, repeated the comments that he had already addressed to Alexander and Pound. Its essence was the following declaration:

It becomes the prime duty of the British Mediterranean Fleet under Admiral Cunningham to stop all sea-borne traffic between Italy and Africa by the fullest use of surface craft, aided so far as possible by aircraft and submarines. For this all-important objective heavy losses in battleships, cruisers, and destroyers must if necessary be accepted ... Every convoy which gets through must be considered a serious naval failure. The reputation of the Royal Navy is engaged in stopping this traffic.

When, after the war, Churchill reread this Directive before it was printed in his history of the war, he added: 'All this was easier to say than do.'

While these tense signals and papers were circulating, the destroyers of the 14th Flotilla were in action from Valletta. Operational difficulties were considerable. Firstly, as we saw in the previous chapter, the German air force had, by mid-April, gained air superiority over Malta and the destroyers could only attempt convoy interception at night. Secondly, the enemy convoys were routed close to the Tunisian coast, 160 miles west of Malta. This required the destroyers to steam at high speed for six hours before an interception became possible, and they had then to be back under Malta's air cover before daylight. This left little time in which to locate and attack an enemy convoy. Finally, once off the Tunisian coast everything then depended on visual sighting since none of the destroyers was equipped with radar, nor had any of the few reconnaissance aircraft been fitted with airborne search radar.

It was hardly surprising, therefore, except perhaps to Churchill, that the first two attempted interceptions on the nights of 11/12 and 12/13 April failed. The latter convoy was located and attacked by a force of Swordfish, but no hits were made.[20] When Churchill read a signal from Maynard in Malta about the failure of the air attack, he dictated an indignant ACTION THIS DAY minute to Alexander and Pound. 'This is a serious <u>Naval</u> failure. Another deadly convoy has got through. We have the right to ask why did not the Navy stop them. It is the duty of the Navy to stop them.' Success, however, was the reward of a further sortie when Captain Mack's destroyers, in a moonlight attack in the early hours of 16 April, sank five merchant ships and their three Italian destroyer escorts. HMS *Mohawk* was torpedoed and sunk in shallow waters, but the other three destroyers safely returned to Valletta.[21] When, on 17 April, Alexander gleefully reported this to Churchill, adding, 'I think you will agree that the action shows that the officers out there are straining every nerve to deny the enemy the achievement of his purpose', he received the rather grudging reply, 'Yes: brilliantly redeemed. But what about the next?'[22]

Despite the outstanding success of the 16 April attack, the very real difficulties of intercepting the Italian supply convoys had been voiced by the Admiral Phillips, the Vice Chief of Naval Staff (VCNS), at a COS meeting on 12 April.

He wished to emphasise once again that the Mediterranean Fleet could not cut or seriously interfere with the enemy line of communication from Italy to Libya. They could harry that line and cause casualties, but could not expect to stop it unless the whole fleet could be based at Malta.[23]

Two weeks later, Admiral Cunningham echoed this in a signal to Admiral Pound: 'I feel we should be blind to facts if we imagine that six destroyers or for that matter sixteen can be quite sure of intercepting Libyan convoys unless they have proper air support to enable them to work by day.'[24] Moreover, the destroyers at Malta had other tasks to perform. After carrying out repairs and reloading with ammunition and fuel, the 14th Flotilla on 19 April escorted a convoy of empty merchant ships towards Alexandria. Two of the destroyers then joined the Fleet for the bombardment of Tripoli, which is described later. Afterwards, these two, joined by two others, HMS *Jaguar* and *Juno*, returned to Malta, followed on 24 April by the cruiser HMS *Gloucester*. On that day the destroyers, while searching for another southbound convoy, attacked and sank an Italian auxiliary cruiser. Four days later, major naval reinforcements for the Mediterranean Fleet brought to Valletta six destroyers of the 5th Flotilla, commanded by Captain Lord Louis Mountbatten. The Admiralty suggested the retention of all ten destroyers at Malta, but Cunningham replied that the destroyers of the 14th were urgently needed at Alexandria. Admiral Pound had also raised the possibility of basing a battleship at Malta. Cunningham said that he was not opposed to this in principle, but thought that the risks of air attack on and around Malta were so great that 'the battleship will be so harassed both at sea and in harbour that she will be unable to fulfil her function'.[25]

We must now turn our attention to the efforts made to increase the aerial offensive from Malta's battered airfields. Despite Admiral Cunningham's complaint that the Air was not doing enough, Churchill recognised the difficulties at Malta and ordered that fighters should have priority in the use of airfields, not least in order to protect the destroyers of the 14th Flotilla. Nevertheless, since the vital port of Tripoli was now out of range of the RAF's Egypt-based bombers, it was essential that it be attacked from Malta. Consequently, at first six, and later nine Wellingtons of 148 Squadron were sent back to Luqa from where they attacked Tripoli at night between 13 and 20 April. The Swordfish of 830 Squadron, carrying bombs or mines to lay in the harbour approaches, joined them on several nights.

It was these two squadrons that provided the prelude to one of the most contentious naval operations of this period: the naval bombardment of Tripoli by the whole Mediterranean Fleet in the early hours of 21 April 1941. Such was the concern in London about the flow of German troops and supplies into Tripoli that Churchill and Pound pressed Cunningham either to sacrifice one of his few battleships to block the harbour entrance, or to carry out a full scale bombardment. Cunningham strenuously objected to the former proposal, fearing losses to mines or air attack that he could ill afford. He eventually, under protest, accepted the second choice put to him. Zero hour for the bombardment was fixed for 5.00 a.m. on 21 April, and from 3.30 to 4.15 a.m. the port was bombed by eight of Malta's Wellingtons. They were followed in the next fifteen minutes by 830 Squadron's Swordfish carrying 250-pound bombs. The subsequent naval bombardment lasted for forty minutes from 5.00 a.m., the Fleet's battleships and cruisers being screened by destroyers including two of the destroyers of the 14th Flotilla from Valletta. To Cunningham's great surprise and relief, the Fleet was not attacked from the air, and suffered no damage from mines or from inaccurate and belated coastal artillery fire.

Nevertheless, the results were disappointing, and Tripoli was only put out of action for one day.[26]

Air attacks from Malta on enemy convoys at sea continued to be hampered by inadequate intelligence, and by the lack of modern strike aircraft. Several more of the Glen Martin 'Maryland' reconnaissance aircraft had been flown to the island in the early months of the year, but these aircraft, too, suffered on the ground from German air attacks, and there were never more than four of them serviceable at any one time. On 29 April, the Admiralty passed on to the Air Ministry an urgent request from Vice-Admiral Ford at Malta for three long-range reconnaissance aircraft fitted with airborne search radar (ASV) to work with the destroyers at night. However, Wellingtons equipped for this purpose did not arrive in Malta until much later, as we shall see.

It had long been the Air Ministry's intention to send a flight of Beaufort torpedo-bombers to Malta to reinforce the Swordfish of 830 Squadron. They had been promised 'in principle' as early as January and in the early days of April after Rommel's advance several references to the imminent arrival of these aircraft have already been quoted. However, after the decision by the Admiralty to send the 14th Destroyer Flotilla to Valletta, the composition of the air forces at Malta's three heavily bombed airfields required review. After Churchill's Directive on 14 April that fighters must have priority, Portal, on the next day, signalled to the AOC-in-C in Cairo:

> Assuming that naval forces are again based on Malta in immediate future for purpose of cutting enemy sea communications with Tripoli, the defence of the naval base against air attack will be primary objective of Air Forces stationed in Island. Request you consider what force can best achieve this object using all aerodromes to the full and accepting consequent risk of damage to aircraft from bombing. I suggest retaining from Dunlop enough Hurricanes to form two or three full squadrons and also raising Glen Martins to full squadron for reconnaissance and day bombing of Sicilian aerodromes. Under new circumstances propose not, repeat not, send Beauforts at present and would agree Wellingtons returning Egypt unless you would require them for night bombing of Sicilian aerodromes. Signal your views.

The reply, two days later, recommended two full Mark II Hurricane squadrons, with 150 per cent reserves, and the retention of a flight of Wellingtons. The Marylands were considered unsuitable for daylight bombing. The signal then added: 'C-in-C Mediterranean will press for torpedo bomber aircraft.'

The C-in-C Mediterranean did indeed protest. In a signal to the Admiralty of 22 April, Admiral Cunningham, after stating that 'We are finding our present commitments rather more than we can deal with efficiently', went on to write:

> To me it appears that the Air Ministry are trying to lay their responsibilities on Navy's shoulders and are not helping us out here on naval side of the war as they should. I draw your attention to latest decision not to send Beauforts to Malta. This will serve to perpetuate the present conditions where enemy can freely move his convoys by day without fear of air attack whereas, even within a few miles of our own coast, ours are only free from that danger on dark nights.[27]

When, however, on the following day the COS considered what more could be done to strengthen the offensive air capability in Malta, ACM Portal told his colleagues that 'a flight of Blenheim aircraft could be sent as an experiment to carry out daylight attacks on ships bound for Tripoli'.

Churchill then decided that Cunningham's signals of 22 and 25 April required a detailed response. This was in part reprimand, in part advice, and in part congratulation. He first pointed out, with reference to Cunningham's claim that bombing of Tripoli would have been more effective than the naval bombardment, that it would have taken a full Wellington squadron at Malta ten and a half weeks to drop as much high explosive on Tripoli as the Fleet fired in forty-two minutes. 'You should obtain accurate information, because no judgement can be formed without it.' He also rejected Cunningham's complaint against the Air Ministry: 'The main disposition of forces between the various theatres rests with the Defence Committee, over which I preside, and not with the Air Ministry, who execute our decisions.' He then continued:

> Your remarks about our withholding the Beauforts from Malta show that you do not appreciate the fact that the primary aim of the Air Force in Malta is to defend the naval base against air attack, in order that your surface craft may operate against enemy convoys with their decisive power as so successfully demonstrated. This policy may be right or wrong, it may prove too costly in ships, but we think it ought to be tried. For the purposes of TIGER, apart from what comes from DOUBLE WINCH, we are sending 15 Beaufighters to Malta, and also to supplement the efforts of the surface forces to interrupt ships between Italy and Tripoli, we are sending out today 6 of the specially trained Blenheim bombers which have been doing so well against coastal shipping here.[28]

Churchill's signal went on to inform Cunningham about the effect on the Mediterranean of the assistance now being given in the Atlantic by the US Navy. He concluded by writing: 'I have taken the pains to give you this full account out of my admiration for the successes you have achieved, your many cares, my sympathy for you in the many risks your fleet has to run, and because of the commanding importance of the duty you have to discharge.'

Although Cunningham may well have been irritated by the content and tone of this signal, he decided to seize the opportunity offered to explain in detail to the Prime Minister the difficulties that faced the Navy in the Mediterranean.[29] Cunningham's principal contention was that, unless British air forces were massively increased, 'to reach some measure of parity with those of the enemy we may have to face some very unpleasant alternatives'. With regard to Malta he made two observations. He first deplored the fact that the island's promised scale of defences had never been achieved. 'Malta,' he declared, 'has always been hazardous for warships and few have emerged undamaged.' Secondly, he disagreed with the decision to make RAF Malta's primary duty the defence of the island. Offensive air operations were equally vital. 'This second string to our bow is of the highest importance to interlock with efforts of our surface craft.'

Parenthetically, it is puzzling to read in Cunningham's post-war memoirs that, alluding to Churchill's signal of 26 April, he wrote: 'I need not refer to the rest of the message, to which I did not reply. We were far too busy with our other commitments.' In fact, he devoted the next two pages of his book to paraphrasing, often word for word, his lengthy reply of 29 April, from which the above extracts have been quoted.[30] This is how historical myths are created and then perpetuated by later writers who ignore documentary evidence.

Churchill did not print Cunningham's reply in his memoirs, or even refer to it, but the influence of this cable, together with Cunningham's earlier cable to the Admiralty of 25 April, cannot be doubted. For at 1.30 a.m. on 30 April, Churchill dictated his Directive of that date which has been discussed in the previous chapter. Paragraph 2 of that Directive bears repeating:

'Winch' and 'Double Winch' have succeeded, and 'Triple Winch' is in preparation, but this is not enough to get us out of the accusation of 'driblets'. An operation similar to 'Tiger' must be planned for the Air.

The 'accusation of 'driblets' came at the end of Cunningham's signal of 25 April where he wrote: 'Driblets merely get swallowed up as has been only too clearly shown in Greece and Malta.' It is also clear that Cunningham's cables had led Churchill to enquire about the current state of Malta's AA establishment for his Malta papers contain a handwritten note from General Ismay, dated 26 April. This states that 94 of the planned 112 heavy guns, and 52 of the 72 light guns had been installed, and that the remainder were on their way. As we have already seen, this Directive set in motion the operations referred to by Churchill as 'Jaguar', which transformed the RAF's strength in Malta and the Middle East, although not before the Navy had suffered further grievous losses in the evacuations from Greece and Crete. It says much for Cunningham's ability and his determination to speak his mind that it took his warnings, rather than those of ACM Longmore, the AOC-in-C Middle East, to galvanise Churchill and the COS to face up to the consequences of British air weakness in the Mediterranean theatre.

It is not surprising, therefore, to find that Churchill replied to Cunningham's forthright signals in more generous terms. On 1 May, he told Cunningham of the major fighter reinforcements of Malta and the Middle East that he had ordered for Operation 'Jaguar'. Referring then to the evacuation of the Expeditionary Force from Greece, he continued: 'I also congratulate you on the brilliant and highly successful manner in which the Navy once again succoured the Army and brought off four-fifths of the entire force.' Finally, after stressing the need to 'fight hard for Crete ... and for Malta as a base for flotilla action against the enemy's communications with Libya', he concluded:

> But above all we look to you to cut off seaborne supplies from the Cyrenaican ports and to beat them up to the utmost. It is in our power to give you information about enemy transport movements to these ports. It causes grief here when we learn of the arrival of precious aviation spirit in one ship after another. This great battle for Egypt is what the Duke of Wellington called 'A close-run thing', but if we can reinforce you and Wavell as proposed by Operations TIGER and JAGUAR and you can cut off the tap of inflow, our immense Armies in the Middle East will soon resume their ascendancy. All good wishes.[31]

Cunningham's reply, thanking the Prime Minister for the 'heartening news of aircraft', suggests that this frank exchange had cleared the air, and given Churchill a better idea of what was required.

Meanwhile at Malta, Vice-Admiral Ford was confronted with three growing problems. As the air attacks on Malta rose to new levels of intensity, Ford signalled to Cunningham: 'Harbour is becoming untenable by ships at night without the gravest risk and it will be necessary to send Gloucester and the 5th Destroyer Flotilla to sea nightly in spite of shortage of fuel whether a convoy has been located or not.' Secondly, the *Luftwaffe* had for several months been dropping mines around Valletta, and Ford had found it increasingly difficult to clear these with a dwindling number of sweepers. In a signal to Pound on 3 May, which Churchill will have seen, Cunningham expressed his own concern:

I am worried to death about Malta and the mining situation there. We are so short of sweepers. I have only two working here and four being fitted out, the gear having only just arrived. VAM [i.e. Ford] has two sets not yet fitted to ships ... Of course the morale of the dockyard workmen there is going down I believe and I expect he has trouble to get divers. They are having a bad time; never a let off from continual bombing ... I think we shall have to take Gloucester away. I hope to keep the destroyers there as their mere presence hampers the convoys and they may get a better chance in the moonlight.[32]

The almost inevitable consequence was that when, on 2 May, the 5th Flotilla returned to Malta from an unsuccessful convoy interception, HMS *Jersey* struck a mine and sank, blocking the entrance to the Grand Harbour. Two of the destroyers and HMS *Gloucester*, unable to enter, were ordered to Gibraltar.

Admiral Ford's third difficulty was a growing shortage of fuel oil as stocks were depleted by the high-speed steaming of the destroyers and the continual refuelling of other warships calling at Malta on other duties. The naval supply ship HMS *Breconshire* had brought in the first of her many cargoes for Malta while the Fleet was bombarding Tripoli, but much more was needed. Cunningham, therefore, decided to add two tankers and *Breconshire* to the four cargo ships he intended to escort to Malta when he sailed to meet the 'Tiger' convoy. The passage of this vital convoy, and its arrival at Alexandria with the loss of only one of its five tank-carrying merchant ships, has been noted in the previous chapter. Meanwhile, the seven ships bound for Malta, including the two tankers loaded with 24,000 tons of fuel, also arrived safely. Dropping depth charges from harbour launches to detonate the mines cleared a channel through the minefield, and the convoy was then swept in by the corvette HMS *Gloxinia*. The clearance of the harbour entrance also allowed the departure of the remaining three destroyers to join the 'Tiger' escort. In addition, Malta provided long-range air cover as the 'Tiger' convoy sailed south of Malta in the shape of the Beaufighters of 252 Squadron, which had been specially flown out to the island for this purpose.

However, although the safe passage of the 'Tiger' convoy was watched with great relief in London and Cairo, the enemy traffic to North Africa could not be ignored. Moreover, intercepted signals in late April showed the German intention to make greater use of Benghazi to supplement Tripoli's unloading facilities. Benghazi was not only several hundred miles closer to Rommel's front line, but the sea passage to it down the Greek coast was further removed from interception from Malta. This information prompted an aggrieved minute to the COS from Churchill:

Is it not rather strange that, when we announced that the port of Benghazi while in our occupation was of no use, and, secondly, that on our evacuation we had completely blocked it, the enemy are using it freely?[33]

This undoubtedly prompted the Admiralty signal to Cunningham on 1 May. 'The necessity,' they wrote, 'for interrupting the communications to Benghazi is so urgent that Their Lordships trust you will review the situation and if possible provide a force to operate against the Benghazi communications between now and TIGER.' Cunningham must have despaired at the unreality of this signal, but restrained his anger in his reply of 2 May:

No one can be more alive to implication of Benghazi situation than we are out here but I suggest I must be allowed to be judge of what can or can't be done as regards keeping units of the fleet at sea. If no action is taken to give a brief lull to man and machinery in light craft we shall find ourselves with a collection of crocks ... The most essential thing now is safe and timely arrival of TIGER and on that I must concentrate.[34]

He concluded this signal by promising to do 'all that is possible to embarrass this line of supply during and after TIGER'.

Accordingly, on the Fleet's passage west to meet the 'Tiger' convoy, the cruiser HMS *Ajax* and three destroyers were, on 7 May, detached to bombard Benghazi, and succeeded in sinking two ammunition ships in the harbour approaches. Four days later, on the night of 10/11 May, Captain Lord Mountbatten led the 5th Destroyer Flotilla from Malta to shell the port again. However, the destroyers caused little damage before withdrawing under continual dive-bomber attack. Cunningham was far from pleased with this operation, signalling Pound on 18 May: 'I was a little disappointed with the 5th Flotilla when they shelled it. They were dive bombed by moonlight and legged it to the northward. If they had gone South in accordance with their orders I think they would have picked up the four ships which arrived at Benghazi the next day.'[35] On 21 May, however, the 5th Flotilla left Malta to rejoin the Mediterranean Fleet as it carried out the dangerous and costly evacuation of British and Commonwealth forces from Crete. Two days later, fifty miles south of Crete, HMS *Kelly* and *Kashmir* were caught and sunk by German dive-bombers although HMS *Kipling* picked up 279 survivors, including Captain Lord Mountbatten. HMS *Gloucester*, which had briefly operated from Malta, was also lost.

The departure of this destroyer force, six weeks after its arrival, left further offensive operations from Malta for the immediate future in the hands of the 10th Flotilla submarines, the Swordfish of 830 Squadron, and the RAF's strike aircraft. Their operations and other developments in Malta are examined in the next chapter, but it will be convenient to review here what the island's offensive forces had achieved in the first five months of 1941. The bare statistics show that these forces had sunk twenty-five merchant ships with an aggregate tonnage of 96,067 tons. Fifteen of these were sunk by submarines, six by surface ships, and three by aircraft. An additional ship succumbed to a combined submarine and air attack. Thirteen of these ships, aggregating 57,550 tons, were sunk in April and May after the arrival of the 5th Flotilla and the reinforcement of the submarine force. In addition to these enemy losses, it should be borne in mind that Rommel was also deprived of the supplies in ships that were damaged and unable to reach North Africa, and in others whose passage was delayed for fear of attack. Nevertheless, despite these growing successes, post-war Italian records reveal that only 6 per cent of the supplies sent to North Africa during the first five months of 1941 failed to arrive, although losses rose to about 8 per cent in April and May.

If Churchill had been aware of these figures at the time, he would undoubtedly have been keenly disappointed. However, a more favourable picture of the effects of the naval and air attacks on the convoy route soon emerged. From late April numerous intercepted *Luftwaffe* signals expressed growing concern about the restriction of operations caused by the shortage of aviation fuel. Whether German army units were also suffering from supply shortages could only be surmised since the army Enigma ciphers had not then been broken. Enlightenment came when British Intelligence read a signal sent to Berlin from General Paulus on 2 May, a signal that had, fortunately, been transmitted in the air force cipher. Paulus had been sent to North Africa by the German High Command to review the state of Rommel's campaign, and his signal followed Rommel's unsuccessful attempt to capture Tobruk. Paulus reported that Rommel's position was weak, that his troops were thoroughly exhausted, and that his supply position was insecure. He had, therefore, ordered Rommel to go on to the defensive until his force had been reorganised and resupplied. This signal, quickly laid before the Prime Minister and his commanders, was read with relief in London and Cairo. It eased anxieties about an early invasion of Egypt, but it also revealed just how fragile Rommel's supply line was.[36] If he was in difficulties after losing only 6 per cent of his shipments, there was every incentive for the intensification of the naval and air attacks from bases in Malta and elsewhere.

But to achieve this objective much more needed to be done. More long-range reconnaissance aircraft, equipped with airborne search radar, more anti-ship strike aircraft, and more medium bombers were essential if the RAF were to cause the enemy more severe losses. The naval forces at Malta also needed to be strengthened. The increasingly effective submarine force required reinforcement by surface ships, also radar-equipped for night interception, if more Axis ships were to be found and destroyed. But above all it was essential that the air and naval bases in Malta be afforded better protection against air attack. By the middle of May, it had become clear that a major reorganisation and reinforcement of RAF Malta was imperative. That, despite all the dangers and difficulties, so much was achieved in the early months of 1941, when the *Luftwaffe* had achieved air superiority over the island, was a tribute to the courage and determination not only of the servicemen based there, but also of the many thousands of Maltese who shared these dangers in the dockyard, at the guns, and in carrying out numerous civil defence duties. As noted earlier, almost 500 civilians lost their lives or were seriously injured in the first year of the war at Malta.

In these early months of 1941, as the powerful German army and air forces inflicted one defeat after another on the British and Commonwealth forces in the Mediterranean, the records leave no doubt about Churchill's influence on decisions and actions. Never one to be disheartened by setbacks, he issued a stream of directives, minutes and telegrams, all designed to stimulate the greatest possible attack on the enemy. Malta became the focus of his attention when the threat posed by Rommel to the British position in Egypt had become apparent. That threat could be blunted if Rommel were starved of supplies, and Malta was ideally placed to apply the pressure if only sufficiently powerful forces could operate from the island. Hence the insistent demands that Churchill made on the Navy to take more vigorous action against the enemy convoys. But it took several blunt warnings from Admiral Cunningham to make Churchill and the Chiefs of Staff realise that little could be achieved without adequate air cover for ships and bases, and without better reconnaissance. Courage and determination could only achieve so much against a foe which had, in mid-1941, attained a high degree of military efficiency. The outlook for the months after the loss of Crete looked bleak. But Hitler had already made, and was about to implement, a decision that changed the character of the war and of the fighting in the Mediterranean.

REINFORCEMENTS AND ATTACK
SUMMER 1941

I take this opportunity to congratulate you on the firm and steadfast manner in which you and your devoted garrison and citizens have maintained Malta inviolate against all attacks for more than a year.
Churchill to General Dobbie, Governor of Malta, 3 August 1941.

On 6 June 1941, the Prime Minister found in his morning box of papers a copy of a lengthy telegram from General Dobbie in Malta, sent on the previous day. The German capture of Crete by the end of May, and the losses incurred by the Royal Navy in rescuing a large part of the garrison, raised in the Governor's mind the prospect of a 'German Airborne attack probably supported by a subsidiary seaborne attack'. In order to be confident of defeating such an attack, the Governor requested two additional infantry battalions, more field and anti-tank guns, and substantially more personnel. He also urged the formation of a third fighter squadron. Three days earlier he had written to General Dill, the CIGS, and on 14 June Churchill received a copy with Dill's note: 'I think you might like to see this letter from Dobbie that I got yesterday.' After beginning, 'It is extraordinary how quickly the situation and outlook change in this amazing war', the Governor went on to say that he was making plans to meet a German airborne attack. He continued:

As I wrote to Admiral Cunningham, one thing is axiomatic – and that is Malta holds on whatever happens elsewhere. The supply situation is not too bad. We have had some drastic R.A.F. changes here and these have done much good and will do more. I am confident about the future, and in a few months we will be able to look back with great thankfulness and see how God has brought us through a very difficult period.

After reading Dobbie's telegram, but before seeing the letter, Churchill at once sent the following signal to the Governor:

I am entirely in agreement with your general outlook. The War Office will deal in detail with all your points. It does not seem that an attack on Malta is likely within the next two or three weeks. Meanwhile other events of importance will be decided, enabling or compelling a new view to be taken. You may be sure we regard Malta as one of the master-keys of the British Empire. We are sure you are the man to hold it, and we will do everything in human power to give you the means.[1]

One can only imagine that Dobbie's letter confirmed Churchill's confidence in the Governor.

General Dobbie may have wondered about the meaning of the fourth sentence of Churchill's signal, but it conceals a growing expectation in London that Germany was in the final stages of preparing a massive surprise attack on Russia. In a detailed and fascinating chapter of his history of British Intelligence, Professor Hinsley has documented the growing evidence from Enigma decrypts and other sources of the German build-up in Eastern Europe. However, the various British Intelligence agencies were, he considers, 'slow to reach agreement on the conclusion that Germany would make an attack on Russia, an undertaking which she had been preparing throughout the previous winter'.[2] The Government Code & Cypher School (GC&CS) at Bletchley Park and Air Intelligence (AI) had become convinced of this German intention by the middle of May, but it was not until early June that the Foreign Office and Military Intelligence (MI) with some hesitation accepted this interpretation of the evidence. As late as 31 May, a COS telegram to the Dominion Prime Ministers about the overall situation concluded: 'Invasion of United Kingdom probably remains Germany's 1941 objective. Apart from Battle of the Atlantic enemy's main effort is now directed to capture of Egypt.'[3] However, Churchill himself had, since late March, been inclined to believe that Germany would attack Russia, and was angered when his warning to Stalin on 3 April was not delivered to him by Stafford Cripps, the British Ambassador in Moscow, until 19 April. It was in the expectation of this imminent German attack, expected in mid-June, that Churchill advised the Governor that an early attack on Malta was unlikely.

But if there had been differing views in Whitehall about the possibility of the German attack, there was almost unanimous agreement that Russia, if attacked, would be defeated in a matter of weeks. Moreover, Germany's military power was thought to be so overwhelming that it would not be seriously weakened by such a campaign. Consequently, she would then be free, within a few months, to return to the possible invasion of Britain. The War Cabinet, therefore, gave instructions to the commanders in Britain that plans were to be made for a possible German invasion attempt at any time after 1 September. A renewed attack on the British position in the

Middle East was also likely, in which case Malta might only enjoy a brief respite.

Before we consider the response of the COS to General Dobbie's request, it should be noted that the German planning staff had, as early as February, devised a plan for the invasion of Malta, and, moreover, judged this to be more important than the seizure of Crete. This order of priority had the support of Admiral Raeder, but Field Marshal Goering objected, pointing to the difficulties that would be caused to an airborne attack by Malta's close network of stone walls. Hitler then ruled that the invasion of Malta be postponed until the autumn after the conclusion of the Russian campaign.[4]

The Governor's signal was discussed by the COS at a series of meetings in mid-June. Admiral Pound expressed the general view on 18 June that 'we should make a big effort and try to give Malta all that the fortress required to keep it going for the next six months'.[5] The Joint Planning Staff (JPS) were instructed to make the necessary plans and quickly accepted the contention of Admiral Cunningham that any reinforcement convoy must come from the west, given the threat to an eastern convoy posed by new German airfields in Crete. On 25 June, three days after the German invasion of Russia, Col. Hollis reported to Churchill what the COS had decided. They had concluded that a major reinforcement of Malta should be undertaken 'while the Germans are occupied with Russia', and proposed to send from the west a convoy comprised of one troopship and six fast merchant ships. In addition to 50,000 tons of supplies, these would carry two infantry battalions, sixteen heavy and sixty light AA guns, and thirty field guns. The large consignment of light AA guns had been urged by Portal in a memorandum to the COS on 3 June. Since, he argued, the enemy could always assemble more aircraft for an attack on Malta than the RAF could base on the island, stronger AA defences were essential. He thought that as many as 250 light Bofors guns were needed rather than the 72 that had been allocated to the island. Otherwise, he continued, 'I see no reason why the enemy should not take Malta in the same way as Crete as soon as he wishes and can spare the forces.'[6]

The army reinforcements, Col. Hollis explained to the Prime Minister, would total 4,610 men. In addition, 710 RAF personnel would be embarked to allow the formation of an additional fighter squadron. The convoy, designated Operation 'Substance', would sail on 12 July and reach Malta on the 24th. Churchill approved these plans at a Defence Committee meeting on 25 June.[7] However, the COS resisted Churchill's pressure to include in the convoy another ship carrying 100 more tanks to Egypt after General Wavell's attack on Rommel on 15–18 June – Operation 'Battleaxe' – had been thrown back with considerable tank losses. Churchill accepted this decision, but complained: 'We were too much inclined to play for safety until a great emergency arose.' On 25 July, after the safe arrival of the 'Substance' convoy, Churchill minuted to General Ismay:

> Let me have, on one sheet of paper, the exact strength and details of the reinforcements and stores which got into Malta, and also the previous strength of the Malta garrison.[8]

Ismay sent him the required information later that day. His note revealed that the garrison had risen to 22,297 men, that 112 heavy and 118 light AA guns were now available to the gunners, that military supplies would last for a further eight months, and civilian supplies for seven and a half months. Unfortunately, for reasons explained later, one infantry battalion, one light AA regiment and 665 RAF men had been left behind at Gibraltar.

In his letter of 2 June, General Dobbie had referred to 'the drastic R.A.F. changes here', and we should now consider what was done to rebuild the strength of RAF Malta. In Chapter V we examined the steps that had been ordered in London to send to Malta the first of a growing number of Mark II Hurricanes, and to strengthen the ground organisation. These measures included more maintenance personnel, several experienced controllers, the establishment of a fighter control room, and the installation of more effective VHF air communications. We have also seen that at the end of May AVM Maynard was relieved as AOC Malta by AVM Lloyd, whose simple instructions from Portal were: 'Your main task at Malta is to sink Axis shipping sailing from Europe to Africa.'[9]

In some respects Lloyd was lucky, a quality much admired by Napoleon. Although the first fighter reinforcements had enabled Maynard to form a second squadron in May, the number of Hurricane II aircraft arriving in June grew significantly. On 6 June, Lloyd received, in Operation 'Rocket', another complete squadron from Fighter Command, No. 46 Squadron, while in Operations 'Railway I and II' at the end of the month a further fifty-five Hurricanes landed, some armed with four 20 mm cannon. When Churchill in early July suggested a repetition of 'Railway', he was told that Malta and the Middle East were now well supplied with modern fighters and experienced pilots. Moreover, in view of these transfers, Fighter Command needed to be strengthened to meet the possible German invasion attempt in the autumn. Apart from these fighter reinforcements, Lloyd also received additional Marylands, more Blenheims to augment the first five that had arrived in May, more Swordfish, and the return of a Wellington flight. Lloyd was quite familiar with the capabilities of the Blenheim low-level anti-ship strike aircraft since his previous appointment had been Senior Air Staff Officer (SASO) at 2 Group in Bomber Command, which operated these aircraft against German convoys in the North Sea.

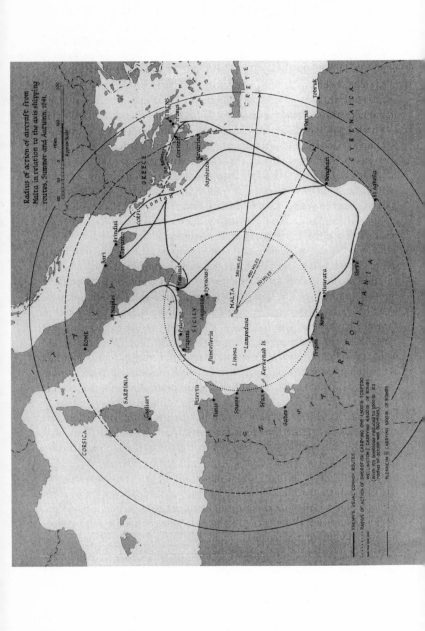

Radius of action of aircraft from Malta in relation to the axis shipping routes, Summer and Autumn, 1941.

CRETE

CYRENAICA

Derna

Tobruk

Benghazi

El Aghelia

Sirte

Misurata

TRIPOLITANIA

Homs

Tripoli

Kerkenah Is.

Gabes

Sfax

Sousse

TUNISIA

Tunis

Bizerta

Cagliari

SARDINIA

CORSICA

ROME

ITALY

Naples

Bari

Brindisi

Taranto

Palermo

Trapani

SICILY

Messina

Augusta

Syracuse

Pantelleria

Linosa

Lampedusa

MALTA

480 MILES

250 MILES

ATHENS

Piraeus

Corinth (on isthmus)

GREECE

Navarino

Sapienza

CORFU

Ionian Is.

Miles
0   50   100   200
Approx Scale

----- ENEMY'S USUAL CONVOY ROUTES.
.... RADIUS OF ACTION OF SWORDFISH CARRYING ONE 1,500 lb TORPEDO
WELLINGTON [CARRYING 4,500 lb OF BOMBS
(WITH ITS BOMBLOAD REDUCED TO 1,000 lb ITS
RADIUS OF ACTION WAS 960 MILES).
BLENHEIM [N] CARRYING 1,000 lb OF BOMBS

8. An attack on an Axis supply ship. Between 1940 and 1943, Malta's air and naval forces sank over 200 enemy supply ships with a combined tonnage of 852,000 tons.

But the most fortunate development was the departure of *Fliegerkorps X* from Sicily. Many of their aircraft had already been diverted to support Rommel's advance in North Africa, but the demands of the Greek campaign and the forthcoming attack on Russia shifted the focus of the German Air Force in the Mediterranean to the east. By early June it had become clear that all the remaining *Luftwaffe* squadrons, including Müncheberg's ME 109s, had left Sicily and had been replaced by Italian squadrons. Admiral Ford at once advised Admiral Cunningham that 'the scale of enemy air attack has greatly reduced'. It was, therefore, under a diminishing weight of attack that Lloyd was able to organise his growing defensive and offensive aircraft, and to improve the ground arrangements.

Lloyd acted quickly, seeing that the most urgent priority was to provide better protection on the ground for his growing force of aircraft. His experience in England taught him that this meant the removal of all aircraft from the airfields. 'In Britain,' he later wrote, 'there was a craze for dispersal.' In a letter to Portal of 20 June he wrote:

As regards the dispersal of aircraft I regret to report that it is in a very sorry state. Much has been done and is being done. I have had considerable difficulty in obtaining labour owing to the Public Shelter Scheme. However, all that is now satisfactory. It will be eight weeks before I shall be satisfied. My first problem has been to move aircraft off the aerodromes. That is now done but considerable development is necessary to ensure adequate dispersal.[10]

He added that 'the Fighter Squadrons are doing well; their morale is excellent'.

With this essential task under control, Lloyd's next problem was that of keeping as many of his aircraft as possible in serviceable condition, a problem exacerbated by the growing number and types of aircraft arriving on the island. He had expected these difficulties to be eased by the arrival of 700 or so airmen in the seven-ship 'Substance' convoy, which has been described above. Unfortunately, all the airmen were embarked on the troopship *Leinster*, and she ran aground outside Gibraltar on 20 July. As soon as he heard of this mishap, Lloyd signalled the Air Ministry on 26 July to explain the difficulties resulting from the loss of these stranded airmen.

He first pointed out that his total ground staff, including those sick, amounted to 1,630 men, 'less that any bomber station in England'. He currently had 174 aircraft on the island, while a further 193 had passed through in June alone, all requiring refuelling and, in some cases, repairs as well. He went on to warn that, on average, only thirty out of eighty-four Hurricanes were serviceable, and only five out of twenty-one Blenheims. On some days only two or three Blenheims were available. 'Many operations,' he continued, 'were almost ruined through aircraft becoming unserviceable in the air and depleted forces going on to achieve a half success.' He had too few petrol bowsers, and he urgently needed 200 bicycles to enable the ground staff to save time in getting to the now widely dispersed aircraft. But, he concluded, when the missing airmen arrive, 'all will be well'. This urgent telegram was placed before the COS on 27 July, and Admiral Pound at once agreed to send the airmen on from Gibraltar to Malta as quickly as possible, employing cruisers for this purpose.[11] This was successfully carried out in Operation 'Style', and a total of 1,700 men, including all the stranded airmen, arrived at Malta on 2 August. General Ismay, in a memorandum of 27 July, had kept Churchill advised of this problem and its solution and on this Churchill wrote: 'I spoke to 1SL [First Sea Lord] and cordially approve his proposal.'

Consequently, when ACM Sir Edgar Ludlow-Hewitt, the Inspector General of the RAF, visited Malta in the middle of July he was able to report to Portal on 21 July: 'This place I find in much better form than I expected. Lloyd has and is working wonders. Everyone here is singing his praises, and he has certainly got a move on.' He told Portal that he had heard some criticism of Maynard, Lloyd's predecessor as AOC, but thought this unfair given the limited resources which Maynard had available. He went on to recommend a fourth fighter squadron and a flight of Beauforts. 'The Blenheims are doing splendid work,' he assured Portal, 'but the torpedo is a much more effective weapon and the Swordfish have insufficient range not to speak of speed.' The letter ended with a handwritten postscript: 'Dobbie and Ford are splendid. In the absence of the Germans this island is just a pleasant seaside resort. The Italian air raids are just childish.'[12] The civilian population of Malta and the growing garrison might have read these comments with some disbelief.

Mention may be made here of the Italian naval attack on the Grand Harbour on the night of 25/26 July, since the target was the recently arrived cargo ships of Operation 'Substance'. A force of motor boats packed with explosives and a number of manned torpedoes attempted to break through the boom defences into the Grand Harbour. But their approach had been detected by radar, and the Maltese-manned harbour defences sank most of these craft, the rest being destroyed by aircraft as they attempted to escape. Among Churchill's Malta papers is a War Office Note describing this action which concluded:

> The accuracy of the RMA shooting and their determination gives proof of long practice and hard training. The success of this regiment in their first test should act as a powerful deterrent against future enemy sea attacks against Malta.

A notation on this paper read: 'It is understood that the Prime Minister wishes to make a reference to this in his speech.' In the event, the debate on production in the House of Commons on 29 July took a different course, and Churchill found no opportunity to mention this attack on Malta. The British newspapers carried full accounts of this action, but the COS, at a meeting on 8 August, criticised the failure to give 'proper credit to the Maltese gunners'. However, Churchill, when recording this attack in his memoirs, did give full credit to the Maltese gunners.[13]

We have followed in some detail Churchill's scrutiny of the reinforcement and rearmament of Malta. But, in his eyes, the purpose of all this effort and its attendant risks was to enable Malta's forces to strike heavier blows at the enemy, and it is to this overriding theme that we must now turn our attention. The failure of General Wavell's 'Battleaxe' attack in Cyrenaica on 17 June was for Churchill a 'most bitter blow'. He later wrote that, having gone down to Chartwell, 'Here I got reports of what had happened. I wandered about the valley disconsolately for some hours.' His Private Secretary, John Colville, also recalled that afternoon at Chartwell:

> After a long sleep the P.M., in a purple dressing-gown and grey felt hat, took me to see his goldfish. He was ruminating deeply about the fate of Tobruk since the failure of BATTLEAXE and contemplating means of resuming the offensive.[14]

When Churchill returned to London his disappointment and frustration led him, on 20 June, to send a minute to the COS. After urging the preparation of a further attack on Rommel, and the dispatch of another 100 tanks through the Mediterranean, he continued:

> The alternative is to remain on the defensive ... The Admiral has abandoned all hopes of blocking Tripoli and perhaps Benghazi also with [HMS] ANSON. Every single one of our plans has failed. The enemy has completely established himself in the central Mediterranean. We are afraid of his dive bombers at every point. Our ships cannot enforce any blockade between Italy and Cyrenaica, apart from submarines. The Air Force are plainly unable to stop them reinforcing. Have we really got to accept this?[15]

Having got this off his chest, he decided on the following day that changes in command were necessary, and General Auchinleck was appointed to replace General Wavell as C-in-C Middle East.

The decisions affecting Malta in the long, hot summer months of 1941, and the operations that resulted from them, can only be understood in the context of the Middle East situation as it appeared after Hitler's attack on Russia on 22 June. In London and Cairo all were agreed that this gave an opportunity to strengthen the British position in the theatre before a renewed German attack developed later in the year after the defeat of Russia. However, a fundamental disagreement quickly emerged about what could and should be done in the western desert. Churchill and the COS believed that the growing British and Commonwealth forces in the Middle East would be strong enough, after the conclusion of the Syrian campaign in mid-July, to mount a successful offensive against Rommel in September. This would have the twin objectives of relieving Tobruk, and of recapturing the Cyrenaican airfields to allow the Navy to recover control of the central Mediterranean. General Auchinleck disagreed, not about the desirability of such an offensive, but about its timing. He was convinced that the need for extensive reorganisation and training, especially of the armoured formations, ruled out any possibility of a successful offensive before November. Telegrams having failed to change his mind, he was summoned home at the end of July to argue out the whole matter.

At a five-hour meeting of the Defence Committee at Chequers on 1 August, the Middle East C-in-C faced the full weight of Churchill's formidable powers of persuasion.[16] The Prime Minister emphasised that intelligence information revealed that Rommel was facing serious supply difficulties. These could be made worse by stronger air and naval attack on his supply route, 'but it would be wrong to ask them to take even greater risks if the Army was not prepared to take advantage of the situation by fighting a battle'. As the minutes recorded, the Prime Minister continued:

> He thought that it was a frightful prospect that nothing should be done for four and a half months at a time when a small German army was having the greatest difficulty in so much as existing. The Army should establish closer contact with the enemy at Tobruk and in the Western Desert and set to work to make the enemy fight. He was ready to authorise quite exceptional measures if by any means a battle could be brought on earlier than November. But if there was no prospect of such a battle then he must reserve the right to withhold the brigade of the 1st Armoured Division.

Despite this fierce onslaught, Auchinleck refused to budge. With marked misgivings, therefore, Churchill accepted that the offensive in the desert could not be renewed before November. Other accounts indicate how tense a meeting this was. Oliver Harvey, Eden's Principal Private Secretary, recorded what Eden had told him: 'PM very rude but General very calm and answered well … The meeting broke up in some confusion, PM grumbling and growling – purple in the face and with streaming eyes.'[17] General Ismay was also concerned about the course of this meeting. In his memoirs he described a lengthy private meeting with Auchinleck that weekend at Chequers. He had known Auchinleck for twenty years and he did his best to explain to him the character of the Prime Minister and the pressure he often placed on his commanders. Ismay concluded by telling Auchinleck:

> [Churchill] was not prone to harbouring grievances, and it was a mistake to take lasting umbrage if his criticisms were sometimes unduly harsh or even unjust. If I had done so, I should never have had a moment's happiness.[18]

Three days later on 4 August, Churchill, with a large party, embarked on the new battleship HMS *Prince of Wales* at Scapa Flow on a voyage to meet President Roosevelt at Placentia Bay in Newfoundland. Before he left he sent two signals. The first went to Admiral Somerville, Commander of Force H at Gibraltar:

> I must not fail to congratulate you upon the skill and resolution with which the extremely difficult and hazardous operations of conducting the troop convoys to Malta were carried out by you and all ranks and ratings under your Command. This is only the latest of a long series of complicated and highly successful operations for which you and Force H have been responsible.[19]

The second signal went to General Dobbie in Malta:

> Now that the convoys have reached you safely with all their stores and
> reinforcements, I take this occasion to congratulate you on the firm and
> steadfast manner in which you and your devoted garrison and citizens
> have maintained Malta inviolate against all attacks for more than a
> year, and to express my confidence that with the help of God our cause
> will continue to prosper, and that the contribution of Malta to the final
> victory will add a noble chapter to the famous story of the island.[20]

The acceptance of a further three-month stalemate in the desert meant
that both sides would use these months to strengthen their forces. Whether
Rommel could do this more rapidly than Auchinleck across the relatively
short sea crossing to Italy and Greece, and then strike first, might determine
the security of Egypt. Much, therefore, would hang on the ability of the naval
and air forces at Malta to reduce or delay the flow of enemy supplies to North
Africa, and it is to these operations that we must now turn our attention.

On 30 June, Churchill sent a brief, sharp minute to the COS through
General Ismay:

> Although we take a heavy toll, very large enemy reinforcements are
> crossing to Africa continually. The Air Force only stop perhaps a fifth.
> You are no doubt impressed with the full gravity of the situation.[21]

After the Chiefs had considered this, Admiral Pound, on their behalf,
replied that they were indeed 'fully impressed with the gravity of the
situation'. He sent Churchill a four-page Naval Staff analysis of the
difficulties that would be faced by a surface force attempting to operate
in the central Mediterranean. Such ships would be outside fighter cover
and therefore vulnerable to dive-bomber attack from *Luftwaffe* bases in
Crete and Cyrenaica. The analysis concluded that only submarines and
aircraft could, with any assurance of success, attack the enemy supply
routes, but admitted that such operations 'are intermittent and do not
achieve complete stoppage of the supply line'. Pound added that, in
May and June, fifty-two enemy ships had been sunk or damaged, and he
thought this a 'creditable effort on the part of our naval and air forces'.
Churchill's reaction to this memorandum cannot be read since the bottom
half of the memorandum is missing, with the notation, 'Torn off by the
Prime Minister'. If, as seems possible, his initial reaction was critical, he
presumably decided not to pursue the matter. Nevertheless, he approved
the dispatch of further submarines and strike aircraft to Malta, convinced
that they were better employed there than in attacking the smaller German
ships in the North Sea.

Operations to starve Rommel of additional men and supplies became, consequently, the task of the Mediterranean submarines and air forces, and of those based at Malta in particular. We will look first at the submarine offensive. Admiral Pound had sent to Cunningham virtually all the available British submarines, and these were supplemented by several Dutch boats. They were distributed among three flotillas. The 1st Flotilla at Alexandria operated largely in the eastern basin and along the Greek and Cyrenaican coasts, while the 8th Flotilla at Gibraltar concentrated on targets in the Tyrrhenian Sea between Sicily, Italy and Sardinia. It was the task of the U-class submarines of the 10th Flotilla at Manoel Island to attack ships sailing between Italy and North African ports. The submarine patrol areas had been affected by the German capture of Greece, Crete and Cyrenaica, other than Tobruk. Axis convoys were, therefore, able to follow a new route, well clear of Malta, down the west coast of Greece to the western tip of Crete before crossing to Benghazi or Derna. However, since these ports could not handle all the necessary supplies, the earlier route from western Sicily to Tripoli along the Tunisian coast, and then to Benghazi was still heavily used.

The overall disposition of the submarine fleet, which had increased from twenty boats in March to twenty-nine in September, lay with Cunningham as C-in-C, but Cdr. Simpson, in collaboration with Admiral Ford, the

9. The submarine base at Manoel Island to the north of Valletta, showing several of the U-class submarines of the 10th Flotilla which was based there.

Senior Naval Officer at Malta, gave directions to the individual captains. This task was made easier in the summer of 1941 by Bletchley Park's breaking of an Italian machine cipher, referred to by Hinsley as 'C38m'.[22] This carried details of all forthcoming convoys to North Africa, and the number of signals sent in this cipher rose from 600 in August 1941 to nearly 4,000 in July 1942. These decrypts were sent directly to Ford and Simpson on a special secure link and enabled them to build up a picture of Italian convoy operations. Their use in directing operations was, however, subject to strict controls to maintain the secrecy of this vital source of information. Particular difficulties could arise when it was necessary to signal new convoy information to a submarine already on patrol. On at least two occasions Cdr. Simpson received a severe reprimand from Admiral Pound for signalling to one of his distant submarines the precise location of a convoy, rather than a general area of search. 'This is a matter,' Pound signalled, 'in which we cannot afford to have any, repeat any, slips.'[23]

The submarines of the 10th Flotilla at Malta, their captains now more experienced in convoy attack and directed by accurate intelligence, were able to sink ten ships with a tonnage of 73,246 tons between June and September 1941. Others were damaged and forced to return to port. Among those sunk were two 20,000-ton liners, *Neptunia* and *Oceania*, both pressed into service to carry Italian troops to North Africa. HMS *Upholder*, under the command of Lt-Com. Wanklyn, had been directed by a C38m decrypt to the course of these ships and sank both on 18 September. But this and other successes were not accomplished without loss; three 10th Flotilla submarines were lost in July and August.

The RAF in Malta was also the beneficiary of the C38m breakthrough. AVM Lloyd, having, as we have seen, acquired a growing number of aircraft and taken steps to improve security and servicing on the ground, turned his attention to his principal task, the attack on Axis convoys to North Africa. He, too, received the intelligence material directly and was able, in collaboration with Admiral Ford, to plan reconnaissance flights and anti-shipping strikes in conjunction with submarine attacks. Lloyd also benefitted from another British technical development – the installation of Air-to-Surface-Vessel (ASV) radar in a number of Swordfish. This short-range radar equipment could locate ships at night or in poor visibility, although the actual attacks needed to be illuminated by flares dropped by other aircraft. A further development came in October when, after a suggestion to Churchill by Lord Cherwell, three Wellingtons equipped with a long-range ASV arrived at Malta. These were able to search over a sixty-mile stretch of water and they were also equipped with means to enable the Swordfish to home onto them when a target was located.

With the help of these intelligence and technical advances, Lloyd was able to plan and execute a programme of shipping attacks. The Blenheim low-level bombers were his principal weapon until the losses suffered by these aircraft against strongly escorted convoys began to cause concern. ACM Freeman, the Vice Chief of the Air Staff (VCAS), suggested, on 27 August, the dispatch of two additional Blenheim squadrons to Malta, and wrote to AM Tedder, the AOC-in-C in Cairo: 'I expect Lloyd to employ these forces with greatest determination against enemy lines of communication.'[24] On 1 October, however, Portal told Tedder and Lloyd: 'I am becoming rather anxious about the strain that is being imposed on the Blenheims at Malta.' He went on:

> The trouble is that one sends out a squadron composed of a few real leaders and the rest good followers, but not leaders. Soon the leaders get killed and then there is no one with the necessary heart to take on what is, after all, an extremely tough job, and so the efficiency of the attacks wanes and morale wanes with it.[25]

After noting that eighteen Blenheim crews had been lost in the previous three months, he recommended that the Blenheim squadrons be rotated between Malta and Egypt. He also recommended that attacks should not be made against strongly escorted convoys. Lloyd reminded him that in August he had refused to direct his Blenheims against such convoys, telling Tedder that this was 'sheer murder'. However, he added that Admiral Cunningham had rebuked him for this statement, and Freeman's comment has been noted above. Nevertheless, it was agreed in mid-October that Blenheims should only be directed against unescorted ships.

The daytime Blenheim attacks were supplemented by the night operations of the Swordfish of 830 Squadron, reinforced in October by 828 Squadron flying Albacore torpedo-bombers, a later version of the Swordfish with a greater range. These aircraft concentrated on the sea route along the Tunisian route to Tripoli. In addition to the interception of merchant shipping, Lloyd's secondary objective was to destroy and damage goods and installations at the loading ports in Italy and at the unloading ports of Tripoli, Benghazi, Derna and Bardia. For this purpose he controlled a squadron of Wellington medium bombers, assisted at times by Marylands, when not engaged on reconnaissance work. RAF and Italian records show that these aircraft bombed Tripoli seventy-two times between mid-June and mid-October 1941, reducing port capacity at times by as much as 50 per cent. Bombing raids on North African ports were at times ordered when C38m decrypts indicated the arrival of a convoy. On one such occasion, on 25 September, a raid on Benghazi resulted in the destruction of a ship carrying the entire stock of one type of bomb.[26] On 8 October, Portal suggested that the port area of Naples be attacked with 4,000-pound bombs, to which Tedder in Cairo responded by confirming that this had been given priority.

10. Three Albacore torpedo-bombers in flight, each carrying a 1,600-pound torpedo. Despite their slow speed and limited range, these aircraft were effective in night operations against enemy convoys.

The damage caused by these bombing raids could only be estimated in general terms, whereas the sinking of merchant ships could be more precisely recorded. Between June and October 1941, Malta's air and submarine forces sank thirty-six ships with an aggregate tonnage of 204,145 tons. Ten of these, as noted earlier, were accounted for by the 10th Flotilla submarines, and twenty-five by aircraft. Another was shared between the two services. In terms of lost Axis supplies, post-war Italian records reveal that, out of a total of 493,000 tons dispatched to North Africa, 80,500 tons were lost at sea, an overall loss rate of 16 per cent in the June–October period as a whole. However, as attacks intensified, the loss rate rose to 28 per cent in September and stood at 20 per cent in October.

Churchill followed these developments closely, and did so by two means. As noted earlier, his daily dispatch boxes contained copies of all the most important service telegrams, together with the papers of the COS and the service departments. But perhaps more valuable to him in this period, when the position in North Africa was so critical, were the contents of his daily buff-coloured box. This contained a selection made for him by 'C', the Head of the Secret Intelligence Service (SIS), of the most revealing of the decrypts of enemy signals. From July 1941 this selection included a growing number of C38m decrypts, and some examples of these will be examined in the next chapter. It is important to recognise that this priceless source of information enabled Churchill to see in considerable detail how the attacks made by Malta's air and submarine forces affected Rommel's supply position and his ability to resume the offensive. In the late summer months of 1941 the easily read *Luftwaffe* Enigma, supplemented after mid-September by some German Army signals, indicated that Rommel was having difficulty in establishing adequate reserves to enable him to launch an attack on Tobruk as a prelude to the invasion of Egypt.

While the assault on the enemy supply lines intensified, the need to keep Malta supplied could not be ignored. The arrival of the 'Substance' convoy at the end of July provided no more than a breathing space of a few months. Consequently, on 28 August, Admiral Pound, conscious of the anticipated return of German forces to the Mediterranean, told the COS that plans were being made to send another large convoy from the west.[27] This became Operation 'Halberd', a convoy of nine fast merchant ships, led by HMS *Breconshire*, which passed through the Straits of Gibraltar on the night of 24/25 September. The ships carried 85,000 tons of civilian and military supplies, while 2,800 service reinforcements were distributed among the merchant ships and their escorts. A powerful battleship escort frightened off a threatened attack by an Italian battleship force, but the *Imperial Star* succumbed to an Italian torpedo-bomber attack. The other eight ships reached Malta safely on 28 September to an enthusiastic reception in the Grand Harbour. These supplies were intended to be sufficient to last until May 1942, with the exception of coal, kerosene, and animal fodder.

The problem of providing fodder for the island's horses and donkeys, widely used for local transport, had been partially met by the arrival of the *Empire Guillemot* on 19 September. She had made an independent passage, wearing various disguises as she sailed along the African coast, and had then, unlike her predecessor, the *Parracombe*, passed unharmed through the Sicilian minefields. However, she was later sunk on the return passage to Gibraltar. Limited supplies of much-needed aviation fuel were brought in from time to time by the larger submarines from Alexandria and Gibraltar, and the value of this 'Magic Carpet' service became more apparent in the following year. Churchill's earlier signal of congratulation to Admiral Somerville has been quoted above, and was richly deserved. In the period from May to September 1941, twenty-two merchant ships had been safely escorted to Malta from the west, and only one had been lost. The garrison of the island and its military effectiveness had been substantially increased, and the stocks of food and essential supplies for the civilian population built up to levels which removed immediate anxiety.

We may end this chapter by noting a discussion about the publicity to be given to Malta's offensive operations. This discussion was initiated by a telegram from the Governor on 26 September. He pointed out that, contrary to the policy adopted during earlier months, increasing publicity was being given by the press to offensive operations, and that the Air Ministry and the Admiralty had sent representatives and official photographers to Malta for this purpose. There was also an American press representative in Malta. The Governor was worried that this might provoke heavier enemy attack on the island, for which the Maltese people would hold the government responsible. He himself, he added, favoured 'the maximum amount of offensive activity from Malta with the minimum of publicity'. AM Tedder in Cairo was of the same view. The Governor, therefore, asked for guidance on this matter.

On his copy of this telegram, Churchill asked Col. Hollis to request a report on the Governor's signal from the COS. They had earlier, as we have seen, criticised the failure of the British newspapers to publicise the success of the Maltese gunners in repulsing the Italian naval attack on the Grand Harbour. The Prime Minister, who, he once reminded Admiral Pound, had been a journalist for many years, was well aware of the conflict between secretive service departments and newspapers eager for news to print. In England this dilemma had only been satisfactorily resolved when Churchill had appointed his old friend, Brendan Bracken, a former newspaper editor, as Minister of Information in July 1941. The COS, as instructed, considered the question at two meetings in early October. Portal shared the Governor's reluctance to see wider publicity, but could not convince his colleagues. The COS, therefore, reported to the Prime Minister on 3 October that they favoured a more relaxed publicity policy subject to strict guidelines. They argued that 'attacks on Malta will continue to be governed by purely military considerations and not by the extent or nature of our propaganda'. On the other hand, they thought that favourable publicity for Malta's successes would boost the morale of the garrison and the civil population. They submitted to the Prime Minister a draft telegram to the Governor, which concluded:

> We realise that this [new publicity] policy may give rise to the feeling that if Malta is attacked it is because of the publicity given to your operations, but we do not consider that this is so, and are agreed that the propaganda value outweighs the security aspect provided above safeguards are applied.[28]

Churchill accepted this advice without further comment, and this became the new policy. The result was much wider press coverage in England and the USA of operations carried out by Malta's forces. These were soon to be significantly increased.

FORCE K JOINS THE ATTACK
AUTUMN 1941

Will you please consider the sending of a flotilla, and, if possible, a cruiser or two to Malta, as soon as possible.

Prime Minister to First Sea Lord, 22 August 1941

On 12 August 1941, Churchill and President Roosevelt, meeting in Placentia Bay, Newfoundland, agreed the terms of 'The Atlantic Charter', a declaration of the principles 'on which they base their hopes for a better future for the world'. After a brief stop in Iceland, the Prime Minister arrived back in London on 18 August and, on the following day, briefed the War Cabinet on his discussions with the President. Despite the latter's difficulties with Congress, he had assured Churchill that 'he would wage war, but not declare it, and that he would become more and more provocative'.[1] He gave clear evidence of this determination two weeks later when, after a request from Churchill, he agreed to provide sufficient US Navy transports to move 20,000 British troops to the Middle East.

Before leaving for Newfoundland, Churchill had made arrangements to receive all important papers, including 'an assortment of Boniface', the word Churchill always used to refer to decrypted enemy signals. He was, consequently, able to keep in touch with major Mediterranean developments during his two-week absence from London. Nevertheless, upon his return he worked his way through a larger accumulation, among which were several signals relating to Axis supplies to North Africa. This prompted, on 20 August, a minute to General Ismay requesting details of these shipments since July. Two days later, Ismay told him that in July 265,000 tons of supplies had been received by the German-Italian forces in North Africa, and a further 194,000 tons in the first twenty days of August. Included in these figures were 1,650 vehicles.[2] These figures, it should be stated, cannot be reconciled with the official post-war Italian naval records. These reveal receipts of only 62,000 tons of general cargo and fuel in July, and no more than 84,000 tons in the whole of August. At that time, it should be noted that Rommel required approximately 70,000 tons of supplies per month to maintain his forces, before building reserves for an offensive.[3]

Nevertheless, whatever their source, these exaggerated figures served their purpose in alarming Churchill sufficiently to send a comprehensive minute to Admiral Pound on 22 August. This important document, with its implications for Malta, deserves to be quoted in full:

> Prime Minister to First Sea Lord. General Ismay to see.
> Further to my minute about supplies reaching Tripoli from Italy will you please consider the sending of a flotilla, and, if possible, a cruiser or two to Malta, as soon as possible.
> 2. We must look back to see how much our purpose has been deflected. There was the plan, considered vital by you, of blocking Tripoli harbour, for which *Barham* was to be sacrificed. There was the alternative desperate proposal by the C.-in-C. Mediterranean to bombard it, which was afterwards effected without the loss of a man or a single ship being damaged. There was the arrival of Mountbatten's flotilla in Malta. All this took place several months ago. It would be well to get out the dates. How is it that the urgency of this matter has declined? How is it that we are now content to watch what we formerly thought unendurable, although it is going forward on a bigger scale against us?
> 3. The reason why Mountbatten's flotilla was withdrawn from Malta was less because of the danger there than for the needs of the Cretan affair, in which the flotilla was practically destroyed. We have thus lost sight of our purpose, on which there was such general agreement, and in which the Admiralty was so forward and strong.
> 4. Meanwhile three things have happened. First the Malta defences have been markedly strengthened in the air and A.A. guns, and the German air forces have been drawn away to some extent to Russia. Secondly, the Battle of the Atlantic has turned sharply in our favour, we have more anti-U-boat craft, and we are to expect a substantial relief through American action west of the 26th meridian, affecting our destroyers and corvettes. Thirdly, General Auchinleck is disinclined to move before November.
> 5. Are we then to wait and allow this ever-growing reinforcement, mainly of Italians and of supplies, to pile up in Libya? If so, General Auchinleck will be no better off, relatively to the enemy, when at last he considers himself perfectly ready, than he is now.
> 6. I shall be glad to hear from you over the week-end, and we could discuss it at the Staff meeting on Monday night.[4]

In his memoirs, Churchill followed the quotation of this minute by writing: 'The policy was accepted, though time was needed to bring it into force.' The truth of the matter is that Admirals Pound and Cunningham at that time both strongly resisted Churchill's request for a surface force at Malta. We must now consider why this was so, and how the impasse was eventually broken. Before we do so, however, the reader should keep two matters in mind since they will help to explain the differences that arose in the coming months between Churchill and the Admiralty.

The first matter relates to the acceptance of risk in war. We have already seen instances, notably when the 'Tiger' convoy and the naval bombardment of Tripoli were under consideration, when Churchill thought, and said, that the Admiralty were being too cautious. Churchill himself could never have been accused of caution. His personal acceptance of risk and danger had been evident since he had first heard bullets whistle past his head in Cuba in 1895. His moral courage was more often conspicuous in his political career, most notably in the Abdication crisis in 1937, when he had been shouted down in the House of Commons, and in his long, and often solitary, opposition to Neville Chamberlain's appeasement policies. Since he had become Prime Minister the mainspring of his leadership had been his determination to attack the enemy whenever and wherever possible. It is scarcely surprising, therefore, that he was often suspicious and frustrated when he read nicely calculated analyses written by Staff College-trained officers which too often concluded that nothing at all could be done. What these papers, in his view, failed to take into account was the extreme uncertainty of war.

Churchill expressed his frustration at the element of caution in the conduct of affairs to his son, Randolph, and later to Harold Macmillan. To his son he complained in October 1941: 'The Admirals, Generals and Air Marshals chant their stately hymn of "Safety First" ... In the midst of this I have to restrain my natural pugnacity by sitting on my own head. How bloody!'[5] A year later, in a discussion with Harold Macmillan, who had praised the Chiefs of Staff system, Churchill protested: 'Why, you may take the most gallant sailor, the most intrepid airman, or the most audacious soldier, put them at a table together – what do you get? *The sum of their fears!*'[6] Although allowance should be made for a degree of exaggeration in these scathing comments, it is pertinent to point out, as David French has shown, that the German commanders shared this view about the caution of British generalship.[7] In a word, Churchill was by nature a fighter, and he may at times have wondered whether some of his senior military advisers shared this essential war-winning quality. It comes as no surprise to learn that Churchill admired Nelson, Napoleon – and Rommel.

The second point to be borne in mind is the effect on his behaviour of the immense and growing weight of his responsibilities during a period when one setback followed upon another, especially in the

Mediterranean. On the day of Churchill's return from Newfoundland, his Private Secretary, John Colville, noted in his diary that he, Churchill's brother Jack, and Desmond Morton had voiced their concern about the growing offence which Churchill's impatient behaviour was causing in the House of Commons.[8] There are also many accounts of his rude and overbearing treatment of ministerial and military colleagues, treatment which they bore, partly because they also saw, at other times, his qualities of generosity and magnanimity, but largely because they recognised that he was indispensable. If, therefore, in the following pages Churchill's impatience and harshness of expression are more evident than his more admirable qualities, the stress of events, and the supreme importance of defeating Rommel, might be advanced in his defence.

Upon receipt of Churchill's minute, Admiral Pound at once signalled Cunningham in Alexandria.[9] He began by observing that, despite the operations of aircraft and submarines, the enemy were building up supply reserves in North Africa 'to an extent that may prejudice our offensive when it comes off'. He thought it unreasonable to expect greater results from the submarine forces in the Mediterranean, and continued:

[The] question arises whether another attempt should be made to maintain surface forces at Malta in view of the reduced threat from dive-bomber attack at the present time. If you are in agreement with this idea what force could you provide for Malta from the eastern Mediterranean?

He also asked Cunningham to let him know what air cover he would need at Malta to protect his warships. Cunningham replied late on the following day. After disputing the suggestion that Rommel was accumulating reserve stocks, he agreed that the provision of a surface force at Malta 'can and should be done and it is only the question of how to provide the destroyers that has delayed my taking action'. He first explained the difficulty of providing sufficient fuel oil at Malta for warship operations, which he described as 'really the crux of the matter'. There was available in Malta's storage tanks only sufficient fuel to maintain two cruisers and four destroyers for two months. He then went on:

It is as well to emphasize main value for force will be as a deterrent and to delay enemy convoys rather than as a destructive force. Initially we may hope to bag a convoy as did the 14th Destroyer Flotilla at Sfax but thereafter fact that enemy can use wide evasive routeing and can always bring superior force to bear must reduce the prospect of actual damage. Process however should impede enemy supplies.

With regard to air cover, he asked for a squadron of long-range fighters to protect a potential force of two 6-inch cruisers and four destroyers. His signal ended, however, by warning that, as a result of the forthcoming operation to replace the Australian troops at Tobruk, an operation demanded by the Australian government despite Churchill's protests, he could provide no ships before the end of September.

Admiral Pound then had his staff prepare a detailed reply to the Prime Minister incorporating many of the points made by Cunningham.[10] This laid stress on two principal considerations. First, the dangers to a relatively small surface force at Malta from German dive-bombers and the more powerful Italian fleet suggested that the results to be expected from such a force would be limited. Secondly, the memorandum demonstrated, with statistics and graphs, that the Royal Navy had become so short of 6-inch cruisers and fleet destroyers that the diversion of two cruisers and four destroyers to Malta for a task of doubtful and limited value would not, in the Admiralty's view, be justified. This paper was signed by Pound, delivered to Churchill on 24 August, and discussed at a COS meeting on the following day.[11] There he repeated the substance of his paper, declaring that 'a force of the kind which Admiral Cunningham could afford to employ at Malta would be faced with an almost impossible task'. He also reminded the Prime Minister and his fellow Chiefs that the air and submarine operations were already having a significant impact on the enemy supply operations, claiming that 35 per cent of the enemy supply ships sailed to North Africa had either been sunk or damaged. Four more submarines were being sent to the Mediterranean to strengthen these operations, while ACM Freeman added, as has been noted in the previous chapter, that the Air Ministry were hoping to send two more Blenheim squadrons to Malta.

We may pause here to say a word or two about Pound's relationship with Churchill. The Prime Minister clearly liked Pound, and his warm tribute to the Admiral, who died on Trafalgar Day, 21 October 1943, deserves repeating here. After describing their initial meeting when Churchill became First Lord of the Admiralty in September 1939, he continued:

> But from the earliest days our friendship and mutual confidence grew and ripened. I measured and respected the great professional and personal qualities of Admiral Pound. As the war, with all its shifts and fortunes, beat upon us with clanging blows, we became ever truer comrades and friends. And when, four years later, he died at the moment of the general victory over Italy, I mourned with a personal pang for all the Navy and the nation had lost.[12]

There is no doubt that Pound returned this affection and respect, and their relationship was helped in no small degree by the method Pound devised to respond to Churchill's often imperious initiatives. This had first become evident as long ago as 1917 when Pound had written a staff paper about one of Churchill's proposals. His biographer, Robin Brodhurst, has written that Pound, confronted by such a proposal,

> had hoisted in the absolute necessity of not saying a direct 'No'. An objective professional appreciation, in which the advantages were accepted, but the implications were fully explained, was far more likely to be accepted. Churchill was essentially a fair man and usually ready to accept a professional opinion provided that it was not defeatist. These were Pound's tactics in 1917 and they were to be those he was to use in 1939–43.[13]

This technique is well illustrated in the exchange of 25 August 1941, and in his handling of several other Churchillian minutes in the following months.

On this occasion the minutes of the meeting record Churchill's endorsement of the dispatch to the Mediterranean of additional submarines and aircraft, but make no reference to any comment that he might have made about Pound's conclusion that a surface force could not, for the present at least, be sent back to Malta. We can only assume that the Prime Minister, whatever his disappointment, accepted the judgement of his senior naval adviser. Pound confirmed his doubts about the viability of such a force in a letter of 3 September to Cunningham. In this he wrote:

> Personally, I am extremely doubtful whether a weak force of two 6-in cruisers and four destroyers would be able to achieve anything commensurate with their loss in the face of air and surface attack. I do not think the latter can be ruled out as the Italians must be more miserable people than we think if they could allow such a weak force to dominate the Central Mediterranean without any support closer than Alexandria.
>
> My own view is that as we are sending you additional submarines and as the Air Ministry are endeavouring to send two more Blenheim Squadrons to Malta we should see how these additions affect the situation before putting a surface force at Malta.
>
> In any case, I am afraid the force would have to be provided by you and I can't really hold out any hope that we should be able to replace any of these ships which were lost.[14]

There for the moment Churchill left the matter of a Malta surface force, but his anxiety about enemy convoys persisted. This was sharpened, while the above papers were being prepared and debated, when his eye caught in his buff box a C38m decrypt. It has been noted in the preceding chapter that CG&CS had begun to break into this Italian naval cipher, giving details of all North African convoys, in the summer of 1941. In July, Churchill had been briefed about the transmission of this vital intelligence to the naval authorities in the Mediterranean, including Admiral Ford in Valletta. This led to two minutes addressed to Admiral Pound shortly before his departure for Newfoundland to meet President Roosevelt. The first, on 29 July, read: 'I hope Admiral Cunningham realises the quality of this information. If he cannot intercept on this we do not deserve success.' On the following day he added: 'I wish I knew what he *did* when he received these messages.'[15]

This particular decrypt of 24 August gave details of the passage to Benghazi of German tankers, one of which was the *Ossag*. Churchill at once sent an urgent minute to Pound:

What action will the C in C Mediterranean take on this information? Surely he cannot put up with this kind of thing. I see on other papers that the mere rumour of his being at sea has disturbed *Ossag* & Co., but is this true? Is he going simply to leave these ships to the chance of a submarine, without making any effort by his surface forces to intercept them?

Please ask specifically what if anything he is going to do. We are still at war.

To this sarcastic minute Pound replied that he had signalled Cunningham to ask if any action could be taken, but he also reminded the Prime Minister of the 'danger of compromising our source of information, which can easily be done if we send a surface ship out to intercept a ship in an area which our forces do not normally operate in. It is unnecessary to stress what the loss of this information would mean to us.'[16] In this case nothing could be done in the time available, and as a subsequent decrypt on 3 September revealed: 'Tanker *Ossag* to leave Benghazi evening 3 September after discharging cargo of aviation fuel.' Having read this, an exasperated Churchill minuted to Pound: 'Admiral Cunningham sh'd feel sorry about this. It is a melancholy failure.'[17] It seems reasonable to assume that this verdict moved Pound, on behalf of the COS, to signal Cunningham on the following day: 'The interception of enemy supplies to Libya in the next few weeks is a matter of such importance that we are anxious to be in the possession of all information which will enable us to form a true appreciation of the practicability of such interceptions.'

The extreme importance, in Churchill's eyes, of Auchinleck's forthcoming November offensive meant that his attention was closely focused in early autumn on Rommel's supply position. He was able to follow this in detail through intercepted messages that were also being read by Pound, Cunningham and Admiral Ford in Malta. These disclosed in early September that an increasing number of enemy convoys were being directed to Benghazi along the west coast of Greece, a route both safer and shorter than the Tunisian route. In a signal of 30 August, Cunningham expressed concern that the attack on this route would become steadily less effective, partly because it lay outside the range of Malta's Swordfish and Albacores, and partly because the Blenheims were encountering increasingly fierce AA defence. Asked by Churchill for his observations on this, Portal replied that Beaufort torpedo-bombers were being sent to Egypt to replace the Malta-based aircraft. He also claimed at that time that the Blenheims were still achieving successes, but, as we have already seen, he became increasingly worried in October about the mounting losses suffered by these squadrons.

A week later Churchill was once again writing to the First Sea Lord after reading a long signal sent by Pound to Cunningham on 13 September, which set out the Admiralty's view about the naval situation in the eastern Mediterranean. This again confirmed that no further surface ships could be made available from other theatres. Churchill at once wrote to Pound: 'All this looks rather gloomy ... Will it not make the Admiral curl up?' Churchill doubted whether the Italian navy was prepared to fight, and ended by writing: 'Cunningham has not done any fighting since Crete, and there is no chance whatever of the Italians attacking him in the Eastern Mediterranean.'[18] Pound quickly replied to this, disagreeing with the Prime Minister's suggestion that the Italians would not fight, and refuting the implication that the Mediterranean Fleet had not been fully occupied. Although Cunningham had not engaged the Italian fleet, the Syrian campaign and the constant resupply of Tobruk, not to mention the replacement of the Australian troops there, had resulted in further losses. Nevertheless, he admitted, 'I am profoundly dissatisfied with the situation in which we find ourselves of being unable to really stop the flow of reinforcements to Africa.'

Admiral Cunningham at Alexandria fully supported Pound, signalling on 18 September:

> I do not think surface forces from Malta would achieve anything in an attempt to stop supplies coming from Italy down the Greek coast to Benghazi. In fact, far as they would be from any fighter support, I think they might have heavy losses by air attack even if the Italians didn't send a large force to cut them off ... In any case with this Gulf of Suez commitment I now can't spare any cruisers, let alone destroyers.[19]

Naval operations in late September concentrated on the sailing of the 'Halberd' convoy to Malta, after the safe arrival of which, Churchill again pressed Pound. Although decrypts revealed that British anti-convoy attacks in September had slowed the build-up of enemy supplies in Cyrenaica somewhat, there was also some evidence suggesting that, at last, Rommel was preparing to attack Tobruk. On 5 October, Churchill minuted to Pound:

> Is there no possibility of helping the Air Force on the Tripoli blockade with some surface craft, including a cruiser or two? We seem to leave it all to the Air Force and the Submarines.[20]

Pound replied on the same day. Since the matter had been last discussed in late August, he told the Prime Minister, the arrival of several new 'Hunt'-class escort destroyers had eased Cunningham's acute shortage of fleet destroyers a little. At the same time, however, Cunningham had been compelled to divert two cruisers to the Red Sea to provide AA protection against long-range German bombing of the growing number of merchant ships anchored there. On top of all this were the demands imposed by the continued evacuation of all Australian troops from Tobruk and their replacement by British and Polish units. This necessitated no fewer than four night-time operations between August and October, at a further heavy cost to the Mediterranean Fleet. Pound concluded by telling the Prime Minister: 'I am sure Cunningham will send a force to Malta as soon as is possible, but whether it will achieve anything if sent is, in my opinion, extremely doubtful.' On this reply Churchill wrote, after questioning the dispatch of two cruisers to the Red Sea, 'Cunningham seems to be lying low. Is he going to play any part in Crusader?'

This barbed comment gained further sharpness because Admiral Cunningham's younger brother, General Sir Alan Cunningham, had been appointed by Auchinleck to command the recently named 8th Army in the forthcoming desert offensive. On 8 October, Pound replied with a vigorous and detailed defence of all the strenuous work done by the Mediterranean Fleet, adding:

> I am glad that Cunningham has had an opportunity to rest his destroyers a bit, as there is no question that the personnel of these ships were worn out after the continuous operating they have been subjected to.

Nevertheless, Pound assured the Prime Minister that he had 'no doubt that Cunningham will do all he can to help his brother'.[21]

In the light of Pound's continued firm rejection of the re-establishment of a surface force at Malta, it comes as a surprise to read the telegram he sent to Admiral Cunningham only three days after his last minute to Churchill. On 11 October he signalled:

(A) In view of situation in Gulf of Suez it does not seem possible for you to spare any cruisers for Malta.

(B) As it is vitally important to stop enemy reinforcements reaching Africa during the next few weeks it has been decided to send AURORA and PENELOPE to Malta.

He added, however, that it would not be possible to provide destroyers from the west. On the same day, Pound wrote privately to Cunningham and offered this further explanation:

It is with great reluctance that we are sending *Aurora* and *Penelope* to Malta, but I can see that it is quite impossible with the Gulf of Suez situation as it is for you to provide any cruisers. I have no exaggerated hopes as to what these two ships will be able to achieve, and I think it quite likely that at the least we shall get both ships badly damaged but, should CRUSADER fail, which I sincerely hope it will not, then I think there would have been lasting criticism because we had not made any attempt to cut the communications to Africa by surface forces.[22]

Cunningham replied to this on 23 October:

I fully agree with you about Force K. They may not achieve much but their presence should result in the Italians having to put up a much greater escort effort and it may be that they will put an end to this running of Hun soldiers in destroyers from Augusta to Benghazi.

Why had Pound changed his mind? Apart from the above documents there is, unfortunately, a lack of evidence bearing on this question. The establishment of the surface force at Malta did not come before the Defence Committee or the COS at this time, and there is no detailed naval staff analysis, as there was in August, which might shed light on Pound's change of heart. Moreover, all of the official histories are silent on this question. Two possible influences deserve consideration. Firstly, although there are no recorded exchanges between Pound and Churchill after Pound's note of 8 October, it is possible that the Prime Minister put further pressure on the Admiral in a private conversation. In his war memoirs, Churchill wrote that 'the activities of "Force K", which the Admiralty, *at my desire*, had created there, yielded rich prizes'.[23] Moreover, the tone of Pound's communications to Cunningham, especially in his letter of 11 October, suggests that the dispatch of the two cruisers had been made against his better judgement. Perhaps the 'lasting criticism' mentioned in his letter to Cunningham had been voiced by Churchill. It is impossible to exaggerate the importance that Churchill attached to the success of the 'Crusader' offensive. Above all else it was a way of demonstrating to President Roosevelt that his growing and tangible support for Britain was deserved, and also in America's interest. Another British defeat in the desert might seriously undermine the President's faith. Churchill reprints in his memoirs the whole of his lengthy letter of 20 October, which Attlee personally delivered on his behalf to the President. 'All my information,' he wrote, 'goes to show that a victory in Cyrenaica of the British over the Germans will alter the whole shape of the war in the Mediterranean.'[24] The Prime Minister's depth of feeling on this matter must have been clear to Pound, even if there was no discussion.

Secondly, it seems possible that Pound was influenced by disturbing intelligence, which, although difficult to interpret, indicated that Rommel, despite the losses at sea, might be winning the battle of supplies, and might therefore be able to strike before Auchinleck was finally ready. As a result of the switch to the safer Benghazi route, the diversion of *Fliegerkorps X* from bombing Egyptian targets to the protection of the Benghazi convoys, and the increasing dispatch of troops and supplies by air and naval vessels, the enemy supply and manpower position had steadily improved. The German and Italian divisions had been brought up to strength, and two regiments of a new German motorised division had been identified.[25] All this pointed to the ominous possibility that Rommel might be able to strike at Tobruk in late October, unless further damage could be done to his supply position. If a growing anxiety that 'Crusader' might fail influenced Pound's decision, it was vindicated when, on 17 October, the Prime Minister was incensed to receive Auchinleck's signal that he had decided to postpone his attack for another two weeks. This delay seemed to tip the balance of advantage towards Rommel. After several angry signals, the date for 'Crusader' was finally set for 18 November. Whatever the full reasons for Pound's decision on 11 October to send a surface force to Malta, his reluctance to do so, and the doubts which both he and Cunningham shared about the value of this force, were soon shown to have been misjudged. They, but perhaps not Churchill, were surprised by what Force K achieved in the following weeks.

In Pound's memorandum of 24 August, the cruiser HMS *Aurora*, under the command of Captain Agnew, had been shown as being 'employed on the Spitzbergen force', protecting the arctic convoys to Russia. Her sister ship, HMS *Penelope*, was at that time 'working up'. Following Pound's order of 11 October, these two 6-inch cruisers sailed for Gibraltar where they were joined by two destroyers, HMS *Lance* and *Lively*, detached from Force H. They then proceeded to Malta in conjunction with Operation 'Callboy', in which eleven Albacores of 828 Squadron were flown off to Malta from HMS *Ark Royal*. The four ships of the new Force K arrived at Malta early on the morning of 21 October, the first surface warships to be based there since May.

Their arrival was soon known in Rome, but before we examine the operations of this small force, it will be convenient to review briefly the reactions of the Italian and German authorities to their mounting convoy losses. We can now see, with the help of captured enemy documents, the full picture, but much of this was known at the time, or could be shrewdly guessed at, from the flow of signal decrypts. The German naval and air force commands strongly disagreed about the measures necessary to prevent further shipping losses. Admiral Raeder, distrustful of the ability of the Italian navy, suffering from an acute shortage of fuel oil, to provide adequate convoy protection, urged Hitler to order Goering to provide stronger air protection, and to resume the attack on Malta. However, Goering, for the moment at least, successfully resisted this pressure, arguing that the aircraft of *Fliegerkorps X* were required to support Rommel's planned offensive. German air protection was, consequently, restricted to the Benghazi route. Nevertheless, Hitler did order Raeder to send U-boats to the Mediterranean. By the end of October the first six had arrived, eight more followed in November, and a further thirteen in December. These German boats operated in the western and eastern basins of the Mediterranean, leaving the central area to the Italian submarines. Admirals Cunningham and Somerville were aware of this new threat to their fleets as early as September, and it was undoubtedly for this reason that the Admiralty added the two destroyers, equipped with ASDIC equipment and forty-two depth charges each, to Force K.

After the German High Command had released 90,000 tons of fuel oil to the Italian navy, the decision was taken to recommence convoys on the Tripoli route with strong naval escort. C38m soon revealed the enemy's plans to sail a seven-ship convoy to Tripoli, following a route 200 miles to the east of Malta. To protect the source of this information, a reconnaissance aircraft from Malta was directed to the general area in order to make a 'chance' visual sighting, which was duly reported back to Malta. Force K then left Valletta after dark on 8 November. The convoy was detected by radar and by the light of a rising moon, and between 1.00 a.m. and 2.00 a.m. on the following day all seven merchant ships, and two of the six escorting destroyers, were sunk. A covering force of Italian 8-inch cruisers, without radar, failed to intervene in the confused action, and by dawn all the RN ships were back at Valletta, without suffering any damage or casualties. Churchill had followed this action with keen interest, and on 9 November he telegraphed jubilantly to President Roosevelt:

Former Naval Person to President Roosevelt   9 Nov 41
The destruction between Italy and Greece of the Axis convoy destined for Benghazi is highly important both in itself and in its consequences. It is also noteworthy that the two Italian heavy cruisers would not face our two 6-inch cruisers, nor their six destroyers our two.[26]

In the early hours of 18 November, Auchinleck launched his 'Crusader' offensive, and Churchill's attention was then focused on the subsequent rapidly moving and often confused battle in the Cyrenaican desert. He was not, however, oblivious to the enemy's increasingly desperate attempts to sail in more supplies. On 23 November, he was alerted by a German Air Force Enigma signal to the passage of two German freighters bound from Greece to Benghazi. These two ships, the *Maritza* and the *Procida*, were carrying ammunition and aviation fuel for the *Luftwaffe* squadrons in North Africa. The Prime Minister at once consulted Pound and both sent urgent messages to Admiral Cunningham. Churchill's telegram ended by stating that, 'The stopping of these ships may save thousands of lives, apart from aiding a victory of cardinal importance.' Churchill reprinted in his war memoirs the whole of this signal, together with Cunningham's reply.[27]

In Churchill's personal Mediterranean Fleet files there is a note by General Ismay, dated 24 November, which Churchill had instructed him to place on record. This read:

> The Prime Minister had two or three conversations with the First Sea Lord about stopping convoys to Benghazi. As a result, the First Sea Lord:
> (a) sent a personal telegram to C. in C. Mediterranean asking him to consider the possibility of using surface ships to interrupt enemy traffic to Africa;
> (b) sent the following telegrams:
>   (i) To VA Malta ordering Force K to raise steam.
>   (ii) To C. in C. Mediterranean, repeated VAM, saying that unless other arrangements had been made Force K was to be used to intercept PROCIDA and MARITZA, all risks being accepted.

A signal was received from Malta later in the evening reporting that Force K would leave Malta at 11 p. m. the same night.

At 3.30 p.m. on 24 November Force K found the two merchant ships, escorted by only two Italian torpedo boats, and both were quickly sunk, again without damage to Force K. On the following day Churchill was no doubt pleased to read an intercepted German air force signal which reported that the loss of these two transports had placed Rommel's operations in 'real danger', and had forced the Italians to employ all available aircraft and destroyers to deliver fuel to North Africa.[28] Upon hearing this news, Churchill sent a signal to Captain Agnew of the *Aurora*:

> Many congratulations on your fine work since you arrived at Malta, and will you please tell all ranks and ratings from me that the two exploits in

which they have been engaged, namely, the annihilation of the enemy's convoys on November 8 and of the two oil ships on Monday last, have played a very definite part in the great battle now raging in Libya. The work of the force has been most fruitful, and all concerned may be proud to have been a real help to Britain and our cause.[29]

Meanwhile, Cunningham, upon receipt of the signals from Churchill and Pound, had dispatched another force of five cruisers and four destroyers, designated as Force B, along the Cyrenaican coast towards Tobruk to support Force K and to intercept other convoys known to be attempting the passage to Benghazi. Cunningham himself, with his three battleships, also put to sea to provide cover for the two cruiser forces, but on the afternoon of 25 November HMS *Barham* was torpedoed and sunk by U-331, with very heavy loss of life. This was the second heavy blow inflicted by the recently arrived German U-boats since, on 12 November, HMS *Ark Royal*, returning to Gibraltar from delivering a further thirty-four Hurricanes and seven Blenheims to Malta, was sunk by U-205. Despite these grievous losses, the need to increase the attack on the Axis convoys caused Cunningham on 27 November to order Force B, composed of the cruisers HMS *Ajax* and *Neptune*, and the destroyers HMS *Kimberley* and *Kingston*, to join Force K at Malta.

Churchill naturally gave close and anxious attention in the closing days of November to the development of the 'Crusader' offensive, which, after Auchinleck had replaced General Cunningham with General Ritchie, continued to make progress. 30 November 1941 was Churchill's sixty-seventh birthday and he received many messages of congratulation, including one from the King. But perhaps the one that gave him greatest pleasure was the signal from General Auchinleck, which read:

Our supply column reached Tobruk morning of 29th. The commander of XIII Corps' birthday message to you is, 'Corridor to Tobruk clear and secure, Tobruk is as relieved as I am.'

Churchill at once replied: 'I am highly complimented by your message. 13 Corps have fought a great fight in this astounding battle.'[30]

But Churchill also remained fully determined that Rommel should not be given any opportunity to replenish his supplies during the battle, and for this reason, on 28 November, he asked Pound to consider sending another dozen destroyers to the Mediterranean to counter the growing number of U-boats operating there. 'Numbers,' he wrote, 'are the essence of successful hunting, and we ought to get good results.'[31] To the attack on the Axis convoys, Malta's air and naval forces, built up at the Prime Minister's urging during the preceding months, now made a major contribution. These operations, skilfully controlled and co-ordinated from Valletta by Admiral Ford and AVM Lloyd, are described in detail in the official histories and need only be summarised here. On 29 November, Forces B and K sailed together from the Grand Harbour to intercept several reported southbound convoys. One ship had already been sunk by Blenheims from Malta, and, at 3.30 a.m. on 1 December, Force K sank another headed for Benghazi with ammunition and supplies. Captain Agnew's force then raced 400 miles westwards at high speed and, at 6.00 p.m. on the same day, sank the 10,540-ton tanker *Iridio Mantovani* and its destroyer escort, both of which had earlier been damaged by aircraft from Malta. These two successful attacks were facilitated by the guidance given by an ASV-equipped Wellington from Malta, after the routes of these ships had been revealed by C38m intercepts.

Two weeks later, further decrypts, now being read with minimal delay, revealed the sailing of two Italian 6-inch cruisers carrying emergency fuel supplies to Tripoli. Admiral Ford at once made plans to send Force K from Malta to intercept these warships off Cape Bon, but Admiral Cunningham refused permission in view of the dwindling fuel stocks at Malta. However, by a stroke of good fortune, four destroyers, commanded by Cdr. Stokes on HMS *Sikh*, sent by Pound to reinforce the Mediterranean Fleet, intercepted and sank the two cruisers at 2.30 a.m. on 13 December. Later that same day, Malta's submarines were in action. An Italian convoy, with a powerful battleship escort, had turned back towards Taranto, alarmed by a 'planted' signal suggesting that the British battle fleet was also at sea. In the resulting confusion HMS *Upright* sank two merchant ships, two others were damaged in a collision, and HMS *Urge* torpedoed and damaged the battleship *Vittorio Veneto*. The final naval clash of 1941 developed around two convoys. RN cruisers and destroyers from Alexandria and Malta were sailed on 15 December to escort HMS *Breconshire* to Malta with urgently needed fuel oil. This operation coincided with another Italian battleship convoy escorting four freighters to Tripoli and Benghazi. The two forces met in the central Mediterranean on 17 December but, in what was later referred to as 'The First Battle of Sirte', Admiral Vian, commanding the British force, drew off the more powerful Italian force, and *Breconshire* reached Valletta safely on 18 December. That evening three RN cruisers and four destroyers left Malta in an attempt to intercept three ships of the Axis convoy then approaching Tripoli. But at midnight disaster struck. Twenty miles off Tripoli, Force K ran on to a newly laid minefield and the cruiser HMS *Neptune*, as well as the destroyer HMS *Kandahar*, were both lost with very heavy loss of life. Of the 765 crew of *Neptune* only one man survived after clinging to a life raft for five days. HMS *Aurora* and *Penelope* were also damaged but were able to return to Malta. A sombre day for the Royal Navy became even darker when Italian human torpedoes, on the same night, disabled Admiral Cunningham's two remaining battleships at their moorings in Alexandria.

News of these naval calamities in the Mediterranean reached Churchill on board HMS *Duke of York* while steaming through an Atlantic gale towards Washington. For, on 7 December while Churchill was at Chequers with the US Ambassador, John Winant, and Averell Harriman, he had heard on the radio of the Japanese attack on the US Pacific Fleet at Pearl Harbor. He at once resolved to meet President Roosevelt, and on 12 December he set out with a large entourage, arriving at the White House on 22 December.

Before the account of the impact of these events on Malta in 1942 is resumed, it will be appropriate to consider what the island's air and naval forces achieved in the last two months of 1941, and the influence Churchill had brought to bear on these operations. The number of Axis merchant ships sunk by Malta's forces in the June–October months, and the resulting loss of supplies, have been recorded in the previous chapter. In November and December the tempo of destruction accelerated. In these two months, after the arrival at Valletta of Force K, Malta-based forces sank twenty Axis merchant ships, aggregating 86,000 tons. This was 81 per cent of the Axis tonnage sunk in the central Mediterranean in this period. Eleven of these were sunk by Force K, five by aircraft, and three by submarines. The sinking of the 10,500-ton tanker *Iridio Mantovani* was shared between Force K and Malta's Blenheims. Other ships were damaged and forced to turn back, while yet more were deterred from sailing by the mere threat of air or naval attack. Nor must the contribution of Malta's bombers be overlooked. Night after night Wellingtons, Blenheims and Marylands bombed dockyards and supply dumps in Italy and North Africa, destroying and damaging supplies, the amount of which cannot be quantified. The effect of these co-ordinated attacks on the delivery of supplies to North Africa was dramatic. In November, when Auchinleck's 'Crusader' offensive was launched, only 30,000 tons of the 79,000 tons dispatched were landed, a loss rate of 62 per cent compared to 20 per cent in October. In December only 48,000 tons were sent, of which 9,000 tons were destroyed, a loss rate of nearly 19 per cent of a much restricted convoy programme. In these two months, therefore, Rommel received less than half of the monthly amount of roughly 70,000 tons he needed for maintenance without engaging in battle. Consequently, when Col. Montezemolo of the Italian High Command warned on 5 December that only the most essential supplies could be delivered that month, Rommel disengaged his remaining battered forces and withdrew from Cyrenaica. There can be no doubt that this retreat, which marked the initial success of the 'Crusader' offensive, was due in large measure to the loss of supplies caused by Malta's air and naval forces.[32]

This chapter has also investigated in some detail the pressure that Churchill exerted on the Admiralty to strengthen Malta's offensive capability by moving surface ships to Valletta. Contrary to what Churchill subsequently wrote in his memoirs, the evidence clearly shows that Pound and Cunningham were reluctant to send warships to Malta in the early autumn, partly because there was an acute shortage of the necessary ships, but also because they both doubted whether such a small force would be effective. In the event, Force K, taking full advantage of decrypted signals and the co-operation of ASV-equipped Wellingtons, achieved results which justified Churchill's optimism and perhaps strengthened his belief that his senior commanders were at times too cautious. One can only wonder what the effect on the 'Crusader' campaign might have been had Pound agreed to the establishment of Force K in September or October, rather than in November.

Be that as it may, the crippling of Force K, and the other losses suffered by the Mediterranean Fleet in late December, heralded another turning point in the Mediterranean war. Churchill later quoted a contemporary German Staff conclusion: 'The sinking of the *Neptune* may be of decisive importance for holding Tripolitania. Without this the British force would probably have destroyed the Italian convoy. There is no doubt that the loss of these supplies at the peak of the crisis would have had the severest consequences.'[33] But these supplies were not lost. With them Rommel was able to recover the initiative, and Malta entered the darkest months of the war.

THE SECOND GERMAN AIR ATTACK
JANUARY – MARCH 1942

The delays you contemplate will seal the fate of Malta. Moreover, the enemy will reinforce faster than you can.

Churchill's draft message to Auchinleck, 2 March 1942

Churchill's visit to the United States and Canada, during which he addressed the US Congress and the Canadian Parliament, kept him away from London from 12 December 1941 until 16 January 1942. Throughout this period, however, he, Admiral Pound and ACM Portal were in daily contact with London where Clement Attlee acted as Deputy Prime Minister. It was during this visit that Churchill suffered what his doctor, Sir Charles Wilson (later Lord Moran) suspected was a mild heart attack, although he concealed this from the Prime Minister.

Among the many signals that Churchill read in this period was a summary of a Joint Intelligence Committee (JIC) paper of 3 January 1942 which examined the possibility of an Axis invasion of Malta. This possibility, which had not caused much anxiety since the German invasion of Crete in May 1942, had re-emerged because the *Luftwaffe* had returned to Sicily and resumed the bombing of Malta. As we have seen, Admiral Raeder had urged Hitler to order such action the previous October when the Italian supply convoys were being subjected to increasingly heavy attack from Malta. At the time, Goering had resisted such a diversion of his squadrons. However, Hitler subsequently changed his mind and ordered the transfer from the Russian front of *Fliegerkorps II* and the HQ staff of *Luftflotte II* to Sicily and North Africa. He also appointed Field Marshal Kesselring as 'C-in-C South', and ordered him, in accordance with Fuehrer Directive No. 38 of 2 December 1941, to regain control of the central Mediterranean by suppressing Malta. The first German squadrons began to arrive in Sicily in December, while others flew to North Africa to strengthen Rommel's air cover in the desert.

The JIC report forecast a large increase in the German air force in Sicily from an estimated 140 aircraft on 1 January to as many as 550 by 1 February.[1] There would, in addition, be 320 Italian aircraft. This formidable, experienced force could inflict severe damage on Malta's defences and this, the report went on, 'would involve a heavily-increased drain on our reserves of ammunition and other supplies on the island'. Moreover, supply convoys would be 'subjected to heavier attack by German aircraft and U-boats'. The JIC also considered that, although there was no evidence of any accumulation of invasion vessels or of gliders or transport aircraft, a German force of one parachute division, one airborne division, and two seaborne infantry divisions could be ready by the beginning of March 'if events in Russia allow'. There were, in addition, six small Italian parachute battalions of good quality. Nevertheless, while expecting an intensification of air attack, the JIC concluded:

> We believe that a combined operation against Malta would be of such difficulty that it is improbable that the enemy would attempt it, at any rate until he could judge whether the attempt to neutralise Malta by air attack is likely to succeed.

On his copy of this report, Churchill, while noting the 'reassuring' conclusion about a possible invasion, asked, 'Is more being done to reinforce the fortress? How do AA ammunition reserves stand?' We will consider later what plans Hitler and Mussolini made for an invasion of Malta.

It should be mentioned here that it was the growing fear of invasion which prompted the Governor in Malta to order the deportation to Uganda of forty-two persons who had been detained since June 1940 under the provisions of the Malta Defence Regulations. The actual Deportation Order was served on them on 12 February, and they were sent to Alexandria on the following day in HMS *Breconshire*. This decision attracted much criticism at the time, and was later declared by the Maltese courts to be illegal. The Governor had raised the possibility of deportations as early as July 1941 and agreement had been reached in principle that any deportations should be made to Uganda. On 29 January 1942, General Dobbie telegraphed to London requesting authority initially for the deportation of fifty-one people. This was granted, although an emergency Bill had to be rushed through when an appeal to the Maltese courts by some of the deportees was upheld. There is no evidence that Lord Moyne, the Colonial Secretary, raised this matter with Churchill, who had not returned to London from Washington until 16 January. There are no papers on this subject in Churchill's Malta files and it seems clear, therefore, that Churchill was not consulted about, or was even aware of these deportations.[2]

Before receiving Churchill's minute, the COS had considered the JIC report on 5 January, and decided to forward a copy to General Dobbie in Malta for his comments. In their telegram to the Governor they wrote: 'It looks to us as though you are next on the list.' The Governor replied on 10 January, requesting two more light AA regiments, one squadron of tanks and two more infantry battalions, and the COS, at their meeting on 12 January, agreed this.[3] On the same day, however, the Governor signalled urgently to Auchinleck to stress that: 'Essential present convoy should be loaded to maximum capacity with stores. Cannot forego any of these to make room for reinforcements.' Clearly, the Governor's concern about the supply position was growing. The last large convoy, Operation 'Halberd', had reached Malta from Gibraltar at the end of September 1941. In November, two merchantmen, SS *Empire Defender* and *Empire Pelican*, both attempting a solo passage in disguise, had been sunk by Italian aircraft off the coast of North Africa. Reviewing the position in early January 1942, the COS agreed that a convoy carrying 30,000 tons should be sailed in January, followed by monthly convoys each loaded with 45,000 tons. The passage from the east had become safer after the capture of the airfields around Benghazi allowed air cover to be provided all the way to Malta, and a four-ship convoy left Alexandria on 16 January. One of these ships, SS *Thermopylae*, was sunk, but the remaining three arrived in the Grand Harbour on 19 January and unloaded 21,000 tons of supplies. Among these, despite the Governor's signal, were twenty Bofors light AA guns, eight tanks, and two-thirds of one infantry battalion. Churchill's Malta papers include a detailed note setting out the cargoes carried in each vessel, including those lost in the *Thermopylae*. Wheat and other foodstuffs made up the bulk of the stores landed, and lost.

Later in the month, General Sir Alan Brooke, who had succeeded Field Marshal Dill as CIGS on 1 December 1941, sent Churchill a copy of a personal letter he had received from General Dobbie. In this the Governor first observed that, in view of the resumed air attack, it would no longer be feasible to accumulate nine months' stocks of supplies by the end of March, as previously intended. '270,000 persons,' he observed, 'eat no end of a lot.' He accepted the inevitability of heavier air attack on the island, but as regards an invasion attempt, he wrote: 'I am sure he can be dealt with (please God) satisfactorily and given much more than he bargains for.' He concluded on a cheerful note:

> All is well here. The air raids ... have imposed some strain on the populace by interruption of sleep. But I am getting to their heads, and really they are very good. We are making all the preparations we can, both Civil and Service, to counter anything the Hun may attempt.[4]

However, before Churchill had read this letter British fortunes in North Africa had taken a turn for the worse, and the outlook for Malta's survival had become more perilous. As we saw in the previous chapter, Auchinleck's 'Crusader' offensive had by mid-December forced Rommel to withdraw from Cyrenaica into Tripolitania. Ominously, however, the Axis convoy, the attempted interception of which had caused Force K such severe losses on 18 December 1941, had brought twenty-one German tanks to Benghazi shortly before that port was captured by British troops. An additional twenty-three were unloaded at Tripoli. With these new tanks, and others from the repair shops, Rommel struck two heavy blows at 22nd Armoured Brigade on 28 and 30 December, causing the loss of sixty British tanks. In early January both armies lay quiet, building up supplies and re-equipping their units for a renewed attack. Auchinleck, whose supply lines were by now very stretched, did not expect to be able to resume his offensive until mid-February, but Rommel, with characteristic energy, moved more quickly. Further Axis convoys in January, escorted by Italian battleships, brought in more than 200 armoured vehicles and 45,000 tons of supplies. With these reinforcements Rommel struck on 21 January, and by the end of the month, to Churchill's dismay and bewilderment, Benghazi and its airfields had been lost and the 8th Army driven back to Gazala, only fifty miles west of Tobruk.[5]

The consequences of the loss of the west Cyrenaican airfields soon became apparent. A three-ship convoy for Malta sailed from Alexandria on 12 February but on the following day was attacked by German dive-bombers re-established near Benghazi. Two ships were heavily damaged and had to be sunk by the escorting warships, while the third was forced to return to Egypt. The loss of these vital supplies at once led to a flurry of signals between London, Valletta and Cairo. The Governor warned on 18 February that the monthly supplies requirement, even on a 'siege condition consumption' basis, was 15,000 tons. On 21 February the Middle East C-in-Cs gloomily concluded: 'It appears useless to try to pass in a convoy until the air situation at Malta has been restored and the military situation in Cyrenaica improved.' Upon his copy of this signal the Prime Minister wrote 'COS Cttee for report'. On the same day, General Dobbie telegraphed to the Colonial Secretary, Lord Cranborne, telling him that 'a critical point in the maintenance of Malta' had been reached. With regard to conditions on the island he added: 'Inevitably there has already been some deterioration in the morale. That deterioration is not yet alarming and it is naturally important to prevent it becoming so.'

Upon receipt of this telegram, Cranborne sent an anxious memorandum to Churchill. After summarising the Governor's telegram, he went on:

> This is hardly the place to discuss the consequences likely to follow the loss of Malta, not the least of which would be the surrender of 300,000 most loyal British subjects, who would then be verging on starvation, to the mercy of the enemy … I know that the passage of convoys from Egypt, while the aerodromes of Cyrenaica are denied to us, presents the most serious difficulties. But I feel it is my duty to emphasize that unless

supplies can be substantially replenished within the next two months, the fortress will be within measurable distance of falling into enemy hands.

All of these papers were referred to the War Office staff who had already been instructed to examine what the position at Malta would be on 1 May if no further supplies reached the island before that date. Their report of 22 February, 'Supplies to Malta', noted that by 1 May there was likely to remain only eight weeks' supply of wheat and flour, a similar supply of kerosene, used for cooking, but no fodder for the island's animals. The report concluded:

> Clearly we must, in spite of the difficulties, transport to Malta what is really indispensable for the continuance of operations and the maintenance of civilian morale. If we do not do so we must face the fact that operations will probably cease after the end of June.[6]

Brooke presented this stark forecast to his fellow Chiefs on 24 February.[7] Admiral Pound was pessimistic. Convoys from either east or west were not feasible in current conditions. The best that might be hoped for, he thought, was 'to run in one or two ships before the nights shortened'. For Portal, too, the situation was one of great difficulty since air cover could not be provided for a Malta convoy 'until General Auchinleck's armies had won back the aerodromes in N. W. Cyrenaica'. The upshot was, firstly, a decision to advise the Middle East C-in-Cs of the 'need for offensive action in the western desert at the earliest possible date', and, secondly, to instruct the Joint Planning Staff (JPS) to prepare an appreciation showing

> the relative strategic importance of Malta, in comparison with the effort and cost of maintaining it, with particular reference to the latest date by which the offensive in the Western Desert must be launched in order to permit the maintenance of Malta during the summer.

At the same meeting the COS considered a further paper from the JIC reviewing the threat of an Axis invasion of Malta. This confirmed the view they had reached in January that an early invasion attempt was unlikely. In the ensuing weeks the bombing of the island had intensified, and since this had, in the Committee's opinion, 'partially achieved for the time being [the enemy's] object of denying to us the operational use of Malta he may be content to continue these tactics'.[8]

While the JPC were studying the position, Churchill decided to send another telegram to Auchinleck asking about his intentions. He thought that there was a risk that Rommel might 'gain reinforcements as fast or even faster than you', and concluded: 'The supply of Malta is causing us increased anxiety, and anyone can see the magnitude of our disasters in the

Far East.'[9] The reference here to the Far East is important for its bearing on Churchill's subsequent dispute with Auchinleck. On 15 February, the Singapore garrison of 75,000 men surrendered to a smaller Japanese force, a defeat which Churchill later described as 'the worst disaster and largest capitulation in British history'.[10] This disaster, which he saw as a disgrace and a humiliation, was constantly in his mind in the following weeks when Malta, Britain's other major overseas base, was in peril.

The JPS Appreciation was submitted on 26 February in the form of a draft signal to the Middle East C-in-Cs, and discussed by the COS on the next day. The results of their discussion were embodied in the following telegram which, after Churchill had made one or two minor amendments, was sent to the Middle East C-in-Cs, with a copy to the Governor. This is quoted in full since it marked the beginning of a fierce controversy between Churchill and Auchinleck on the value of Malta.

> Our view is that Malta is of such importance both as air staging post and as impediment to enemy reinforcement route that the most drastic steps are justifiable to sustain it. Even if Axis maintain their present scale of attack on Malta, thus reducing value, it will continue to be of great importance to war as a whole by containing important enemy air forces during critical months.
>
> 2. We are unable to supply Malta from the west. Your chances of doing so from the east depend mainly on either reduction of German air strength in Mediterranean or an advance in Cyrenaica. Although we think that Russian campaign will force enemy to recall aircraft from Mediterranean before May we cannot count on this. In any case situation at Malta would be dangerous by that time if no convoys have got through.
>
> 3. We agree with your CS/747 of 20 February that prevention of enemy reinforcements for Libya and probably also ultimate fate of Malta depend on recapture of air bases in W. Cyrenaica. We appreciate that the timing of another offensive will depend on building an adequate tank superiority, and that its launching may necessitate taking considerable risks in other parts of Middle East Command. Nevertheless, we feel that we must aim to be so placed in Cyrenaica by April dark period that we can pass substantial convoy to Malta. It will then be essential not only to send maintenance necessities but to build up stocks well above present critical level. Please let us have your considered views on above.
>
> 4. Meanwhile every effort must be made to keep stocks at least at present level. We suggest the following methods:
>
> (a) A further attempt to pass a convoy in March dark period. No consideration of risk to ships themselves need deter you from

this. During the progress of this operation it should be regarded as our primary military commitment.

(b) Assembling substantial convoy ready to despatch immediately favourable opportunity arises.

(c) Using cruiser for fast regular service to Malta with its own stores and fuel cut down to bare necessities for each trip in order to make room for reasonable loads.

5. Admiralty will signal C-in-C Mediterranean regarding unorthodox methods.

6. In view of difficult supply situation we consider that reinforcement of Malta with army units should be discontinued. Details urgently required by C-in-C Malta should be sent as opportunity offers.[11]

The reader will see that the JPS had not strictly carried out the instruction to compare the strategic value of Malta with other tasks and objectives with which the effort to sustain Malta might conflict, particularly the need to prevent the loss of Egypt. They and the COS simply assumed, perhaps with Singapore in their minds, that there was no choice in this matter. Malta must be resupplied whatever risks might arise elsewhere.

On the very day this signal was sent, the COS and the Prime Minister received a seven-page telegram from Auchinleck setting out his view of the situation and his intentions.[12] The central theme of this signal was that it would take several months to gather a tank force capable of defeating Rommel. This telegram is too long to quote in full, but the following extracts relate to the problem posed by Malta's shrinking supplies:

7. Critical nature of Malta maintenance situation thoroughly understood here. I fully realise need for recovering landing grounds in Cyrenaica as soon as possible irrespective of desirability resumption offensive on wider grounds ...

10. [It] is clear that we cannot have reasonable superiority before 1 June, and that to launch major offensive before then would be to risk defeat in detail and possibly endanger safety of Egypt.

To sum up my intentions are ...

4. To seize the first chance of staging a limited offensive to regain landing-grounds in area Derna-Mechili, provided this can be done without prejudicing chances of launching major offensive to recapture Cyrenaica or safety of the Tobruk area.

Churchill was, by all accounts, infuriated with this signal and over the weekend of 28 February to 1 March ordered that the matter be brought before the Defence Committee on 2 March. Meanwhile, he dictated an angry draft reply, which was circulated to the Defence Committee with

Auchinleck's appreciation.[13] Although this draft – reflecting, as he later told the Committee, 'the thoughts that had come into his mind' when reading Auchinleck's signal – was never sent, it remains in the records and several extracts are quoted below in order to demonstrate the depths of the Prime Minister's initial anger.

1. Am deeply grieved to receive your appreciation. Armies are expected to fight, not stand about month after month waiting for a certainty which never occurs. I told you last year when you demanded five months to prepare your attack that you would find no certainty of victory ... The delays you contemplate will seal the fate of Malta. Moreover, the enemy will reinforce faster than you can, so that after all your waiting you will find yourself in relatively the same position ...

3. The reputation of the British Army now lies unhappily very low. We do not seem to be able to fight the enemy on even terms or man to man. I was looking to the 8th Army, on which everything has been lavished, to repair the shame of Singapore ...

7. No one is going to stand your remaining in deep peace while Malta is being starved out, while the Russians are fighting like mad and while we are suffering continued disasters in Burma and India at the hands of the Japanese. The whole system of the command will have to be revolutionized. It is imperative that our forces everywhere shall come to grips with the enemy and force him to consume lives, munitions, tanks, and aircraft around the whole circle of his fighting front.

Before we look at the course of the Defence Committee meeting on 2 March, we may briefly note some of the comments made at the time by other people involved, for they demonstrate how angry Churchill was with Auchinleck's appreciation. Sir Charles Wilson, his doctor, pencilled the following note in February:

Found the PM in an explosive mood today. Auchinleck will not be ready to take the offensive in the Desert till June. 'The bloody man does not seem to care about the fate of Malta. Anyway,' said Winston setting his jaw, 'we can't settle this by writing letters.'[14]

In his diary for 2 March, General Brooke wrote:

Another bad Monday ... Found PM had drafted a bad wire for Auchinleck in which he poured abuse on him for not attacking sooner, and for sending us an appreciation in which he did not propose to attack till June!![15]

When Brooke reviewed this entry after the war, he made the following observation:

> Here we have another example of Winston's interference with a commander in the field. Without it being possible for him to be familiar with all aspects of the situation facing Auchinleck he is trying to force him to attack at an earlier date than is thought advisable, and what is more, tries to obtain his ends by an offensive wire. Thank heaven we were able to stop the wire and re-word it.

Nevertheless, it must be said that, as we shall shortly see, the replacement telegram, although less harsh in tone, was equally insistent that Auchinleck's intention to delay his offensive until June was unacceptable, and urged him to reconsider. Churchill's main argument was endorsed by the Committee. His draft was his way of giving vent to his immediate anger and frustration, and he no doubt expected the COS to send a more restrained signal.

At the Defence Committee, which met at 10.00 p.m. on 2 March, much time was spent in a vain attempt to reconcile Auchinleck's complaints about his weak tank position with the War Office figures. In particular, the Committee did not understand why the latest British tanks had so lost the confidence of their crews and commanders that Auchinleck demanded a two to one numerical superiority as a condition for engaging the German armour. Oliver Lyttleton, recently returned from his appointment as Minister of State in Cairo, tried to explain these difficulties, but hardly to the Committee's satisfaction, and Attlee was requested to conduct an enquiry into this matter. When he reported in June, he told his colleagues that, such was the urgency of producing as many tanks as possible, design faults were not identified and rectified before full-scale production commenced.[16] No member spoke in support of Auchinleck's proposed delay, and it was agreed that the COS send a less aggressive telegram in place of Churchill's draft.[17] Auchinleck's biographer has argued that it might have been better to have sent Churchill's angry draft so that Auchinleck could see how deeply offended the Prime Minister had become.[18] Nevertheless, the substance of this was as critical as Churchill's draft had been. It began:

> We are greatly disturbed by your review of the situation. The dominant factor in the Mediterranean and Middle East situation at the present time is Malta. It may not have been known to you when you wrote your review that, if we do not succeed in running a substantial convoy into Malta by May, the position there will be critical. The loss of Malta or even its effective neutralisation will mean that the Axis will be able to

reinforce Libya almost without hindrance and at any rate much faster than we can. Supplies of aircraft to the Middle East will also be seriously affected. A convoy can only be run into Malta if we can use the landing grounds in Western Cyrenaica. Hence the recapture of these in the near future is vital to your whole situation.

The signal went on to observe that, 'Your review seems to us to give a picture heavily biased in favour of the enemy,' and concluded: 'If our view of the situation is correct, you must either grasp the opportunity which is held out in the immediate future or else we must face the loss of Malta and a precarious defensive. Please reconsider the matter urgently and telegraph your views.'[19]

Auchinleck, nevertheless, refused to bow to this intense pressure from Churchill and the COS. In two telegrams of 4 and 5 March, while acknowledging the growing dangers to Malta, he maintained his central position that 'a premature offensive to recapture Cyrenaica within the next few weeks might result in the destruction piecemeal of the new armoured force we are building up and thereby jeopardise the security of Egypt'.[20] However, he also raised a further objection whose validity was soon to be demonstrated:

We would point out that the re-occupation of Cyrenaica is not a complete answer to the problem of supply to Malta. Fighter protection during the reception and unloading of convoys is needed, and other aircraft must be able to operate against enemy surface forces. On the other hand, the scale of attack which enemy can produce from Sicily may make it extremely difficult, if not impossible, for Malta to play its part however much the defences of the island are strengthened.

Auchinleck concluded by saying that the only available course was to run convoys to Malta both in March and April dark periods under 'present conditions of risk'. Although, as one of the three Middle East C-in-Cs, Admiral Cunningham, had put his name to this signal, he was uneasy, as his letter of 15 March to Admiral Pound makes clear. 'I do not find the attitude of the soldiers to this Malta problem much to my liking,' he told Pound and went on to write that, after he had warned that the proposed convoys might not get through, 'I am met with the reply that it is better to lose Malta than Egypt.'[21] This view of priorities, although perhaps implicit in Auchinleck's position, was to re-emerge more clearly later with serious consequences.

These crossed telegrams, with their widely differing conclusions about the action to be taken, persuaded Churchill that Auchinleck should return to London, as he had done in the previous August, to discuss the whole problem. When, however, the Prime Minister telegraphed to this effect on

8 March, Auchinleck simply declined, arguing that the critical situation in the Middle East would not permit his absence. He suggested instead that Brooke and Portal should visit him in Cairo. When Brooke, as he noted in his diary, telephoned the Prime Minister at Chequers to tell him of this response, 'he was infuriated and once again suggested relieving him of his command! Would not agree to Auchinleck's suggestion that I should go out with CAS.'[22]

Churchill then signalled at some length to Auchinleck: 'Your appreciation of February 27 continues to cause deepest anxiety here, both to the Chiefs of Staff and Defence Committee. I therefore regret extremely your inability to come home for consultation. The delay you have in mind will endanger safety of Malta.' He went on to repeat his earlier arguments for an early offensive in the desert, and concluded by telling Auchinleck that Sir Stafford Cripps, on his way to India, would stop in Cairo to discuss the situation. General Nye, the Vice-Chief of the Imperial General Staff (VCIGS) would join him there.[23] It is not difficult to imagine Churchill's reaction to the telegram Cripps sent back to him from Cairo on 21 March – 'very ill-content' was Churchill's post-war phrase. For Cripps and Nye had both accepted Auchinleck's analysis of the situation, and endorsed the C-in-C's conclusion that nothing could be done 'before about mid-May'.[24]

As part of his instructions General Nye had been given a list of twenty questions to which Churchill and the COS sought answers. The first of these asked, if an early offensive were not to be launched, 'what constructive measures are proposed for the maintenance of Malta?' The reply, telegraphed on 22 March, was that a convoy was about to sail with two months' supplies, and another would be sent in April. It concluded that 'all risks are being accepted in the attempts to get the convoys through'.[25]

The entire situation was reviewed once again at a Defence Committee meeting on 26 March.[26] Churchill complained at length that an opportunity to defeat Rommel had been missed, and said 'he could not believe that we stood to gain, on balance, by postponing the offensive'. Other Ministers were equally critical, although Lyttleton reminded the Committee that the 'High Command had lost confidence in the present cruiser tank'. With considerable misgivings the Committee decided that the proposed mid-May target date 'must be accepted'. However, when they telegraphed this decision to the Middle East Defence Committee on 31 March, they did so on the understanding that 'any fair opportunity for action that occurs before then will be taken'. Churchill had the last word:

> The Committee recorded this decision with reluctance on account of the increasing danger to Malta and to the probability that the enemy will receive reinforcements at least as fast as you will during the interval. They consider these are two very great dangers.

How angry Churchill remained is shown in the reply he sent to the COS when they suggested that he send a telegram of encouragement to Auchinleck. 'There is no question,' he wrote, 'of my sending any "friendly telegram" … The situation is too grave for empty compliments.' He was surely further dismayed when he read the next telegram from Cairo, which warned: 'The C-in-Cs cannot bind themselves in any way to launch an offensive on 15th May in spite of the very obvious and urgent need to take the offensive as soon as possible.'[27] This was to light a delayed fuse that was to explode two months later.

It will be evident from this exchange of signals that there was now a deepening rift between London and Cairo, and that the problem and plight of Malta lay at the heart of this dispute. It was the view in London that, if the island were to be sustained so that it could continue to play a vital part in the Mediterranean war, regular convoys were essential. Getting these through appeared to depend on air cover from Cyrenaican airfields. Auchinleck accepted this argument in principle but insisted that any premature attempt to attack would lead to defeat and thus endanger Egypt. It is clear from Cunningham's letter to Pound that Auchinleck, or at least some members of his staff, was beginning to think that Egypt was more important than Malta, although he had not yet said so. He also made the telling point that the recapture of the Cyrenaican airfields would not of itself ensure the safe resupply of Malta since the *Luftwaffe* squadrons in Sicily had recovered air superiority over Malta.

For the time being, therefore, Churchill was compelled to accept Auchinleck's qualified agreement to launch a new offensive in mid-May. But his misgivings about this delay were intensified by the fate of the March convoy to Malta and we should now turn to consider this. After the failure of the February convoy, following the limited supplies landed in January, the March convoy was that much more important. On 20 March, three freighters accompanied by HMS *Breconshire* sailed from Alexandria with as strong an escort as Cunningham could provide in the absence of battleships and aircraft carriers. On 22 March, the convoy, already under air attack, was approached by a powerful Italian naval force led by the battleship *Littorio*. Throughout the afternoon, Admiral Vian fought what was later known as the Second Battle of Sirte, and prevented the Italian heavy ships from getting to the freighters. Nevertheless, as the convoy, now dispersed, approached Malta, SS *Clan Campbell* was sunk by air attack. *Breconshire* was also heavily damaged and, although eventually towed into Marsaslokk Harbour, rolled over and sank in shallow water on 27 March. The other two freighters entered the Grand Harbour on the morning of 23 March, but two days later suffered fierce air attack. SS *Pampas* was sunk and settled on the bottom, while SS *Talabot* was scuttled as a spreading fire threatened the explosion of its cargo of ammunition. By then, in very difficult and dangerous conditions, only 5,000 tons of cargo had been unloaded, although a further 2,500 tons were salvaged later. Much of *Breconshire*'s cargo of oil fuel was also pumped out.

Churchill followed this critical convoy closely and, before the sinking of *Pampas* and *Talabot* became known, signalled Admiral Cunningham on 25 March:

> I shall be glad if you will convey to Admiral Vian and all who sailed with him the admiration which I feel at this resolute and brilliant action ... That one of the most powerful modern battleships afloat, attended by two heavy and one light cruiser and a flotilla, should have been routed and put to flight with severe torpedo and gunfire injuries in broad daylight by the fire of British light cruisers and destroyers constitutes a naval episode of the highest distinction and entitles all ranks and ratings concerned, and above all their Commander, to the compliments of the British nation.[28]

The initial mood of relief in London evaporated when the subsequent loss of the two freighters in the Grand Harbour became known. But before we consider the reaction in London and Valletta to this severe setback to Malta's supply position, we will examine the impact on the RAF in Malta

11. A German air attack on the SS *Talabot* in the Grand Harbour in March 1942. She was sunk at her moorings, and only a limited amount of her cargo was unloaded.

12. The SS *Talabot* on fire after the initial air attack.

13. Heavy damage in Floriana. On the right are the ruins of the King George V Hospital, while the upper works of the partially sunken *Talabot* can be seen on the left.

of the mounting German air attacks since it had now become clear that, as Auchinleck had feared, the *Luftwaffe* had gained air superiority over Malta.

Hitler's decision to transfer *Fliegerkorps II* to Sicily, and the warning from the JIC in January that this was taking place, have been described at the beginning of this chapter. AVM Lloyd could, therefore, expect a heavy air attack carried out by experienced pilots. More worryingly, it soon became apparent that the German fighter squadrons had been re-equipped with the latest ME 109F aircraft, which outclassed Malta's Hurricane IIs. Consequently, Lloyd at once requested large reinforcements, including five squadrons of Spitfires. After some discussion in the Air Ministry about the servicing and maintenance problems arising from the introduction of a new fighter type to Malta, Portal agreed to this in February. 'We must gamble on the Spitfire being a success,' he wrote on 6 February to his DCAS, ACM Freeman.[29] Two weeks later, Churchill and the COS received an anxious signal from Cairo.

> We are seriously concerned at air situation in Malta. We realise you have this very much in mind but should be grateful for any measures you can possibly take to augment and accelerate arrival of reinforcements of fighter aircraft.

On his copy of this telegram Churchill wrote, 'CAS. What action is proposed?' Portal explained that Spitfire reinforcements were being arranged with the Admiralty since these aircraft could only reach Malta from an aircraft carrier as in 1941. A first attempt failed on 27 February when it was found that the necessary long-range fuel tanks were defective. However, a fly-off at dawn on 7 March from HMS *Eagle* was successful, and fifteen Spitfire Vbs, armed with two cannons and four machine guns, arrived safely at Malta later that morning. A further sixteen arrived in two flights at the end of March, while Tedder from Egypt sent another ten Hurricane IIs.

Despite these valuable reinforcements the numerical superiority of the German air forces was such that the number of Lloyd's serviceable aircraft steadily fell. The weight of the German air attack in these early months of 1942 is illustrated by the following figures of the tonnage of bombs dropped over Malta:

January	February	March	April	May
669	1,020	2,170	6,700	520

These raids, concentrated on the dockyard and the three airfields, were supplemented by frequent low-level strafing attacks aimed at aircraft on the ground and at airfield defences and installations. At a COS meeting on 23 March, Portal referred to AM Tedder's plea for more Spitfires, but Pound pointed out that HMS *Eagle* was about to go into the dockyard for repairs to her steering gear, and would not be available for another four weeks. In this emergency Portal could only suggest that the US Navy be asked to lend one of their large carriers. After it had been established that one of these could carry as many as fifty erected Spitfires, Churchill was asked to send a telegram to President Roosevelt. This he did on 1 April, after having his draft cleared by Portal and Pound. Churchill reprinted this important signal in his memoirs, and it need not be repeated here in full.[30]

After describing the heavy air attacks on Malta, Churchill explained what had been done to fly in Spitfire reinforcements. He pointed out that *Eagle* was in the dockyard for a month, that *Argus* was too small for such an operation, and that the lifts on *Victorious* were too small for Spitfires. There was, therefore, the prospect that Malta would receive no more reinforcements for a whole month. He then continued:

3. Would you be willing to allow your carrier Wasp to do one of these trips provided details are satisfactorily agreed between the Naval Staffs? With her broad lifts, capacity, and length, we estimate that Wasp could take fifty or more Spitfires …

4. Thus, instead of not being able to give Malta any further Spitfires during April, a powerful Spitfire force could be flown into Malta at a stroke and give us a chance of inflicting a very severe and possibly decisive check on enemy. Operation might take place during third week of April.

The President agreed to this request, and we will follow in the next chapter the results of the two operations carried out in April and May by USS *Wasp*.

Malta's growing weakness, both in terms of diminishing supplies and faltering defence against air attack, led the JIC to review once more the danger of an invasion of the island, and they presented their appreciation to the COS on 2 April.[31] As before, they found no evidence of any assembly of landing craft or transport aircraft in Sicily. Moreover, they thought that an attempt to invade Malta would be 'a more formidable undertaking than on Crete', and would require as many as 800 aircraft. On the other side, they recorded, 'there has been a recrudescence of reports that an assault on the island has been planned, some of the reports mentioning April as the probable time'. They also noted the arrival in Rome of a senior parachute general, who had been involved in the invasion of Crete, while another 'reliable report' indicated that Hitler had given his approval for an invasion. The JIC were clearly in two minds, but, forced to make a judgement, concluded that, although the danger of an invasion attempt had increased, 'On balance, however, we think that neutralisation is more likely than assault.' The COS were equally dubious about German intentions, but recognised 'that there was little we could do to reinforce the garrison during the next few weeks beyond the action already taken by the Prime Minister to obtain the use of an American carrier'.

We may conclude this chapter by briefly noting the impact in the first quarter of 1942 of the mounting Axis air attack upon the island's offensive capability, which had become so important in the closing months of 1941. The Royal Navy struggled to maintain a reduced Force K at Valletta, now suffering increasing damage. Only one light cruiser and several destroyers could be maintained there, and this was too weak a force to challenge the strongly escorted Italian convoys to North Africa. However, the U-class submarines of the 10th Flotilla sank six merchant ships, and shared in the destruction of three others. The RAF's bomber operations and the torpedo-bomber attacks of the FAA became progressively more difficult, and those aircraft that were not lost on operations, or on the ground, were eventually sent to North Africa. Despite these difficulties, the RAF and FAA sank another four ships in addition to the three shared with the submarines. In total, Malta's forces sank thirteen enemy cargo ships, aggregating 59,384 tons, in the first three months of 1942. This compares with the sinking of twenty-seven ships, with a tonnage of 119,710 tons, in the last three months of 1941, a reduction of one half in Axis shipping losses. The result was that in January and February 1942 virtually all the enemy supplies shipped to North Africa arrived safely, and only in March did the loss rate briefly rise to 17 per cent. It was this steady flow of supplies that fuelled Churchill's anxiety that continued delay on Auchinleck's part would allow Rommel, once more, to strike first. Events were soon to show that the Prime Minister's fears were only too well grounded.

THE GEORGE CROSS
AND A NEW GOVERNOR

*I am deeply anxious about Malta under the increasing bombardment of
450 first-line German aircraft.*

Churchill to President Roosevelt, 4 April 1942

It was in the month of April 1942 that the people and garrison of Malta
suffered most grievously from Kesselring's ferocious bombing attacks
designed to eliminate the island as an operational base. The number of
air raids, the weight of bombs dropped, the loss of life, and the scale of
devastation surpassed all previous experience.[1] At the same time stocks of
civilian and military supplies relentlessly fell since no relief convoy reached
the island. But the mounting concern in Malta, Cairo and London about
the island's plight was not the only anxiety that weighed on Churchill
and his colleagues during this most difficult period. In order, therefore, to
understand correctly the decisions taken to sustain Malta in the second
quarter of 1942 it will again be necessary to set these decisions in a wider
framework, for difficult choices had often to be made.

The growing threat from Japan was the most ominous development.
Even before the fall of Singapore, Japanese forces had, in mid-January,
invaded Burma and by the end of March the remaining British forces had
withdrawn to the borders of India. At the same time a powerful Japanese
naval task force, comprising no fewer than five aircraft carriers and four
modern battleships, entered the Indian Ocean and carried out heavy
bombing raids on the ports of Colombo and Trincomalee in Ceylon. The
weaker British naval force in the area was ordered to avoid an engagement
with this powerful enemy fleet, but the aircraft carrier HMS *Hermes* and
the heavy cruisers HMS *Cornwall* and *Devonshire* were sunk, together with
116,000 tons of merchant shipping. Meanwhile, in order to protect the vital
Cape reinforcement route to the Middle East and the Persian oil fields, the
British government, with Roosevelt's support, determined to occupy the
Vichy French island of Madagascar – Operation 'Ironclad' – and opposed
landings began on 5 May. The Royal Navy was stretched to the limit by

these eastern commitments, but could send only limited reinforcements from home waters since the Arctic convoys, vital to Russia's ability to fight on, required increasingly powerful escort to protect the convoys from the German battleship *Tirpitz* and other capital ships, which had moved into Norwegian waters. Both Roosevelt and Stalin made urgent representations to the Prime Minister to increase the size and frequency of these convoys. It was in the midst of these other pressing demands on limited resources that the needs of Malta claimed equally urgent attention.

As soon as it became clear that only a limited amount of supplies could be salvaged from the sunken *Talabot* and *Pampas*, the Governor, on 1 April, sent two urgent telegrams to London.[2] In the first he stressed the need for 'a really strong fighter force', adding, 'this is a paramount necessity and needs to be fully met without delay. We must control the skies over Malta.' The Governor went on to ask if transport aircraft, fast warships and submarines could be employed to send in smaller quantities of emergency supplies. In the second signal he set out in detail the remaining amounts of civilian and military supplies. Wheat and flour stocks were sufficient to last only until early July, while AA ammunition would be exhausted within 1½–3 months, depending on the weight of air attack.

After studying these telegrams, Churchill, on 3 April, sent a minute to the COS, asking that 'this serious report be considered with a view to action. Are we to understand,' he continued, 'that they are entirely meatless? or

14. The mine-laying submarine HMS *Rorqual* leaving Manoel Island. She could carry significant amounts of emergency supplies in her mine deck.

have they cattle they can kill, and if so how many?' While noting that there were no transport aircraft available he asked whether fast ships and submarines could help to ease the problem.[3] The COS considered the Prime Minister's request on 4 April, pending a more detailed analysis by the War Office.[4] At this meeting Admiral Pound told his colleagues that 'in view of the air situation at Malta he had decided that no attempt should be made to run in a convoy during April. Plans would, however, be made to send in convoys during May from each end of the Mediterranean.' Portal reluctantly agreed, observing that by mid-May Malta's fighter defences would be stronger, and that by then some of the *Luftwaffe* squadrons in Sicily might have been withdrawn.

General Brooke presented the War Office's detailed report on the supply position at a subsequent COS meeting on 7 April.[5] After summarising the stock levels reported by the Governor, the report answered the Prime Minister's questions by noting that, although there was no longer any frozen meat, supplies of preserved meat would last until the end of June. There were few cattle remaining on the island and the goats were essential for milk supplies. The report concluded: 'Malta has sufficient stocks of all necessary items to last, without further replenishment, well into June, provided that the present reduced scale of consumption is maintained.' After General Brooke had presented this report, Admiral Pound added that fast warships could not be employed due to the lack of oil fuel at Malta. Colonel Hollis duly reported these findings to Churchill, who, a week later, asked Pound for information about the amounts that could be carried in submarines. The First Sea Lord told him that the larger submarines could carry between 150 and 200 tons of fuel and other stores, and that the largest submarine, HMS *Clyde*, was being modified to carry even more. Such amounts, while useful, could hardly be a substitute for the loads carried by merchant ships.

At the COS meeting on 4 April, Admiral Pound had said that plans were being made to sail convoys to Malta in May from both Gibraltar and Alexandria. However, the demands on the Admiralty noted at the beginning of this chapter now compelled Pound to tell his colleagues on 16 April that the proposed Gibraltar convoy would be too risky.[6] Any such convoy would require battleship and aircraft carrier escort, while the probable weight of air attack from *Luftwaffe* squadrons in Sicily and Sardinia meant that heavy losses might be suffered. As Col. Hollis explained to the Prime Minister, the COS 'do not consider that the risk to these valuable ships should be accepted'. The abandonment of this eastbound convoy would also enable the battlecruiser HMS *Renown* to reinforce the eastern fleet in the Indian Ocean three weeks earlier. On Col. Hollis's memorandum Churchill wrote 'I agree', and a telegram to this effect was sent to the Governor on 18 April.

Upon receipt of this unwelcome news, the Governor sat down to write a lengthy reply to the COS and the Middle East C-in-Cs, which he dispatched on 20 April. Since this telegram provides a vivid and sombre account of Malta's growing crisis it will be appropriate to quote extensively from it.[7] The signal began:

> The decision not to run a convoy from West for present is based on general considerations which are outside my sphere. I can only speak for Malta itself and our situation is so grave that it is my duty to restate it in the clearest possible terms. The decision materially reduces our chances of survival not because of any failure of morale or fighting efficiency but because it is impossible to carry on without food and ammunition. When the question of running a convoy from Egypt in March was under consideration I said the problem of maintaining the Fortress had reached a critical point. It has now gone beyond that point and it is obvious that the very worst must happen if we cannot replenish our vital needs especially flour and ammunition and that very soon.

The Governor then explained that existing stocks of flour would last until the latter half of May and that some additional amounts might be provided as long as the flour mills, some of which had already been damaged, were not put out of action. As regards AA ammunition, there remained only one month's supply, and usage had been cut back to maintain protection for vital areas and for arriving convoys. He then continued:

> It follows from the above that we can only be sure of surviving if the May convoy from the East is successfully unloaded. I understand the Naval opinion to be that we cannot rely on more than 50% of the ships reaching Malta. If five ships are run and only two or three arrive it is vital to our survival to ensure that the whole or the major part of their cargo is unloaded. Otherwise we shall at the best be in the same critical position after the operation as we are now. If the convoy fails altogether or we do not succeed in even obtaining a substantial out-turn from two or three ships we shall in all probability not be able to survive. It is for this reason that I consider it imperative that we should have more than one string to our bow, i.e. a convoy from West as well as all possible other subsidiary means.
>
> In order that the convoy may be successful it has not only to reach the neighbourhood of Malta. We in Malta must see that it is protected in the Approaches to the Island and in Harbour and that its cargo is safely unloaded and dispersed. We cannot afford to repeat the experience of the last convoy from which out of a total of 30,000 tons of stores reaching vicinity of Malta we have obtained about 5,000 tons. All but a small

part of our lighters and tugs have been destroyed or severely damaged. The wharfs and transit sheds have been badly knocked about and the services of the Dockyard have been largely put out of action. In the time available there are strict limits to what can be accomplished in repairing lighters and tugs and otherwise preparing for the convoy. All that we can do we will, but what little we can achieve will be further reduced if heavy air raids on the harbour continue to take place several times a day. In order that the convoy may be a success we must secure and retain local air superiority not only while it is here or on the way but also during the period of preparation.

Our needs are more Spitfires in addition to those already arranged for, with regular reinforcements, sufficient supplies of flour, and an adequate replenishment of A.A. ammunition. If Middle East are not in a position materially to increase the amount of ammunition already released for the Eastern Convoy then we must obtain our supplies from the West if not by convoy then by special means. If a convoy cannot be run from the West in May then the number of ships from the East should be increased so as to ensure that even with losses we obtain sufficient flour. But whatever plans are made will fail unless we are adequately reinforced with modern fighters. The primary need is Spitfires and more Spitfires. They must not arrive in driblets but in really big quantities without long intervals between consignments. At all costs we must avoid the danger of our fighter force being worn down before the convoys arrive so that it will not be strong enough to protect it on arrival.

If Malta is to be held, drastic action is needed now it is a question of survival.

Upon receipt of this signal, Churchill gave orders for a special meeting of the Defence Committee to consider all aspects of the worsening position at Malta.

Before we consider the deliberations of the Defence Committee on 22 April, two other matters, each affecting Malta in different ways, deserve examination. The first was the notable and unprecedented initiative taken by King George VI. That his eyes were closely focused on events in the island was demonstrated by the letter he sent to General Dobbie on 3 April:

I have been watching with admiration the stout-hearted resistance of all in Malta, Service personnel and civilians alike, to the fierce and constant air attacks of the enemy in recent weeks.

In the active defence of the Island, the Royal Air Force have been ably supported by the Royal Malta Artillery, and it therefore gives me special pleasure, in recognition of their skill and resolution, to assume the Colonelcy-in-Chief of the Regiment. Please convey my best wishes to all ranks of my new Regiment, and assure them of the added pride with which I shall follow future activities.[8]

The second sentence of this letter is now engraved on the War Memorial of the Regiment in Floriana.

Two weeks later the King decided to award the George Cross to the people of Malta and on 15 April he sent a letter in his own hand to General Dobbie:

> The Governor
>   Malta.
>   To honour her brave people I award the George Cross to the Island Fortress of Malta to bear witness to a heroism and devotion that will long be famous in history.
> > George R.I.
> April 15th 1942

This message is now inscribed on a marble tablet on the wall of the Grand Master's Palace in Valletta.

Although ACM Portal at a COS meeting on 28 March had raised the possibility of some message from the King, and Leo Amery, then Secretary of State for India, suggested to the King's Private Secretary, Sir Alexander Hardinge, on 10 April the award of the Victoria Cross,[9] the final decision

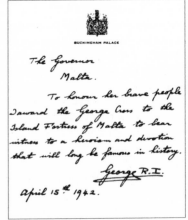

15. The George Cross, awarded by King George VI to the people of Malta, and the King's letter of 15 April 1942.

16. The Governor of Malta, General Lord Gort, presenting the George Cross to Malta's Chief Justice, Sir George Borg, in September 1942.

to award the George Cross was taken by the King. There is no reference to this award in Churchill's Malta papers, or even, more surprisingly, in his post-war memoirs. Nevertheless, it seems likely that he was advised of the King's intentions, perhaps at a weekly lunch with the King, which was a regular appointment in his diary whenever he was not abroad. Apart from the pleasure and pride felt by many people, both in Malta and Great Britain, the award served to make the surrender of Malta unthinkable, a theme to which we shall return later.

The second development was the arrival, even as the Governor was writing the letter quoted above, of a large reinforcement of forty-six Spitfires in Operation 'Calendar'. At about 10.00 a.m. on 20 April, the Spitfires of 601 'County of London' Squadron landed at Luqa, and those of 603 'City of Edinburgh' Squadron at Takali. These two squadrons, equipped with Spitfire VCs mounting four cannons and four machine guns, had flown off USS *Wasp* at dawn. However, German radar had plotted the passage of these aircraft, and within two hours a series of heavy attacks was launched on the airfields. During that day, 272 bomber and 223 fighter sorties were made against Malta's airfields. On 23 April,

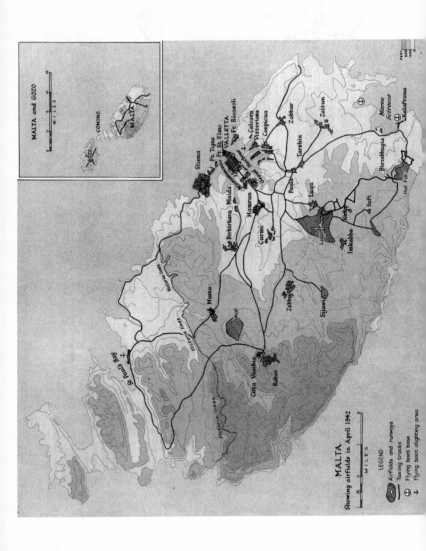

MALTA
Showing airfields in April 1942

LEGEND

⊠ Airfields and runways
⊕ Taxiing tracks
⊕ Flying boat base
⊕ Flying boat alighting area

MALTA and GOZO

17. A Spitfire being serviced in a protective pen. These were built of sand-filled petrol containers and limestone blocks.

the Governor signalled to the Prime Minister to tell him that of the newly arrived Spitfires seventeen had been destroyed in the air or on the ground, and twenty-nine more damaged. Only six were still serviceable. 'Situation demands most drastic action,' the Governor wrote, 'and we must think in quite different numbers of Spitfires than we have envisaged heretofore.' On this telegram Churchill wrote: 'CAS. Please speak to me.'

The defeat of this first major Spitfire reinforcement was perhaps inevitable given the strength and ferocity of the enemy raids, but the RAF's response was weakened by the poor condition of many of the new Spitfires' guns and radios. Moreover, the two squadrons sent on this occasion were not among the best in Fighter Command. Seven of the most experienced pilots of 601 Squadron were posted away from the squadron before it left for Malta, and twelve of its twenty-three pilots had never fired their guns in action. 603 Squadron presented a similar picture, nine of its pilots having had no operational experience. It is no wonder that AVM Lloyd complained strenuously to the Air Ministry about the condition of the aircraft, and the lack of experience of many of the pilots. 'Only fully-experienced operational pilots must come here,' he signalled. 'It is no place for beginners. Casualties up to now have been the beginners.'[10] It should be noted that Churchill had been receiving since early April weekly reports from the Air Ministry on the RAF and enemy aircraft losses over Malta. On 26 April, however, he requested that these be made on a daily basis, prescribing the form in which the figures should be briefly presented. These reports enabled him to see at a glance the course of the air battle in Malta's skies.[11]

On 22 April, the Defence Committee was faced with two difficult decisions. The first was to decide the composition, timing and routeing of the next Malta convoy. The second was whether to accept the recommendation of the Middle East Defence Committee (MEDC) that General Dobbie be relieved as Governor of Malta. This second matter was by no means straightforward, and will be considered later in this chapter. This critical Defence Committee meeting began at noon, and then resumed at 5.30 p.m. after lunch and other engagements.[12] Several papers had previously been circulated to the Committee members, and these will be considered first. The Governor's telegram of 20 April, extensively quoted earlier, was accompanied by the minutes of a meeting of the Malta Defence Committee chaired by Sir Walter Monckton in Valletta on 13 April, and a subsequent memorandum, written after that meeting by a Mr Jackson, a member of Monckton's staff.

Sir Walter Monckton had been appointed as Acting Minister of State in the Middle East after Oliver Lyttleton had returned to London. On 12 April, he and AM Tedder flew to Malta to assess the position for themselves. The meeting of the Malta Defence Committee was convened on 13 April and was attended by the Governor, the Lt-Governor, Sir Edward Jackson, the three Service Commanders on the island, and Mr Jackson. Admiral Leatham reported that only a few submarines remained to intercept enemy convoys to North Africa and these were forced to lie submerged to avoid air raid attack at Manoel Island. General Beak, the General Officer Commanding (GOC) the troops, explained that AA ammunition had been restricted to fifteen rounds per gun per day to conserve stocks to protect the next convoy. He also warned the Committee that the troops 'were not ready for battle ... At least two months' training were required before they would be fit to play their part in defeating an invasion.' AVM Lloyd, speaking before the arrival of the forty-six Spitfires in Operation 'Calendar', described the problems arising from the loss of air control, which have been noted above. Lack of fighters, he conceded, meant that numerous enemy air raids could not be opposed. Sir Edward Jackson spoke about the civilian situation, and noted that, despite anxieties about the shortage of food, 'the civilian population are bearing up well'. There remained only three months' supplies of the principal commodities, which made the safe arrival of the next convoy 'vital'.

Mr Jackson's memorandum, 'Maintenance of Malta', written on 14 April after his return to Cairo with Monckton and Tedder, presented further details of the supply position before examining the difficulties that would arise in unloading whatever merchant ships that might get through. The widespread destruction of the harbour facilities and the shortage of tugs and lighters exacerbated these difficulties. The repair of these facilities, and the provision of more lighters, were urgent necessities. It was also essential, he believed, that the unloading of cargoes continue

18. In April 1942, Sir Walter Monckton and Air Marshal Tedder visited Malta. Shown here in the gardens of San Anton Palace are (from left to right): General Beak; the Lt-Governor, Sir Edward Jackson; Air Vice-Marshal Lloyd; Vice-Admiral Leatham; Sir Walter Monckton; the Governor, General Dobbie; and Air Marshal Tedder.

even during air raids, and in this regard he wrote: 'Action should be taken in Malta to ensure that all men working either voluntarily or compulsorily on the discharge of ships are guaranteed adequate dependent allowances in the event of death or injury. This is of the greatest importance.' He concluded by recommending a convoy of ten merchant ships and a tanker, and assumed that five of these might arrive.

With these papers before them, Churchill and his colleagues spent most of the morning session of the Defence Committee meeting wrestling with the problem of escorting a convoy to Malta, either from Alexandria or Gibraltar, or possibly from both directions at the same time. In all cases the inability to provide effective air cover while the convoys were approaching the island, and during the unloading operation was the most important factor to be considered. In addition, there was the continuing threat posed by the capital ships of the Italian navy. The minutes recorded the Committee's view that 'the last convoy had a very narrow escape, mainly owing to weather conditions. We cannot count on a repetition of this stroke of fortune.' Rather gloomily, the Committee observed that even if the convoy arrived safely, the same problem would arise six weeks later. On only one matter was agreement reached; President Roosevelt must be asked to approve a second delivery of Spitfires from USS *Wasp*.

In preparation for the second session of the meeting at 5.30 p.m., Churchill, after lunch, dictated and circulated a Note with his own appreciation of the difficulties and a plan of action. Since it is not unusual to read in biographies of Churchill that his strategic sense was limited, this Note deserves close attention. The opening sentences grasped the nettle:

No satisfactory solution of the Malta problem is available in May. The island must therefore hold out to the June dark period. This should be possible if rigorous severity of rationing is imposed from now and the supply of Spitfires by WASP and EAGLE is maintained.

The Note proceeded to point out that 'the month gained by Malta holding out till the middle of June and the dropping of the idea of a convoy from the west' would allow time to complete the Madagascar operation, 'Ironclad', and the sailing of a May convoy to Russia. By that time, too, a more powerful fleet of battleships and aircraft carriers would have been assembled in the Indian Ocean. Churchill then continued:

After IRONCLAD is over, it is hoped about May 10, [Admiral Somerville] should work his way north to fuel at Aden in the early days of June. By this time we shall know what has happened to General Auchinleck's offensive. If he has got Martuba or Benghazi, the chances of a Malta convoy getting through from the east will be greatly improved. We shall also know how much of the German Air Force has been drawn away from the Mediterranean to the South Russian front, the actual moves that have taken place or are in progress. We can also judge the situation in the Indian Ocean as it then appears, observing that we cannot fight a Fleet action anyhow except against a minor detachment. The decision can then be taken whether or not to escort the convoy in strength from the east through the Mediterranean or sail southwards again to meet DUKE OF YORK and RENOWN and pick up VALIANT for the Eastern Fleet assembly on June 30.

Should the decision be to make a dart into the Mediterranean and see the convoy through in style, Admiral Somerville should proceed with all three aircraft carriers and WARSPITE with ancillaries through the Canal where the convoy should be assembled. This convoy must be worthy of the effort and risk required to put it through. At least seven supply ships can now be loaded at Alexandria. The four 15-knot supply ships which were considered for the convoy from the west ought to be loaded and sent round the Cape at once. They should be just in time for the mid-June convoy making 12 ships in all with ample escort.

Churchill's Note then concluded: 'It will be necessary to ask the President in the next few days to have a second sting out of WASP.'

The Committee accepted the Prime Minister's plan, although Brooke pointed out that before June Malta would run out of AA ammunition unless special arrangements were made. Anthony Eden remarked that the delay until June 'would mean cutting it very fine in Malta', and Oliver Lyttleton added that, if this failed, Malta would probably be lost. Two signals were then drafted and dispatched. The first, on 23 April to General Dobbie, summarised the Defence Committee's deliberations and explained why 'the passage of a convoy to Malta in May, whether from the West or the East, presents insurmountable difficulties'. The Governor was advised, however, of plans 'to fly in a further big batch of Spitfires from WASP during the early part of May', and that arrangements were being made to send in AA ammunition in a fast minelayer. 'You must,' the telegram concluded, 'hold out with the above slight relief until mid-June.'

Upon receipt of this signal, the Governor at once assured the Prime Minister, 'This will be done.' He then told Churchill and the COS that he had cut the bread ration to 10½ ounces per person per day, but emphasised that this was 'quite definitely inadequate, and will inevitably reduce working capacity ... It cannot be continued indefinitely.' He added that present flour stocks would be exhausted by mid-June, but 'if whole stock of wheat and maize can be milled, we shall be able to last until latter half of July, but this depends on main mills not being put out of action'. It was no doubt with considerable relief that Churchill wrote on his copy of this signal: 'COS Committee. This looks better than we thought.'

The second telegram Churchill sent personally on 24 April to President Roosevelt. On the previous day he had read a memorandum from Portal that stated: 'I attach a copy of a telegram sent by Lloyd to Tedder yesterday. You may wish to use the facts contained in this telegram to strengthen your request to the President for further use of the WASP.' In his telegram to Tedder, Lloyd, after describing the elimination of the first batch of Spitfires, wrote: 'In battle of Britain one squadron of 12 fighters used 60 fighters each 14 days with all resources of Britain on hand ... Must have 100 Spitfires a month to deal with present strength of attack, in fifties every 14 days.' With this information before him, Churchill appealed again to the President:

I am deeply anxious about Malta under the unceasing bombardment of 450 first-line German aircraft. If the island fortress is to hold out till the June convoy, which is the earliest possible, it must have a continued flow of Spitfires. The last flying-off from WASP was most successful, although unhappily the enemy's attack broke up many after they had landed. We are using EAGLE to send in 15 or so at a time. I shall be grateful if you will allow WASP to do a second trip. We will of course escort with RENOWN as before. I do not think enemy have the slightest idea WASP has been in and out of the Mediterranean. Without this I fear Malta will be pounded to bits. Meanwhile its defence is wearing out the enemy's Air Force and effectively aiding Russia.

The President at once agreed, and after thanking him, Churchill asked Portal, 'Now that the President has agreed about WASP, let me know the programme for feeding Malta with Spitfires, week by week, during the next eight weeks.' Portal told him that *Wasp* and *Eagle* would take sixty-two around 9 May, with a further sixteen from *Eagle* around 15 May. Further deliveries would depend on the availability of *Wasp*, about which Portal commented, 'I presume you will not wish to approach the President again until the second operation is completed.' To this Churchill replied, 'No, but then if all's well, certainly.' The departure of the *Wasp* for the Pacific on 15 May removed this possibility.

Churchill's attention now swung to the means of supplying Malta with AA ammunition for which the Governor had made an urgent plea in several signals. Although Pound, earlier in the month, had ruled out the possibility of using a fast warship for this purpose, concerned about the lack of fuel oil at Valletta, he had subsequently had second thoughts about this. Consequently, while Pound was visiting Admiral King in Washington, Vice-Admiral Moore told the COS that a fast minelayer, HMS *Welshman*, would be sent to Malta with the required ammunition. After his return to London, Pound sent the Prime Minister a note about this on 29 April. He explained first that this ship could carry ten times as much as a destroyer. She would be exposed to daylight attack south of Sardinia, but would make the final passage to Malta at night. It was intended, however, that she arrive after the delivery of the next batch of Spitfires so that air cover could be provided while her dangerous cargo was unloaded. His note concluded by warning: 'We are quite likely to lose this ship, but in view of the urgency of getting A.A. ammunition through to Malta there appears to be no alternative.'

We must now return to the meeting of the Defence Committee held on 22 April in order to consider the other disturbing matter that engaged the Committee's attention. On the morning of 21 April, Churchill and the COS received the following telegram from the Middle East Defence Committee:

Lord Privy Seal [Sir Stafford Cripps] is bringing home with him our recommendations:
(A) That General Dobbie should be relieved as soon as possible on grounds that he is a tired man, has lost grip of situation and is no longer capable of affording higher direction and control which is vital (R) vital to present situation.

(B) That a young and vigorous Civil Governor should be appointed in
    his place.

Information received since departure of Lord Privy Seal confirms the
urgency of these recommendations. Request most urgent consideration
of this question immediately Lord Privy Seal arrives and that General
Dobbie's relief should arrive (R) arrive in Malta by 1st May at latest.[13]

Lord Cranborne, who had been appointed as Colonial Secretary in February,
had also received a copy of this telegram, and he at once wrote to Churchill:

> This is a most distressing telegram. I cannot help feeling that the Middle
> East have treated us very badly. I know that Malta only came under the
> Middle East Command on the 11th March; but even so we have never
> heard one word about General Dobbie's unfitness for command since
> that date. On the contrary, I had every reason to suppose that he was
> doing admirably and was in fact the life and soul of the defence of Malta.
> We have indeed in recent weeks played him up as a great national hero.
> And the high level at which the spirit and morale of the people has been
> maintained during these last three months of intensive bombardment
> from the air is in itself a fine tribute to his leadership.
>
>   Now we suddenly hear that he must be replaced immediately. The
> effect both in this country and in Malta at this critical juncture is likely
> to be extremely bad.

Cranborne went on to write that he did not understand the suggestion
of a 'young and vigorous Civil Governor', adding that 'the latest review
of the general situation in Malta contained in the Governor's telegram
of 20/4/42 is a most sensible and balanced exposition, which shows no
trace of any loss of grip at the helm'. He asked the Prime Minister to keep
an open mind on the matter until they had heard what Cripps had to say
when he reached London.

General Sir William Shedden Dobbie was born on 12 July 1879 in India,
where several generations of Dobbies had served in the Indian Army and
Civil Administration. He was commissioned into the Royal Engineers in
1899, served as a 2nd Lieutenant in South Africa during the Boer War, and
from 1935 until July 1939 held the appointment of GOC Malaya. Then,
although due for retirement, he was unexpectedly sent to Malta in April
1940 as Acting Governor when the Governor, General Sir Charles Bonham-
Carter, returned to London for urgent medical treatment. The latter,
however, was not able to return to Malta and Dobbie was, in March 1941,
confirmed as Governor and awarded a KCB. Lady Dobbie accompanied
him to Malta, and their daughter, Sybil, joined them in October 1940.
From the following January she acted as her father's secretary.[14]

What distinguished General Dobbie, in every sense of the word, was that, while still a cadet at Woolwich, he had joined the Plymouth Brethren, a strict Evangelical religious sect whose first congregation was established at Plymouth in 1830. This gave him a deep religious belief coupled with a high and strict standard of personal morality and behaviour. These personal qualities and beliefs made him an excellent choice as Governor of an island whose people, then as now, shared his religious beliefs, albeit in the Catholic faith. General Dobbie, consequently, shared with the people of Malta from the very outset the hazards and sorrows of the war launched on the island in June 1940. A number of his communications with London have been quoted in earlier pages, but he was well known in Malta for his constant and inspiring presence throughout the island and for his many radio broadcasts.

Cranborne's memorandum to Churchill referred to the recent change in Dobbie's relationship with the Middle East C-in-Cs. The Governor of Malta had always been a senior military officer, and he carried dual responsibilities. As Governor of the colony, reporting to the Colonial Secretary, he was responsible for the administration of the island and the welfare of its people; as C-in-C of the garrison, under the direct control of the War Office, his duty was to defend the island. Nevertheless, although the GOC reported to the Governor, the AOC and the Vice-Admiral Malta reported to their respective C-in-Cs in Egypt. This arrangement meant that the Governor could not give direct orders to the air force and naval commanders, nor could the Middle East C-in-Cs give orders to the Governor. In February, General Brooke proposed that the GOC also report to Egypt, but after objections from the Colonial Office, supported by Churchill, it was agreed that the Governor should be placed under the direct control of the C-in-Cs.[15] However, when advising the Governor on 3 March of this decision, the COS went to some lengths to 'make it clear to you beyond all doubt that nothing could be further from our minds than lack of confidence in you. We are all deeply conscious of magnificent fight you have put up and of inspiration which your leadership has given to Malta garrison and colony.'[16]

It should be noted, however, that this change coincided with other changes in the Middle East command. At the end of March, Admiral Sir Henry Harwood had succeeded Admiral Sir Andrew Cunningham as C-in-C Mediterranean, while the Minister of State, Oliver Lyttleton, had returned to London in February, leaving Sir Walter Monckton as Acting Minister. General Auchinleck, under heavy pressure from London, but with considerable misgivings, was preparing for an offensive about mid-May. It fell, therefore, to Tedder to carry the main weight of concern for Malta as the air attacks intensified. In these circumstances it seems doubtful whether the March change in the Malta command structure had the benefits that were intended, especially because Churchill and the COS in London were bound to take a close interest in all that was happening on the island.

At their own meeting on 22 April before the Defence Committee met, the COS quickly registered their objection to the suggestion of a civilian Governor, and Brooke proposed that General Lord Gort, then Governor at Gibraltar, succeed Dobbie at Malta. In his diary, Brooke noted that Churchill was initially opposed to the relief of Dobbie. 'PM would not agree at first,' he wrote, 'but called me up after lunch to say that he had come round and agreed.'[17] The second session of the Defence Committee Meeting at 5.30 p.m. on 22 April was devoted to this matter. In addition to the papers already mentioned, Cripps, who arrived in London in time to attend the meeting, circulated an 'Aide Memoire: Higher Direction of the War, Malta'.[18] This explained in more detail the background to the recommendation in the MEDC telegram. This emphasised that the necessity for General Dobbie's relief had become apparent to Monckton and Tedder when they visited Malta on 12–13 April. This view was shared not only by the three military commanders at Malta, but also by the Lt-Governor, Sir Edward Jackson. Nevertheless, Cripps wrote, 'General Dobbie commands the affection and respect of the Malta population to a remarkable degree and it will inevitably be a shock to them when he is relieved.' Therefore, he continued, 'General Dobbie's relief must be presented to the population [in such a way] as will cause the minimum of disquiet. General Dobbie himself is well aware of the possibility that the solution may be for him to withdraw and is generously disposed to assist in every possible way.' Cripps's note concluded by writing that the MEDC also proposed the retention of the three Service Commanders in Malta, but added that 'as soon as the present phase of the battle for Malta has been completed, the AOC, RAF, Mediterranean, should be relieved'. This recommendation was made 'purely on the grounds that it would be militarily unsound to ask any Commander to continue to exercise his command for too long a period under the conditions now obtaining in Malta'. However, other possible reasons for this recommendation will shortly appear.

Churchill began the evening session of the Defence Committee meeting, according to the minutes, by meditating upon the matter:

> At first, he had been shocked at this proposal to pull down General Dobbie at a time when the gallant resistance of Malta and its Governor were exciting the admiration of the world. On further thought, however, he was inclined to agree with the view expressed to him by the CIGS that the reports from the Middle East seemed to show that General Dobbie's immediate subordinates and superiors had lost faith in his ability to continue to control and stimulate the resistance of the Fortress.

Lord Cranborne confessed that he was still 'bewildered by the reports that General Dobbie had lost his grip on the situation', but Cripps responded that the Acting Minister and the C-in-Cs 'were most definite that General Dobbie was tired out'. The Committee then agreed that General Gort should succeed Dobbie, and various telegrams were then drafted to this effect.

However, before these could be enciphered and dispatched there was a startling and unwelcome development. Lord Cranborne received a telegram from General Dobbie, dated 23 April. This began:

> The following telegram was sent on 21st from Mabel Strickland to Lord Louis Mountbatten. Begins. Reference our last conversation. That removal now vitally essential and urgent. Ends.
>
> I sent for her and invited her to explain. She said that she was urging a change of Governorship owing to alleged lack of co-ordination, which was responsible for disaster to the last convoy …
>
> Apart from the merits or demerits of her suggestion, I naturally take the strongest exception to this back-STAIRS [sic] intrigue. I can only assume that Mountbatten, a serving officer in no way connected with this matter, was an unwilling recipient of these advances. But I think it is necessary to invite an explanation from him.

Mabel Strickland was the daughter of Lord Strickland, a former Prime Minister of Malta, and she was then the influential and well-connected editor of the Strickland daily newspaper, the *Times of Malta*. This telegram from Dobbie was almost immediately followed by a second. This read: 'Following telegram has been received in Malta addressed to Mabel Strickland. Begins. Arrangements made as requested. Lord Louis Mountbatten. Ends. Presume this is the answer to her telegram quoted [earlier]. If so strongly resent latter's interference in matters which do not concern him.'

Copies of both telegrams were at once forwarded by Cranborne to Churchill. Although there is no account of his immediate reaction to these, it is not difficult to imagine that he was angered at what seemed to be foul play against a man for whom he had clearly formed a high opinion since Malta had been under attack. This regard is clear in the signal he immediately dictated and sent to Dobbie on 24 April:

> You may be quite sure that there shall be no intrigue where you are concerned. Nothing but the public interest must be considered. Mountbatten has not been consulted or had the slightest influence on War Cabinet discussions. His telegram quoted in your 159 [telegram] had no authority.

Naturally we are gravely anxious about Malta. I am therefore sending Lord Cranborne at once by air to talk everything over with you. He will be accompanied by a staff officer to go into your needs in stores in detail.

In all circumstances you may be confident of the gratitude of your countrymen.

To this Dobbie replied: 'Many thanks for your telegram of 24th. Entirely agree only public interest must be considered. You can rely on me doing all I can to further it with no thought of personal considerations.' Churchill placed the matter before a meeting of the War Cabinet later that day. Cripps observed that 'the vital question was the relation of the Governor to the three military commanders', and Brooke added, 'what was wanted was a Governor who was in command of the fortress rather than a *locum tenens*'. The Committee then agreed that it would be more appropriate that Mr Richard Casey, recently designated as the new Minister of State in the Middle East, rather than Lord Cranborne, should investigate General Dobbie's complaint. When advising Dobbie of this, Churchill concluded: 'All our hearts are with you in your hard battle.'

Unaware of these developments, but anxious about the delay, Monckton himself telegraphed on 24 April: 'Please expedite decision as to Governorship of Malta. Days even hours will count now in sphere of civilian control. If no decision in day or two I must go and try to co-ordinate as Acting Minister.' As soon as he saw his copy of this telegram, Churchill wrote out on the bottom of the telegram the following peremptory reply: 'Prime Minister for Monckton. Casey is starting for Malta to report to Cabinet. (Stop) Governor has complained of Strickland intrigue. (Stop) Matter is one of high importance. You should remain in Cairo.'

Such was the 'high importance' of this enquiry that several further cables were sent in which irritation and exasperation lay not far below the surface. These need only be summarised. First, Monckton responded on 25 April to the brusque Churchillian message quoted above. He admitted, rather surprisingly, that he had known something of the 'Strickland intrigue' before his mid-April visit to Malta, but had avoided meeting Mabel Strickland during his stay there. It was from his own observations that he had concluded that the 'Governor had lost grip of the situation and his colleagues'. He regretted the further delay that would arise before Casey's arrival, and concluded that this procedure implied 'a complete lack of confidence in me'. Churchill quickly replied on the following day. The delay that had arisen in resolving this matter was entirely Monckton's fault. Instead of telling London of his misgivings about the Governor while he was still in Malta, or upon his return to Cairo, it was not until 21 April that the War Cabinet and the COS were advised of the problem that had arisen.

Moreover, the initial information given to the War Cabinet led them to believe that the Governor 'was himself a consenting party to his dismissal', a view contradicted by the Governor's protests. In these circumstances, Churchill told Monckton, 'we felt bound to reassure ourselves by a personal visit of a Member of the War Cabinet'. A chastened Monckton replied to this rebuke on 27 April. While endeavouring to explain the reasons for his delay in bringing the issue to the War Cabinet's attention, he conceded that he should have telegraphed earlier, 'and I regret that I did not do so'.

While the Governor's relief was being discussed in these terms he telegraphed a two-page situation report, the last two paragraphs of which, with their tribute to the Maltese people, deserve quotation:

9. While it has been possible to make arrangements to meet any difficulties which have so far arisen, the outlook remains very difficult. Growing shortage of food is serious and the effect of the cut in the bread ration cannot yet be foreseen. Extreme shortage of fodder is also causing difficulties. I am confident, however, that we shall see our troubles through.

10. With all we have had to put up with both in bombing, in restriction and scarcity of food, bearing and morale of the public has remained admirable. I cannot too highly praise the fortitude and endurance which they have shown under the most severe test to which they have been subjected. Without that spirit we could not have carried on.[19]

Casey's departure for Malta was delayed for several days by bad weather, but before he left London on 29 April, Churchill gave him an aide-memoire summarising several key points, mostly related to the next Malta convoy and Auchinleck's plans for an offensive in Cyrenaica. However, since Casey would stop briefly at Gibraltar, Churchill instructed him to alert Gort to the possibility of a sudden transfer to Malta. He also gave Casey another memorandum to give to Gort, and this will be examined in the next chapter. But if, Churchill wrote, 'when you get to Malta you decide to recommend Dobbie staying on he must be given adequate powers over the Service Commanders, and you will no doubt recommend to us the form that it should take'. After his stop in Gibraltar, Casey arrived at Malta during the night of 1 May. He spent the next two days in detailed discussions with the Governor, the Lt-Governor, and the three Service Commanders, before telegraphing on 3 May his findings and recommendations to Churchill. The key paragraphs of this long signal were as follows:

3. I have no doubt that Dobbie should be replaced by Gort as soon as possible.

4. Dobbie is a man of courage and high character who has set example of steadiness and devotion to duty. He has gone out of his way to make my task easy for me by his generous attitude. I hope his services and high quality will be publicly recognised.

5. But the team here are not working together and the main reason is that Dobbie is no longer capable of vigorous leadership. He has little grasp of the situation or power of decision and lacks the knowledge and drive which would enable him to guide and where necessary impose his will on the forceful commanders under him. Although respected by the civil population he is not giving them adequate lead and has failed to get anything like the maximum out of them. For example with population of 300,000 it should have been possible to organise large body of adult male labourers to work under discipline in support of services. Accomplishment in this field has been totally inadequate. Situation today is regrettable. It would become menace if shortage of food or threat of invasion put population under further strain. Dobbie's departure will be regretted by people of Malta but his own view with which I agree is that it will not be more than 9 days wonder.

The rest of this telegram related to decisions that Gort would be faced with, and these will be related in the following chapter.

Churchill informed the War Cabinet on the evening of 4 May of Casey's telegram and its unambiguous recommendation. Ministers accepted this, and Churchill at once signalled to General Dobbie. This is a fine example of Churchill's distinctive and memorable writing on such occasions:

Pursuant on the report received from Minister of State we have decided that your long and gallantly borne vigil at Malta entitles you to relief and throws new honour on the Island's record (stop) Lord Gort has been ordered to take over from you at the earliest (stop) I take this occasion of expressing on behalf of His Majesty's Government the high regard in which your conduct of this historic defence stands at home (stop) I shall take the opportunity immediately upon your return of submitting your name to His Majesty for a signal mark of his favour (stop) Let me also thank you for the selfless and high-minded spirit in which you have viewed the situation including your own and for your devotion to the public interest.

To this Dobbie replied: 'Your telegram of 4th [May] received. Very grateful for your kind words which I deeply appreciate. Trust I may report to you personally on my return.' Churchill agreed that he should do so, adding, 'We shall arrange for you to keep in close touch with Malta affairs during the progress of the siege.'

General Gort flew in from Gibraltar on the evening of 7 May and was sworn in as Governor at Kalafrana in the middle of an air raid. After a private discussion with the new Governor, General Dobbie left with his family on the flying boat that had brought Gort. Such was the secrecy of the handover that General Dobbie was not able to broadcast a farewell message to the people of Malta but a message from him was read out later. He also broadcast to the island after his return to London. After a brief stop in Gibraltar, where his daughter Sybil was struck by the abundance of food, Dobbie arrived home on 10 May. To his surprise he was met at the airport by an official welcoming party led by Lord Cranborne, Admiral Sir Dudley Pound, and representatives of the War Office and the Air Council. In a World Broadcast later that day, Churchill paid Dobbie this warm tribute: 'Today we welcome back to our shores General Dobbie, for nearly two years the heroic defender of Malta. The burden he has borne so honourably and for so long entitles him to release and repose.'[20]

On the following day Dobbie called on the Prime Minister, as requested. Although the details of their conversation have not been recorded, it seems likely that Churchill questioned General Dobbie about the command structure in Malta, and, if so, this may have had some influence on the instructions later given to Lord Gort. General Dobbie then had an audience with the King who wrote in his diary:

> I knighted him and invested him with the K.C.B., and for his outstanding services in Malta during the last months I invested him with the G.C.M.G. … He is a God-fearing man, and lives with the bible in one hand and a sword in the other. He looks very old and tired after his ordeal.[21]

A few days later Dobbie collapsed from exhaustion and entered hospital for an operation from which he made only a slow recovery.

The warmth of the reception that General Dobbie received upon his return to England, where the press acclaimed him as 'Dobbie of Malta', his private meeting with the Prime Minister, and his audience with the King all ensured that his term as Governor of Malta during its darkest days ended with the tributes and the honours he richly deserved. It is, therefore, a matter of regret that his final weeks in office were clouded by a suspicion that he was forced out by an 'intrigue', and it is to Churchill's great credit that, as soon as he became aware of this, he ordered a full enquiry to be carried out by a War Cabinet Minister with no prior knowledge of the situation.

Casey, when he first met Dobbie on 3 May, must have been struck at once by the Governor's physical condition although, somewhat surprisingly, he did not specifically refer to this in his report. For the Governor, like all those in Malta at that time, was half-starved. A photograph of him standing

alongside Monckton and Tedder during their mid-April visit to Malta
clearly shows the effect on his 6-foot, 2-inch frame of the restricted Malta
diet. The War Cabinet in June were to be given a worrying report about
the effects of Malta's food shortage. This lack of adequate nourishment
undermined his mental as well as his physical capacity, inducing lassitude
and an inability to make decisions. This fully explains Casey's conclusion
that 'he was no longer capable of vigorous leadership'. When Churchill
met Dobbie upon his return to London he would have seen for himself
what Casey meant, and the King's comment has been quoted above.

But Casey also concluded that, quite apart from Dobbie's poor health, he
had also lost the confidence of the island's military commanders. It seems
probable that behind the alleged 'Strickland intrigue' lay, in particular,
a growing rift between the Governor and the AOC, AVM Lloyd. Tedder
has recalled that Dobbie wrote to him in early April requesting Lloyd's
relief, describing him as 'a difficult person to absorb into a team'.[22]
Tedder, however, refused to do so at the time, although he decided that
Lloyd should be relieved before too long, a decision recorded in Cripps's
previously quoted aide-memoire. Lloyd himself had also telegraphed
to Tedder complaining in strong terms about the failure to unload the
Pampas and *Talabot* before they were sunk in late March, although the
unloading of ships was primarily a naval responsibility. Mabel Strickland's
reference to this in her meeting with the Governor on 22 April appears to
reflect Lloyd's views. In passing, it should be mentioned that, many years
later, Mabel Strickland also made the allegation that General Dobbie had
been prepared to surrender the island. This can be set aside, for not only
would any attempt by Dobbie to do so have been immediately disowned,
but such action was wholly inconsistent with his character and record
as Governor. His many telegrams to London, while not disguising the
seriousness of Malta's condition, show that his courage and resolution
were undiminished, as Cranborne had remarked to the Prime Minister.

What had become clear was that too much had been asked of a man,
no longer young, in circumstances without parallel. He had steered the
island through the first Axis onslaught of 1940–1941, had presided over
the recovery in late 1941, before enduring the even fiercer attack in the
spring of 1942. An invasion of the island seemed then only too likely.
Although his sense of duty kept him to his task, his physical and mental
reserves were, by the end of April 1942, exhausted, and he was entitled,
as Churchill expressed it, to 'release and repose'. Nevertheless, General
Sir William Dobbie fully deserves his place of honour in the island's long
history.

We may appropriately conclude this account of a harrowing month by
quoting from a speech delivered by Churchill to the House of Commons.
Throughout the war the debates of the House continued to be published,

but on five occasions the House went into secret session to listen to a speech by the Prime Minister which gave Members more information than it seemed wise to publish. On these occasions no officials were present and no record of what the Prime Minister said was made. However, Churchill's extensive notes allowed these speeches to be reconstructed and published after the war as 'a complete and accurate record of what he almost certainly said'. One such speech – the longest he made – was delivered on 23 April 1942.[23]

The greater part of the speech described the fall of Singapore and subsequent developments in the Far East and the Indian Ocean. He then turned to the Middle East. After telling Members of the loss of Benghazi and the effect of this on the resupply of Malta, he continued:

> For now nearly two years Malta has stood against the enemy. What a thorn it has been in their side! What toll it has taken of their convoys! Can we wonder that a most strenuous effort had been made by Germany and Italy to rid themselves of this fierce, aggressive foe. For the last six weeks over 450 German first-line strength in aircraft, and perhaps 200 Italian, have been venting their fury on Malta. An unending intermittent bombardment has fallen on the harbour and city, and sometimes as many as 300 aircraft have attacked in a single day. The terrific ordeal has been borne with exemplary fortitude by the garrison and people.

He then went on to explain the consequences, for the *Luftwaffe* as well as for the RAF, of the fierce air battles over Malta, and he concluded:

> Therefore, every day that the air battle for Malta continues, grievous as it is to the island, its defenders and its gallant inhabitants, it plays its part in our general war effort and in helping our Russian allies. It may be that presently the German air force attacking Malta will have to move eastward to sustain the impending offensive against Southern Russia. If so we shall have topped the ridge. Meanwhile the struggle at Malta is very hard. It is still too early to say how it will end. But all the time we watch with admiration and gratitude this protracted, undaunted, heroic conflict.

Thus did Churchill deliver to the House of Commons in secret session his tribute to the courage and endurance of the garrison and people of Malta during a period of unprecedented hardship.

SPITFIRES AND THE GROWING FOOD CRISIS APRIL – JUNE 1942

We are determined that Malta shall not be allowed to fall without a battle being fought by your whole army for its retention.
                    Churchill to General Auchinleck, 10 May 1942

When Richard Casey, the new Minister of State in the Middle East, flew to Malta to see General Dobbie, he stopped briefly at Gibraltar. There he explained to Lord Gort the position that had arisen in Malta, and also handed him a personal letter and an aide-memoire from the Prime Minister. The letter read as follows:

                                                        25 April 1942
My dear Gort,
    I avail myself of the Minister of State's journey through Gibraltar and Malta to send you these few lines. It may be that – as he will explain to you – a change will be required at a most critical juncture in the Command of Malta. If this should be so, we all feel you are the man of all others to render this vitally important service. You may be sure that I shall do everything in my power to carry a heavy convoy of supplies into Malta in the latter part of June, and that meanwhile the supply of Spitfires from the West will be continued.
    I am delighted with all the reports we get of the splendid way in which you have organised Gibraltar and maintained the high morale of its garrison. Should you be required for this further service, you will be equipped with ample powers and will carry with you the full confidence of His Majesty's Government and of
                    Your sincere friend,
                    Winston S. Churchill.[1]

The three-page aide-memoire enclosed with the letter summarised for Gort all the essential information about the situation in Malta, and the decisions that had been taken to sustain the island. These decisions have all been examined in the previous chapter and need not be repeated here. The aide-memoire concluded by affirming that, if the War Cabinet decided to relieve General Dobbie, 'it would be their wish that General Lord Gort should proceed to Malta at the earliest possible moment to take full charge of the Island. The War Cabinet felt that this would give Malta, the Empire and the World the best assurance possible that Malta would be held.'[2] It should be noted that there are no documents to support the allegation that has sometimes been made that Gort had secret instructions to surrender Malta.

After the War Cabinet had received and accepted Casey's recommendation that General Dobbie be relieved, Churchill, after thanking Casey for 'giving such clear-cut advice', at once telegraphed Gort:

> You should proceed forthwith to Malta and assume command as Governor, Commander-in-Chief and Supreme Commander in the island (stop) Every effort must be made to prolong the resistance of the fortress to the utmost limit (stop) We recognise you are taking over a most anxious and dangerous situation at a late stage (stop) We are sure that you are the man to save the fortress and we shall strive hard to sustain you.

Gort flew to Malta on 7 May, as we have seen, and was sworn in as Governor that evening. Such was the urgency of Gort's transfer to Malta that he did not bring with him, as had been intended, the George Cross that the King had awarded to the island on 15 April; it was sent on later. Churchill announced Gort's appointment in his broadcast of 10 May after welcoming General Dobbie home. He told his listeners that, although 'for the moment the terrific air attack on Malta has slackened', other perils remained, 'and I know of no man in the British Empire to whom I would sooner entrust the combating and breaking-down of those perils than Lord Gort'.

Churchill, whose own bravery had been amply demonstrated in India, the Sudan, and in South Africa, always held in high esteem those who had acted with courage in the face of the enemy, and none more so than the holders of the Victoria Cross. Lord Gort had won the VC in the First World War, alongside three DSOs and the MC, and he had later risen to become the head of the army as CIGS, before being appointed in 1939 to command the British Expeditionary Force (BEF). Most historians now accept that it was only Gort's decision on 25 May 1940 to order the retreat to Dunkirk, in defiance of the War Cabinet's orders, that avoided the complete loss of the BEF. After a period of frustrating inactivity, Gort was appointed as Governor of Gibraltar in May 1941 and a year later, at the age of fifty-five, found himself amid the devastation of Malta.[3]

There was at the outset of his Governorship an important matter of command to be resolved. Although a Directive written by Churchill on 7 May made him Supreme Commander, it also stated that, except in the event of invasion, the Service Commanders in Malta would remain under the command of their respective C-in-Cs in Egypt. Gort, perhaps heeding advice given him by Dobbie in their private meeting on the evening of 7 May, objected strongly to this. On 9 May he telegraphed to Churchill:

Malta is in a serious plight calling for much organisation and closest co-operation. I cannot feel happy that local Commanders are empowered to communicate with and receive instructions except on purely administrative questions otherwise than through the Supreme Commander in Malta, who receives his guidance on policy from Middle East Defence Committee.

On his copy of this signal Churchill wrote: '<u>COS Cte.</u> I consider Lord Gort should have supreme powers in Malta. Pray consider recommendations.' Although the COS thought that the Directive gave him the necessary powers in an emergency, Churchill, who had by then also seen General Dobbie in London, amended the Directive to meet Gort's objection on 15 May. He thus signalled to Gort: 'With effect from receipt of this telegram you are appointed Supreme Commander of the Fighting Services and Civil Administration in Malta until further notice.' The responsibility in Malta of the Middle East C-in-Cs was confined to purely administrative matters.

Before we examine in detail how the new Governor of Malta tackled the task he had suddenly inherited, we must turn to consider another significant development, which seemed to reduce the prospect of the island's survival. We have seen in the previous chapter that a fierce disagreement had arisen in March between Churchill and General Auchinleck about the timing of a renewed offensive to recover Cyrenaica. It was only with the greatest reluctance, and with no little ill-temper, that the Prime Minister had eventually accepted a date of 'about 15 May' for this attack, although Auchinleck had tried to warn Churchill that he could not be irrevocably committed to this date. On 4 May, Auchinleck, concerned about the Japanese threat to India, telegraphed to suggest that he stand on the defensive in Cyrenaica in order to allow the transfer of some of his troops to India. Churchill, however, would have none of this, replying on 5 May that 'the greatest help you could give to the whole war at this juncture would be [to] engage and defeat the enemy on your western front'.[4] He and the COS were still expecting such an attack to be made about 15 May.

However, on the morning of 7 May, Churchill and the COS were handed copies of a further telegram sent on the previous evening by Auchinleck and the Middle East C-in-Cs.[5] This presented an Appreciation of the proposed offensive and the early paragraphs analysed in detail the comparative tank strengths of the opposing forces. Although Auchinleck now considered that a superiority of three-to-two, rather than his earlier demand of two-to-one, would be acceptable – due to the arrival of the new American Grant tanks and 6-pounder anti-tank guns – he did not expect to achieve this degree of advantage before the end of May. He therefore concluded:

> In view of the above, we do not repeat not consider an offensive would be justified before 15 June. To start earlier would incur risk of only partial success and tank losses and might in the worst case lead to a serious reverse the consequences of which in present circumstances are likely in our opinion to be extremely dangerous.

Auchinleck also voiced his concern about his air support position, particularly if some of Tedder's squadrons had to be diverted to his northern front. Brooke recorded in his diary that Churchill, when he read this alarming signal, had been 'very upset about the whole business, wishing to bring Alexander back to take over half of Middle East! Luckily, news from Madagascar was better again and this took the edge off the trouble!'[6] The COS met on the morning of 8 May to agree the advice they would give to the War Cabinet, and Brooke presented this when the War Cabinet convened at 3.00 p.m. The COS believed, Brooke told Ministers, that Auchinleck had not paid sufficient attention to the situation in Malta, but, nevertheless, as the minutes recorded, they 'thought it would be wrong to give General Auchinleck a direct order to attack on, say, 15th May. At the same time the COS thought it would be right to tell General Auchinleck that his attack should be carried out in such a way as to provide the maximum support for the convoy to Malta in the June dark period.' In the general discussion that followed there was a broad consensus that the advantages of postponing the attack were 'more than offset by the disadvantages of delay. In this connection, great importance was attached to the position at Malta.' Churchill then summed up. After remarking that 'battles are not won by arithmetical calculations of the strength of the opposing forces', he proposed to tell Auchinleck that the War Cabinet 'were of the opinion that an attack ought to take place in the latter half of May'. Auchinleck was then sent the following telegram on 8 May:

> The Chiefs of Staff, the Defence Committee, and the War Cabinet have all earnestly considered your telegram in relation to the whole war situation, having particular regard to Malta, the loss of which would be a disaster of first magnitude to the British Empire, and probably fatal in the long run to the defence of the Nile Valley.

We are agreed that in spite of the risks you mention you would be right to attack the enemy and fight a major battle, if possible during May, and the sooner the better. We are prepared to take full responsibility for these general directions, leaving you the necessary latitude for their execution. In this you will no doubt have regard to the fact that the enemy may himself be planning to attack you early in June.[7]

If Churchill thought this had settled the matter, he was mistaken. While he was spending the weekend at Chequers a further telegram arrived from Auchinleck. Churchill at once gave orders that a War Cabinet meeting be convened in London that evening to consider this latest telegram. The principal paragraphs of a long signal read as follows:

3. First in regard to Malta. We realise its importance, but do not repeat not, in the light of the most recent information in our possession, consider that its fall (much though this would be deplored) would necessarily be fatal to security of Egypt for a very long period if at all, provided our supply lines through the Indian Ocean remain uninterrupted. In its present almost completely neutralised state, Malta has very little influence on the enemy maintenance situation in North Africa though it is containing large enemy air forces. The regaining of Cyrenaica by us, though it would greatly assist the movement of our ships to and from Malta in the Eastern Mediterranean can not repeat not of itself guarantee the restoration to Malta of its offensive power in the event of the enemy continuing to devote large air forces to its neutralisation. This is merely an expression of opinion.

4. Secondly. It would be most dangerous to assume that, having launched an offensive in the latter half of May, we can count on being able to operate aircraft from landing grounds near Benghasi [sic] before the end of June or even later, depending on the degree of resistance offered by the enemy, and the tactical results obtained on the battlefield, neither of which can be foreseen.

5. Thirdly. We feel that to launch an offensive with inadequate armoured forces may very well result in the almost complete destruction of those troops, in view of our experience in the last Cyrenaican campaign ... We still feel that the risk to Egypt incurred by the piecemeal destruction of our armoured forces which may result from a premature offensive may be more serious and more immediate than that involved in the possible loss of Malta, serious though this would be.[8]

Brooke, summoned to London from a weekend at his Hampshire home, noted in his diary that Auchinleck 'has again stuck his toes in and was refusing to attack till a late date, and had sent in a very bad telegram in which he entirely failed to realize the importance of Malta and overestimated the danger to Egypt in the event of his being defeated'.[9] Major-General Kennedy, Brooke's Director of Military Operations (DMO), later wrote that Auchinleck's view about the importance of Malta was 'an incredible misconception', and had lost him the confidence of both the Cabinet and the Chiefs of Staff.[10]

Churchill opened the War Cabinet meeting that evening by observing that 'the telegram of 9th May gravely under-estimated the importance of Malta', before inviting Brooke to give the views of the COS.[11] Brooke then proceeded to rebut Auchinleck's signal paragraph by paragraph. With regard to Auchinleck's paragraph 3, he first declared that 'it would be a disaster to sacrifice the garrison in the fortress'. Moreover, it was only lately that the island had 'fallen into disrepair' and, with a change in the situation, Malta might soon regain its offensive power. Even in its current condition the island retained its value as an air staging route. Portal interjected to say that 300 aircraft had already passed through Malta in the first four months of 1942, 163 of them in the last month. Brooke accepted Auchinleck's argument in his paragraph 4 that it would take time to advance as far as Benghazi, but argued that the mere commencement of the attack would provide a diversion that would assist the June convoy to Malta. Finally, with regard to Auchinleck's paragraph 5, Brooke judged that the C-in-C had overestimated the danger to Egypt should the offensive fail. Summing up, the CIGS said that the advice of the COS was that Auchinleck's attack should be timed so as to provide an effective diversion for the June convoy to Malta.

Ministers had little to add to this expert military assessment, and a telegram in the following terms was quickly agreed and dispatched that evening:

Prime Minister to General Auchinleck   10 May 1942

The Chiefs of Staff, the Defence Committee, and the War Cabinet have again considered the whole position. We are determined that Malta shall not be allowed to fall without a battle being fought by your whole army for its retention. The starving out of this fortress would involve the surrender of over 30,000 men, Army and Air Force, together with several hundred guns. Its possession would give the enemy a clear and sure bridge to Africa, with all the consequences flowing from that. Its loss would sever the air route upon which both you and India must depend for a substantial part of your air reinforcements. Besides this, it would compromise any offensive against Italy, and future plans such as 'Acrobat' and 'Gymnast'. Compared with the certainty of these disasters, we consider the risks you have set out to the safety of Egypt are definitely less, and we accept them.

2. We therefore reiterate the views we have expressed, with this qualification – that the very latest date for engaging the enemy which we could approve is one which provides a distraction in time to help the passage of the June dark-period convoy.[12]

There followed an uneasy silence from Cairo. After a week Churchill cabled Auchinleck: 'It is necessary for me to have some account of your general intention in the light of our recent telegrams.' Auchinleck then confirmed his intention to carry out the instructions of 10 May, merely seeking confirmation that what the War Cabinet intended was not simply a diversion to assist the Malta convoy, but a full-scale offensive designed to destroy the Axis armies. To this the Prime Minister replied: 'Your interpretation of the instructions contained in mine of May 10 is absolutely correct. We feel that the time has come for a trial of strength in Cyrenaica, and that the survival of Malta is involved.' It is clear that Auchinleck still had serious doubts about what he had now been ordered to do, but it is also clear that the relevance of this argument had been overtaken by events. There was growing evidence that Rommel would launch his own offensive well before mid-June; he struck in fact on the night of 26/27 May.

The telegrams, minutes and papers quoted in these pages reveal the differences between London and Cairo, and between Churchill and Auchinleck, about the strategic value of Malta. By refusing, as requested, to return to London for discussions, Auchinleck denied himself the opportunity to judge at first hand the factors that made the survival of Malta so important in the eyes of the Prime Minister and his colleagues. Malta's military value, as seen from London, was clearly explained to him but it was also essential, in the aftermath of the ignominious surrender of Singapore, that Britain's willingness to fight to the last man, if necessary, be demonstrated to her allies. As Churchill had expressed it in his 8 May telegram, the loss of Malta 'would be a disaster of first magnitude to the British Empire'.

But there was another factor pulling in the same direction, and this was the unique place that Malta held in British history and sentiment, a feeling that was particularly strong in Churchill's case. His four pre-war visits to the island on official and private occasions gave him memories which enabled him to understand and sympathise with the dangers and hardships confronting the island's people and garrison as the bombs rained down during March and April of 1942.[13] Lord Moran, his doctor, later wrote that 'the plight of Malta had become an obsession with him', while the Conservative MP, Harold Nicolson, entered in his diary on 25 June, 'How the public would stand the loss of Malta I cannot conceive.'[14] It is difficult to understand why Auchinleck did not see, particularly after the King's

award of the George Cross on 15 April, that the abandonment of Malta
was unthinkable, and that nothing would be left undone that might sustain
the island's resistance. Perhaps General Ismay caught Churchill's mood
best. During the war no one stood closer to the Prime Minister, and it
was he who often sat up with Churchill in the small hours of the morning
while the Prime Minster talked out the difficulties of the unique burden he
carried. Ismay surely echoed Churchill's feelings when he later wrote:

> The loss of our great base at Singapore had been a bitter blow; but she
> was far away and historically speaking a comparative upstart. Malta
> was near at hand, and almost one of our kith and kin. To lose her would
> be almost as painful as to lose a part of England itself.[15]

Rommel's decision to attack on 26/27 May ensured that any help that
the 8th Army might be able to give to the June convoy to Malta would be
determined on the battlefield. The 'trial of strength' had come later than
Churchill had wished, but before Auchinleck felt fully prepared.

While these tense exchanges between London and Cairo were taking
place, all thoughts in Malta were concentrated on the absolute necessity
of receiving and safely unloading the substantial convoy promised in June.
While Casey was still in Malta considering whether to recommend General
Dobbie's relief, he held a meeting with the Governor, AVM Lloyd and
Vice-Admiral Leatham, and on 4 May he cabled Churchill his summary
of the situation and his recommendations. The paramount need to recover
air control over Malta had already been stressed by the Governor and
the AOC, but Casey made the point that that even the unloading of four
merchant ships – the most that Valletta's damaged dock facilities could
handle – would probably take fourteen days. 'During this period,' he
signalled, 'they would present targets which would inevitably be destroyed
under present circumstances.' He was aware of the impending arrival of
sixty more Spitfires, and stated that, thereafter, fifty more per month would
be required. He also urged that consideration be given to the bombing of
Sicilian airfields, a task that would need to be undertaken by bombers
from outside Malta since the island's three airfields would be required for
the Spitfires. If the June convoy failed, he concluded, reserves of food and
AA ammunition would be exhausted 'some time in July'. This cable had
the merit of making clear that any solution to Malta's plight must begin
with the recovery of air control and its continuance when the June convoy
arrived and was being unloaded. Much depended, therefore, on the next
batch of Spitfires.

The circumstances surrounding Churchill's second appeal to President
Roosevelt for the services of USS *Wasp* have been described in the previous
chapter. For this second voyage – Operation 'Bowery' – *Wasp* was

accompanied by HMS *Eagle*, the two ships carrying a total of sixty-four Spitfires. These flew off for Malta at dawn on 9 May, and sixty reached the island during the morning. Elaborate arrangements had been made to receive them.[16] As each of the new aircraft landed it was directed to a designated pen where a ground crew refuelled and serviced the aircraft, and a Malta-experienced pilot was strapped into the cockpit. AVM Lloyd's aim was that each aircraft should be ready for action within ten minutes of its initial landing. On this occasion there were fewer complaints about the condition of the aircraft, although the lack of operational experience of some of the new pilots led to the return of several of them to England for their own safety. Churchill followed this second passage of USS *Wasp* closely, and after she had flown off her Spitfires, he cabled: 'Following from Prime Minister to Captain and Ship's Company of USS WASP. Many thanks for all your timely help. Who said a wasp couldn't sting twice?' The reply he received read: 'Captain, Officers and Ship's Company of USS WASP thank the Prime Minister for his gracious message which they much appreciate.'

In the week after Operation 'Bowery', there were daily air battles over Malta in which Lloyd and his Senior Fighter Controller, Group Captain Woodhall, held back the enlarged Spitfire force in order to engage the bombers. It was mentioned in the last chapter that Churchill had called for daily reports about air activity over Malta and these reveal the rising enemy losses after 10 May. His Malta files also contain a note from ACM Portal, dated 20 May, describing the operations since 9 May, and the arrival of a further 16 Spitfires on the 18th. In this note Portal reported and endorsed an assessment made by Gort on 19 May that the RAF had recovered air superiority. He cited enemy losses of 64 aircraft, with 45 more 'probables', and 74 'damaged'. The RAF had lost 14 aircraft and had a further 16 damaged. He concluded by telling the Prime Minister that 'the Germans appear to have given up for the time being serious bombing raids and now resort to strong fighter sweeps with very few bombers'. An immediate consequence of the RAF's recovery of air control was the sharp reduction in the level of enemy bombing. As compared with the 6,700 tons dropped on Malta in April, it was estimated that only 520 tons fell in May.

An obvious target for the German bombers on the morning of 10 May was the warship that had slipped into the Grand Harbour at dawn and was busily unloading her cargo. This was the fast minelayer HMS *Welshman*, under the command of Captain Dennis Friedburger. Admiral Pound had agreed in April that a solo passage by this ship should be attempted, although he warned Churchill that the ship might be lost. However, all went well. Disguised as a French destroyer, *Welshman*, although spotted by German and French reconnaissance aircraft off the Tunisian coast, reached Malta without being attacked. Most of the cargo was AA ammunition, but there were also replacement aero-engines, a variety of essential foodstuffs, and 100 RAF maintenance personnel for the Spitfire force. She also carried smoke generators to obscure the ship while unloading. Despite heavy and persistent air attack during the day, *Welshman* escaped serious damage and, her cargo having been all unloaded by mid-afternoon, she sailed for Gibraltar at 8.00 p.m.

Lloyd's task was eased to a degree by a reduction in the *Luftwaffe* force in Sicily. Churchill and the COS had anticipated that this might happen as the 1942 German spring offensive in Russia got under way. Rommel, too, would demand increased air support for his forthcoming offensive in Cyrenaica. However, the first hard evidence Churchill received of the German moves came in a decrypted German Air Force Enigma signal on 26 April, confirmed by others in the following days, which indicated which units were being withdrawn.[17] What Churchill did not know was that Field Marshal Kesselring had on 10 May advised the German High Command that Malta had been effectively neutralised as an offensive base against the Axis supply line to North Africa, thus allowing the reduction in the strength of *Fliegerkorps II* in Sicily. Nor could Churchill know that Hitler and Mussolini, at a conference at the end of April, had agreed that an invasion of Malta – planning for which, under the German code name of Operation 'Herkules', had proceeded in a half-hearted way for some months – should be postponed until Rommel had captured Tobruk.[18]

Nevertheless, these German transfers did no more than reduce the earlier *Luftwaffe* preponderance, and the air fighting continued to be hard on men and machines. Many young men from Britain, the Commonwealth, and the USA lost their lives in this struggle and their names are among the 2,300 inscribed on the Commonwealth Air Forces Memorial outside the walls of Valletta. On 14 May, Portal told Lloyd that he would receive 48 more Spitfires in May, and possibly a further 48 in June. In his reply of 16 May, Lloyd pointed out that the continuous fighting of the previous week had reduced his serviceable Spitfires to 25, and he insisted that he must have a minimum operational force of 60. He concluded: 'If convoy is to arrive June we must repeat must receive more Spitfires than your signal indicates.' On his copy of this signal Churchill wrote: 'CAS/1SL. What can be done?' Portal replied on the next day. He first told the Prime Minister that he and Admiral Pound had arranged to increase the supply of Spitfires. Sixteen aircraft would arrive on 18 May, 32 more on 30 May, and a further 32 on 6 June. This total of 80 aircraft, he pointed out, was 32 more than had been promised earlier. Portal also described plans to deliver more aero-engines and the sending of 18 additional RAF technicians, and he finally listed proposed reinforcements of Beaufighters, Beauforts, Wellingtons, and Hudson reconnaissance aircraft. This was all approved by the COS and signalled to Malta and Cairo on 21 May.

The provision of stronger air defences at Malta was essential, as Casey had earlier emphasised, if any merchant ships that arrived in June were to be unloaded safely, but the larger problem was to escort these ships to Malta from either Alexandria or Gibraltar, or possibly from both ports. The examination of this task proceeded alongside that of the air defence of the island, so that nearly all of the meetings of the COS in May had on their agenda 'Supplies for Malta' as well as 'Spitfires for Malta'. The root of the problem was that the approaches to Malta from either east or west were dominated by German and Italian air force squadrons widely dispersed on airfields to the north and south of the sea passage. Not for nothing was this passage referred to as 'Bomb Alley'. The threat from the air was reinforced by the Italian fleet, which, after recovering from the damage inflicted at Taranto in November 1940, had available at least two modern battleships supported by a powerful force of cruisers and destroyers. Finally, numerous German and Italian submarines were operating in both basins of the Mediterranean. How then were the merchant ships to be protected against this triple threat, given that the Mediterranean Fleet no longer had any battleships or aircraft carriers?

In the previous chapter we examined in some detail a Note presented to the War Cabinet by Churchill on 22 April. In this he raised the possibility that Admiral Somerville, after the completion of the Madagascar landings, might bring his flagship, HMS *Warspite*, and his three aircraft carriers into the Mediterranean to escort a westbound Malta convoy. However, Admiral Pound had been in Washington when this proposal was aired, and, upon his return, he at once expressed his opinion that such a move by Admiral Somerville would be 'strategically and tactically unsound'.[19] Brooke then proposed that the JPC consider the problem in detail, and their Appreciation was presented to the COS on 9 May.[20] This assumed, first, that the Cyrenaican airfields would not have been recovered by mid-June, but noted a JIC estimate that the scale of attack on Malta would be 'substantially less'. The JPC, however, judged that the risks to Somerville's capital ships in the eastern Mediterranean would be 'very great', and they, therefore, advised against this possibility. Instead, they recommended an escort force of 6 cruisers, over 30 destroyers and a screen of 7–10 submarines. In the absence of a battleship the best that was available was HMS *Centurion*, an old, disarmed battleship that had been used as a radio-controlled target ship. This would be disguised to masquerade as a fully-armed battleship. Nevertheless, despite the size of the proposed naval escort, it was not strong enough to face an Italian battleship force, and much, therefore, hung on the ability of the RAF not merely to defend the convoy against air attacks, but also to hold off any approaching Italian warships.

Pound discussed this Appreciation with the Prime Minister who, on 9 May, sent the COS a Minute in which he outlined two possible plans.[21]

Plan 1 would require the transfer to the Mediterranean of Somerville's capital ships. Under Plan 2 the escort would be limited to *Centurion* and the force of cruisers and destroyers. After the COS had considered this, they confirmed their preference for Plan 2. Meanwhile, the C-in-C Mediterranean, Admiral Harwood, had on 15 May cabled his own analysis of the problem from the naval perspective. He noted the plans for additional Beaufighters to provide long-range fighter cover, and for Beaufort and Wellington torpedo-bombers to strike at the Italian fleet, but regretted the Air Ministry's decision not to provide any long-range heavy bombers for ship attack. He concluded by cabling:

> I must emphasise that the scale of air attack that the German Air Force can bring against a convoy, combined with the number of aerodromes from which they can operate, makes the scale of defence which we can bring against this, even with the proposed reinforcements, inadequate. All we can hope for is that the above minimum proposals may form a deterrent, but they will in no way ensure against heavy losses.

On this Churchill wrote 'CAS please report to me on this', and Portal's response was given in his Note of 18 May, which has been mentioned earlier.

Despite all these air force reinforcements, both at Malta and in Egypt, the Middle East C-in-Cs remained apprehensive, and several further telegrams warned of the high risks to an eastern convoy. Casey supported this in his own personal telegram to the Prime Minister on 20 May, in which he argued the case for a western convoy as a safer option. The situation was made worse by Rommel's offensive on 26 May, after which the resulting heavy fighting in the desert naturally commanded the attention of the RAF in Egypt. During the first week of this battle, Auchinleck and Ritchie managed to hold up Rommel's first attack, and the latter then withdrew to what became known as the 'cauldron' to regroup and rearm. During this pause in the desert, Churchill, on 2 June, reminded Auchinleck and Tedder:

> There is no need for me to stress the vital importance of the safe arrival of our convoys at Malta, and I am sure you will both take all steps to enable the air escorts, and particularly the Beaufighters, to be operated from landing grounds as far west as possible.[22]

Despite the reservations expressed in Cairo, the COS ordered that preparations for the eastern convoy be continued, and on 7 June they cabled to the Middle East C-in-Cs:

Malta cannot be allowed to surrender owing to a lack of supplies without an effort being made to run in the Eastern Convoy.

2. An attempt therefore must be made to run the Eastern Convoy.

3. It is accepted that heavy losses may be incurred. The day on which the convoy sails must be left to the discretion of the C-in-C Mediterranean as he will have better information regarding the military and air situation, the movements of enemy surface forces and the weather prospects than we have.

However, they sought to mitigate these risks in two ways. First, a smaller convoy, Operation 'Harpoon', consisting of six merchant ships, would be run from Gibraltar in an attempt to divide the Axis air and naval threat. Secondly, an appeal was made to General Marshall, through Field Marshal Dill in Washington, for the temporary use of a force of USAAF Liberators, which had been sent to Egypt to make an attack on the Ploesti oil fields in Romania. After an initial refusal, General Marshall then agreed that this force, after the completion of the Ploesti raid, could be retained in Egypt to strike against the Italian fleet should it threaten the eastern convoy. Churchill had been ready to approach the President directly on this matter, and had drafted a telegram, which read in part: 'If we cannot get this convoy through to Malta the doom of the fortress cannot long be deferred.' However, Marshall's acquiescence made this gloomy signal unnecessary.

Full accounts of the two June Malta convoys are given in the official histories and need not be repeated here in detail. The western convoy, Operation 'Harpoon', comprising five merchant ships and a tanker, the American-built *Kentucky*, passed Gibraltar on the night of 11/12 June. It then came under heavy and persistent air attack as it approached Sardinia, before being threatened south of Pantelleria by a force of two Italian cruisers and five destroyers. Two of the freighters were sunk by air attack, while a third and the *Kentucky* were disabled and later sunk by the escorting destroyers. AVM Lloyd later wrote that 'our own forces should not have sunk the tanker'[23] and when, during the next convoy, the tanker *Ohio* was similarly disabled, bolder action was taken, as we shall see. Only *Troilus* and *Orari*, with a total of 15,000 tons of supplies, reached Valletta safely on the evening of 15 June, although HMS *Welshman*, which had raced ahead of these ships, also reached Malta with a further cargo of AA ammunition. As was noted earlier, Casey had warned that it might take as long as fourteen days to unload four ships, but the two June arrivals were unloaded within 48 hours by a large force of seamen and soldiers working around the clock. Although the decision to sail this western convoy was designed to split the Axis air and naval threat, it also inevitably divided the defensive forces as well. Moreover, AVM Lloyd and Admiral Leatham in Malta agreed that the eastern convoy should be given priority if both convoys came under attack at the same time. In these circumstances, since the decisive action took place at the very limit of the Spitfire's operational range, it was a considerable achievement to escort two of the six merchant ships to Malta. This was to have its effect on the planning of the next convoy. It is also worth observing that a subsequent convoy report in June from RAF Malta judged that 'with a good dive bomber capable of carrying 1000 lb. bombs there is not the slightest doubt that enemy cruisers would not have molested 'Harpoon' and would have made off at the first attack'.[24] The RAF had no such aircraft.

The eastern convoy, 'Vigorous', comprised of eleven merchant ships, left Alexandria on 11 June, but this, too, was soon subjected to heavy air attack from Crete and Cyrenaica. Two ships were sunk and two others forced to turn back before, at dawn on 15 June, reconnaissance aircraft reported the approach of an Italian battleship force. Wellingtons and Beauforts were scrambled from Malta to strike at this force, but, although the heavy cruiser *Trento* was torpedoed by a Malta Beaufort, and later sunk by the submarine *P.35*, and the battleship *Littorio* was hit by a bomb from a USAAF Liberator, the Italian force held on towards the convoy. Admiral Vian was

19. A Bofors anti-aircraft gun position looking from Valletta towards Senglea in June 1942. By this time, enemy aircraft faced a fearsome AA barrage around the Grand Harbour.

quite unable to protect the convoy from an imminent attack by such a superior force, and he gave orders for the convoy to reverse course. Late in the afternoon, as the Italian force itself turned north, Admiral Harwood questioned whether the convoy might still seize a 'golden opportunity' to make for Malta, but Vian replied that the escorts were by then too low on fuel and ammunition to face further air attack. The remaining seven ships of the convoy returned to Alexandria on 16 June.

In these early June weeks, Churchill's principal concern was for the course of Auchinleck's desert battle with Rommel, and he reprints in his post-war memoirs some of the signals that passed between him and Auchinleck during this period. But he also followed closely the passage of the two Malta convoys, and it so happened that the crisis in the attacks on these convoys fell shortly after Rommel, on 12/13 June, had inflicted a defeat on the 8th Army, compelling Auchinleck to order a general withdrawal of his remaining forces. Churchill's Malta files contain the principal signals relating to the 'Vigorous' convoy, upon which the main hope for the relief of the island rested. When he received news of Vian's decision to turn the convoy back to Alexandria he asked about the reasons for this. The Admiralty then sent over a copy of Admiral Harwood's signal of 16 June. This explained that the convoy had been subjected to almost continuous air attack, and that the air strikes against the approaching Italian battleships 'had no decisive results'. His signal concluded:

> I will venture to do all I can to remount VIGOROUS as soon as ships are re-fuelled and re-ammunitioned but facts are clear. We are outnumbered both in surface and Air Force and very gallant endeavour of all concerned cannot make up for the unfortunate deficiency.

On his copy of this signal Churchill drew a circle around this last sentence, and when his Private Secretary asked whether he wished any further enquiries to be made, he wrote, 'No'.

On 15 June, the Prime Minister presided at a meeting of the COS, and told the Chiefs: 'The surrender of Malta, which would have a most heartening effect on the Italian people and might well bring them back effectively into the war, could not be contemplated before every effort to relieve the fortress had failed.' Both Pound and Portal made clear that plans for the next convoy were already under study.[25] On the following morning, Churchill dictated an ACTION THIS DAY minute to the COS, which read as follows:

> 1. It will be necessary to make another attempt to run a convoy into Malta. This can only be from Gibraltar, though a feint from Alexandria will be useful. The fate of the island is at stake, and if the effort to relieve it is worth making, it is worth making on a great

Action. this day.

PRIME MINISTER'S 302
PERSONAL MINUTE

SERIAL No. __M 26/2__   Indexed

FIRST LORD,
FIRST SEA LORD,
GENERAL ISMAY FOR C.O.S. COMMITTEE.

1.   It will be necessary to make another
attempt to run a convoy into Malta.   This can
only be from Gibraltar, though a feint from
Alexandria will be useful.   The fate of the
island is at stake, and if the effort to relieve
it is worth making, it is worth making on a great
scale.   Strong battleship escort capable of
fighting the Italian battle squadron and strong
Aircraft Carrier support would seem to be required.
Also at least a dozen fast supply ships, for which
super-priority over all civil requirements must
be given.

2.   The improved situation in the Indian Ocean
enables a delay to be accepted in the movement of
RODNEY.   In any case ANAKIM does not happen till
later on in the year.

3.   I shall be glad to know in the course of
the day what proposals can be made, as it will be
right to telegraph to Lord Gort, thus preventing
despair in the population.   He must be able to
tell them: "The Navy will never abandon Malta."

W.S.C.

16.6.42.

20. Churchill's minute of 16 June 1942 ordering the planning of the 'Pedestal' relief convoy of August 1942.

scale. Strong battleship escort, capable of fighting the Italian battle squadron and strong Aircraft Carrier support would seem to be required. Also at least a dozen fast supply ships, for which super-priority over all civil requirements must be given.

2. The improved situation in the Indian Ocean enables a delay to be accepted in the movement of [HMS] RODNEY. In any case ANAKIM [i.e. Burma] does not happen till later on in the year.

3. I shall be glad to know in the course of the day what proposals can be made, as it will be right to telegraph Lord Gort, thus preventing despair in the population. He must be able to tell them: 'The Navy will never abandon Malta.'

On the evening of 17 June, Churchill flew to Washington for a further conference with President Roosevelt.

We may conclude this chapter by noting, as Churchill knew only too well, that during these critical months of March–June 1942 Malta's ability to interfere with the flow of enemy supplies to North Africa had been sharply diminished. The offensive aircraft that had not been lost were flown away to make room for Spitfires. In addition, the dangers to the submarines of the 10th Flotilla, particularly from mines laid around the Grand Harbour, had become so great that, on 26 April, the remaining boats were ordered to Alexandria. In this difficult period, three British submarines were lost, including HMS *Upholder*, commanded by Lt-Com. Wanklyn, VC, on what was to be the last of her twenty-five patrols. Post-war statistics reveal that Rommel, as he prepared for his offensive, received 150,000 tons of supplies in April, and a further 86,000 tons in May, compared with an average monthly total of only 60,000 tons in the first three months of the year. In March, Malta's forces sank six ships, with an aggregate tonnage of 25,110 tons, but only two ships of 9,700 tons in April, and none in May.

Nevertheless, despite Kesselring's undoubted success in protecting Rommel's supply line, Malta's continuing strategic value was demonstrated in two ways. First, as Portal had told the War Cabinet on 10 May, the bomber aircraft urgently needed in the Middle East and in India had continued to fly through Malta at night with very little interruption. Secondly, the growing force of Spitfires had forced Kesselring to retain in Sicily aircraft that might otherwise have reinforced Rommel in the desert, or the German armies in Russia. Moreover, he had lost many of these aircraft. Post-war records again show that during May the number of serviceable German fighters in Sicily fell from 88 to 36, and the bomber force from 52 to 42. Consequently, despite Malta's parlous internal situation at the end of June 1942, and the elimination of her offensive threat, Churchill and the COS were in no doubt that Malta's continuing strategic value was such that a supreme effort must now be made to resupply the island.

THE 'PEDESTAL' CONVOY
AUGUST 1942

We are absolutely bound to save Malta in one way or the other.
Churchill to Attlee and Eden, 17 June 1942

Despite Auchinleck's defeat in Cyrenaica and the safe arrival in June of only two of the seventeen ships that had sailed to the relief of Malta, Churchill felt it was essential to visit President Roosevelt again to discuss and agree Allied strategy for the year ahead. Accordingly, on the night of 17 June 1942 the Prime Minister, accompanied, among others, by Generals Brooke and Ismay, boarded a Boeing Clipper flying boat at Stranraer in western Scotland. Twenty-six hours later they alighted on the Potomac river below Washington, and on the following morning Churchill flew to Roosevelt's home at Hyde Park for private discussions. It was upon his return to Washington on 21 June that Churchill received what he later described as 'one of the heaviest blows I can recall during the war'.[1] For as he was talking to the President a messenger brought in a pink telegram, which the President, after a brief glance, passed to the Prime Minister. It read: 'Tobruk has surrendered, with twenty-five thousand men taken prisoners.' This was for Churchill a profound and, indeed, a humiliating shock: 'It was a bitter moment. Defeat is one thing; disgrace is another.' General Ismay, who was present, later recalled that this 'was the first time in my life I saw the Prime Minister wince'.[2] 'What can we do to help?' was the President's immediate and generous response. This disaster, coming on top of other defeats in the Far East and Burma, prompted a number of Members of Parliament to table a motion of 'No Confidence'. However, after his return to London on 27 June, Churchill vigorously defended himself and the record of his administration, and the motion was defeated by 475 votes to 25.

Even before Churchill had left Washington, the news from the Middle East continued to be bleak. Although he welcomed Auchinleck's assumption of direct command of the 8th Army on 25 June, he was dismayed by the general's decision not to attempt to hold Rommel either on the Egyptian border or, 100 miles further east, at Mersa Matruh. General Brooke recorded in his diary that it was only with considerable difficulty that he was able to deter the Prime Minister from going out to Egypt at once to establish what had gone wrong.[3] The 8th Army, consequently, withdrew to a more defensible position at El Alamein, a mere sixty miles from Alexandria. This retreat, and the danger of German air attack, forced Admiral Harwood to move the Mediterranean Fleet and his HQ further east. These major setbacks appeared to worsen Malta's chances of survival. The RAF's loss of airfields west of Alamein ruled out any possibility of an eastern relief convoy, leaving only the western route through the dangerous waters of the Sicilian Narrows. But there was also a positive consequence of the 8th Army's retreat, for the completeness of Rommel's victory spared Malta an imminent invasion. Although, as noted in the previous chapter, Hitler and Mussolini had agreed on 1 May that Operation 'Herkules', the assault on Malta, should be carried out after the capture of Tobruk and before the advance into Egypt, Rommel, flushed with success, persuaded them to change their minds. He had captured enormous amounts of supplies at Tobruk and in surrounding dumps, including many thousands of vehicles, and he was convinced that the remnants of the 8th Army would not be able to prevent an early advance to Cairo. Hitler, who, after the experience of Crete, had always been doubtful about 'Herkules', persuaded Mussolini to accept Rommel's request to continue his advance, writing: 'The goddess of Battles visits warriors only once. He who does not grasp her at such a moment never reaches her again.'[4] Mussolini accepted Hitler's proposal and, beguiled by the prospect of a triumphal entry into Cairo, left for North Africa on 29 June.

It is against this sombre background of defeat and disarray that we must resume our account of Churchill's continuing anxiety for the relief of Malta. The ACTION THIS DAY minute that he sent to the COS on 15 June has been quoted at the end of the preceding chapter, but as he travelled north to Stranraer on 17 June he dictated a more detailed minute for Attlee and Eden on Malta's plight. A note at the top of this minute states that it was telephoned to Downing Street at 11.00 p.m. just before Churchill boarded the Boeing Clipper for his flight to Washington. This minute, dictated in the relative quiet of his northbound train, deserves to be quoted in full:

DEPUTY PRIME MINISTER   PRIME MINISTER'S
FOREIGN SECRETARY   PERSONAL MINUTE
                D.123/2

1. The First Sea Lord has given me four alternative schemes for a further attempt to victual Malta from the West. You should obtain this paper from him. Of these schemes the first is the most satisfactory, but it depends on American help for which I will ask the President.

Meanwhile I have told the First Sea Lord to begin loading the ten supply ships.

2. Will you please sit with the First Lord and the First Sea Lord and press this matter forward to the utmost. Apparently Admiral Harwood has a plan for a further attempt from the East during the next ten days provided the American Liberators can be made available. Let me have details of this and what is thought of it, so that I can put the point to the President if there is value in it. At first sight it seems rather a forlorn hope with the forces available after what happened last time.

3. We are absolutely bound to save Malta in one way or the other. I should not myself exclude sending two or three of the Carriers and WARSPITE and VALIANT through from the Indian Ocean in the middle of July, if there is no other way. This was the original plan which we reluctantly abandoned owing to the objections of the First Sea Lord. Owing to the Japanese losses in the Pacific, the situation in the Indian Ocean has become less urgent, and a further delay could be accepted in forming the Eastern Fleet. Admiral Cunningham has written, at the request of the First Sea Lord, a paper on this scheme, for which you should also ask. You should if necessary see him. Now that the Italians have shown a readiness to bring their battle-fleet down to arrest a convoy reaching Malta from the East, an opportunity of bringing them to battle might be found, which would have far-reaching effects.

4. I am relying upon you to treat the whole question of the relief of Malta as vitally urgent, and to keep at it with the Admiralty till a solution is reached. Keep me advised so that I can do my best with the President.[5]

There then followed a series of detailed discussions in London with Attlee, as Deputy Prime Minister, presiding at a number of lengthy COS meetings. The results of these were all telegraphed to Churchill in Washington. On 18 June, Attlee reported that the COS, having received a pessimistic signal from Admiral Harwood in Alexandria, were opposed to any attempt to re-launch the eastern convoy in June. They felt that two convoys in July would allow time to provide stronger air defences. The COS also asked the Prime Minister to put to the President a request for the loan of the aircraft carrier USS *Ranger* and of the tanker SS *Ohio*, which was due to arrive on the Clyde on 20 June. She could carry 12,000 tons of fuel, compared with the 4,000 tons that could be loaded on HMS *Glengyle*, the only other ship available. Admiral Sir Charles Little, the head of the British Naval Delegation in Washington, discussed the availability of USS *Ranger* with Admiral King, the US Navy C-in-C. However, King, although willing to send this ship to join the Home Fleet at Scapa Flow to release HMS

Victorious, was not prepared to send her into the dangerous waters of the Mediterranean. When reporting this to the COS on 20 June, Pound told his colleagues that there would be no aircraft carriers available to support a July convoy, but, he added, the latest news from General Gort in Malta indicated that, with some additional restrictions, food supplies should last until September. He was, therefore, turning his mind to an August convoy.

The whole matter was discussed at two COS meetings on 23 June.[6] General Nye, the VCIGS, warned that 'the food situation was so critical and such drastic rationing would be necessary that the fighting efficiency of the garrison would suffer and civilian morale might deteriorate. Everything pointed to the urgency of running in a convoy as soon as possible.' Admiral Pound, nevertheless, saw no possibility of getting a July convoy through. Lord Cranborne, the Colonial Secretary, reluctantly accepted this but he, too, was anxious that 'disturbances would break out as a result of a prolonged period of severe rationing and of the disappointment that there would be no July convoy, and that the resistance of the community to air attack would diminish.' Accordingly, a telegram was sent to the Prime Minister on the evening of 23 June recommending a large relief convoy in mid-August. In the absence of an American carrier, HMS *Indomitable* would be brought back from the Indian Ocean, and the Royal Navy's two 16-inch battleships, HMS *Nelson* and *Rodney*, both due to go east, would be retained to provide a powerful escort capable of dealing with the Italian battle fleet. All that could be done in July was to send some vital food and medical supplies by submarine, and to attempt a further solo passage by HMS *Welshman*. Thus by the time Churchill returned to London on 27 June the basic decision for the 'Pedestal' convoy had been hammered out. It should, perhaps, be added that in none of the many documents relating to this matter is there any suggestion that this relief convoy not be attempted and that Malta should be surrendered. For his part, Churchill, grieved by the humiliating surrender of Tobruk, was adamant that the Royal Navy and the Royal Air Force would fight it out. His military advisers agreed.

On 26 June, the COS were given a first-hand account of the food situation in Malta.[7] Two officials of the Ministry of Food, Dr Drummond and Mr Wall, had recently returned from a visit to Malta, and Sir George Gater of the Colonial Office introduced them to the Chiefs. They observed that the effects of the reduced diet were clearly evident in the military garrison: 'The men were looking fit and hard but were in lean condition.' Their general health, they added, would not be at risk, but they would experience greater fatigue as they worked, and would steadily lose weight. They continued: 'The effect of rationing was not so apparent on the Maltese who were believed to be eking out supplies from their hidden stocks of food. They had been encouraged to lay in stocks during the earlier days of the siege, but these stocks were probably close to exhaustion.' The experts commended the Governor's policy of slaughtering more of the island's livestock since this would provide an extra meat ration to offset the severe cut in the bread ration. Overall, they advised, 'the recent cuts in edible oil, kerosene, sugar and coffee would, it was feared, now begin to have a psychological effect'. They anticipated that there might be a serious decline in morale by mid-August. No mention was made at this meeting of the communal feeding arrangements, the 'Victory Kitchens', but this was raised at a later meeting, as we shall see.

Maltese endurance was put to a further test when, in the first two weeks of July, the enemy air attack on the island was resumed. Mussolini had made the continued suppression of Malta a condition of his consent to defer the planned invasion and both the Italian and German squadrons in Sicily were strengthened at the end of June. RAF losses rose steadily but were offset by the delivery from HMS *Eagle* of 59 more Spitfires in two operations on 15 July (Operation 'Pinpoint') and on 21 July (Operation 'Insect'). It was later established that the RAF lost 36 Spitfires during July, but, with the help of the AA guns, destroyed 65 enemy aircraft. 700 tons of bombs fell in the month, mainly on the three airfields. The easing of this renewed onslaught coincided with AVM Lloyd's departure on 15 July to join Tedder's staff in Cairo, and his replacement by AVM Park, the former Commander of 11 Group of Fighter Command during the Battle of Britain.

None had followed more closely than Churchill the struggle to regain air control over Malta in the early months of 1942. He had read many of Lloyd's signals urging the delivery of more Spitfires, and his response to these has already been described. When he learned of Lloyd's departure from Malta he signalled:

> Following from Prime Minister to Air Vice-Marshal Lloyd
> I congratulate you on your brilliant fourteen months in Malta, and wish you continued success in your new important command.[8]

As noted in an earlier chapter, Tedder had advised Portal in April that he intended to relieve Lloyd before too long. By July his relief was long overdue. When he assumed command as AOC Malta in June 1941, he had been told by Portal, 'You will be on the island for six months as a minimum and nine months as a maximum as by that time you will be worn out.'[9] In the last six months of 1941, Lloyd had built up the strength of RAF Malta and his force had made a significant contribution to the initial success of Auchinleck's 'Crusader' offensive. However, the return of the *Luftwaffe* to Sicily in overwhelming numbers led, as we have seen, to the gradual destruction of Malta's Hurricane force in the first three months of 1942. It was Lloyd's finest achievement to rebuild his command from a growing supply of Spitfire Vs in the face of determined and skilful opposition until air control was re-established by the end of May.

Since this achievement has been overshadowed in some accounts by the claims made for the later successes of AVM Park, it seems appropriate to quote the post-war judgement of the Air Ministry's Air Historical Branch:

> Park's forward interception policy was only possible because of the increased fighter strength in Spitfires at Malta. The new policy saved bombs and crashing aircraft from falling on the Island, but it is an exaggeration to claim, as has been done in some quarters, that the policy of forward interception 'saved' Malta. The battle for Malta had been won before Air Vice-Marshal Lloyd left the Island. After the enemy had called off the Spring '*blitz*' of April 1942 and Rommel became deeply committed to his offensive [in Libya], the existence of Malta as an air and naval base was never seriously threatened by concentrated air attack.[10]

A longer perspective suggests that each of Malta's three wartime AOCs, 'Freddie' Maynard, Hugh Lloyd and Keith Park, made an outstanding contribution to the air defence of Malta. Each faced a different set of circumstances and difficulties, and each succeeded in surmounting them.

Throughout July, Churchill, the COS and the War Cabinet were pre-occupied with strategic decisions, the discussion of which had begun during Churchill's visit to Washington in the previous month. The British and American Chiefs could not agree. General Marshall, who with Admiral King and Harry Hopkins came to London on 18 July, pressed hard for an early landing on the Cherbourg peninsula, code-named Operation 'Sledgehammer'. However, Brooke was vehemently opposed to this and Churchill and the War Cabinet supported him at a meeting on 22 July. It was then that the US Joint Chiefs, with considerable reluctance and misgivings, accepted the British plan for a landing in French North Africa, a decision forced on them by President Roosevelt's insistence that US troops must fight somewhere in 1942. This became Operation 'Torch', the implications of which for Malta are the subject of a later chapter.

While these plans were being debated, Churchill remained fully aware of the difficult conditions in Malta. At the top of his box of papers on 15 July was a memorandum reporting the safe arrival of thirty-two Spitfires, the first of the two batches flown in during July from HMS *Eagle*. The Prime Minister had also learned from Lord Cranborne, the Colonial Secretary, that Gort had written to him urging an early visit to the island. Gort thought that such a visit by a Cabinet Minister would enable the authorities at home to be given a first-hand account of Malta's growing difficulties. This prompted Churchill to signal to Gort on 18 July:

1. I should be very glad to hear from you how you are getting on.
2. It is a great comfort to me to feel that you are in full control of this vital
   island fortress. You may be sure we shall do everything to help you.

To this Gort at once replied on 20 July:

I am most grateful for your signal and I am writing to you. The arrival of
Welshman and her cargo of milk, etc, was most acceptable as a gesture to
Maltese people who remain for present in good spirits. Consumption of
aviation spirit still causes me concern as for last three weeks ending 18th
July we used 235,000 gallons, whereas weekly flat rate to target date must
not exceed 45,000 gallons on the assumption of no replenishments.

Gort expanded on these remarks in a three-page letter of 27 July.[11] He
repeated his admiration for the 'cheerfulness of the Maltese people and their
stoical determination to withstand everything that it is humanly possible
to endure, rather than surrender to the despised Italians'. Concerned about
dwindling stocks of aviation fuel, he questioned again the priority given to
offensive air strikes, fearing that there would not be enough fuel left to
protect the arrival and unloading of the next convoy. He ended by writing
that Lord Cranborne's expected visit would be of great help in sustaining
morale. Churchill no doubt found this first-hand account of the conditions
in Malta helpful, and he wrote on it: 'General Ismay. For COS Cte to see'.
Gort had also written to Cranborne in similar terms and, when Cranborne
sent Churchill a copy of this letter, he drew the Prime Minister's attention
to the paragraph describing the fuel problem. This letter, too, Churchill
sent on to the COS with the notation, 'A very serious letter'.

The COS were naturally well aware of this problem. As early as 1 July,
ACM Portal had told his colleagues that, at the present rate of consumption,
stocks would be exhausted by mid-August. They would, however, last
until October if offensive air operations and the transit of aircraft through
Malta to Egypt were suspended. He thought the best solution was to send
aircraft to Egypt via the Takoradi route across central Africa, noting that
this would only cause a delay of about a week.[12] He undertook to consult
the Middle East C-in-Cs about this, while Admiral Pound agreed that the
two submarines due to sail to Malta in July would carry aviation fuel.
After the receipt of Gort's letter to Cranborne with Churchill's notation,
the COS discussed the matter once again on 30 July.[13] Before then Portal
had received a telegram from the Middle East Defence Committee on 22
July urging that everything possible be done to halt Rommel's continuing
offensive towards Cairo. In particular, they asked that eight more Beaufort
torpedo-bombers be sent to operate from Malta to attack Axis supply
convoys, despite the effect this would have on the island's fuel reserves.

Gort strongly objected to this and signalled the COS on 29 July expressing 'grave anxiety about the continued over-expenditure of aviation spirit'. He asked for an immediate policy decision, pending which, he signalled, he had ordered the suspension of long-range air strikes. Confronted by these conflicting demands, Portal proposed that the transit of aircraft through Malta should cease and that offensive operations be limited to those in the vicinity of the island. He was then reported as saying, 'he considered that the Middle East required guidance in this matter since they were inclined very naturally to view the situation in the light of the present battle in Egypt, possibly at the expense of Malta. He outlined the steps being taken to keep up the flow of Wellington and Halifax aircraft to the Middle East.' Portal's recommendations were accepted and, accordingly, the Middle East C-in-Cs were advised that evening that 'strikes from Malta must be reduced to an absolute minimum, e.g. extremely good chances at close range. Transits, except for Beauforts, will cease.' To offset this restriction of air power, the C-in-Cs decided that the submarines of the 10th Flotilla, which had been withdrawn from Malta on 26 April, should return. The consequences of this decision will be examined in the next chapter.

Plans were now made for Cranborne to fly out to Malta with General Brooke who was on his way to the Middle East. When Churchill advised Casey in Cairo of this visit, he told him: 'Gort had been feeling a little neglected and we think it important that a Minister of Cabinet rank should go and see him without delay.' Brooke and Cranborne flew to Gibraltar on 1 August, and then on to Malta on the next day. Brooke, who only stayed one day, wrote in his diary for that day that he had told Gort about the plans for North Africa. He was then taken on a tour of Valletta and the docks. 'The destruction,' he wrote, 'is inconceivable and reminds one of Ypres, Arras, Lens at their worst during last war.'[14] When, after the war, Brooke reviewed what he had written at the time, he added the further comment: 'I was especially anxious to visit Gort in Malta as I knew he was in a depressed state, feeling that he been shoved away in a corner out of the real war, and in danger of his whole garrison being scuppered without much chance of giving an account of themselves.'[15] Churchill, too, later recalled that when they met in Cairo in late August, Gort had told him that if Malta were forced to surrender he would attempt to sail to Sicily with a part of the garrison, attack the airfields and 'go down fighting there, the survivors taking to the mountains and resisting to the end'. Churchill recorded that he authorised Gort to plan accordingly.[16]

Churchill left London on the day after Brooke and flew, with a brief stop at Gibraltar, directly to Cairo. He remained in Egypt until 11 August, taking the hard decision to replace General Auchinleck as C-in-C Middle East Command with General Alexander. General Montgomery took over command of the 8th Army. Churchill and Brooke then flew to Moscow for five days of difficult discussions with Stalin, before returning to Cairo on 17 August. Since it was on the day that Churchill left for Moscow that the 'Pedestal' relief convoy entered the Mediterranean, the Prime Minister gave instructions that details of its progress be cabled to him immediately in Moscow. It was, consequently, during his meetings with Stalin that Churchill received news of the 'Pedestal' convoy. There are many detailed accounts of this vital convoy,[17] but the following extracts from his Malta files show how the Prime Minister heard the news.

The 'Pedestal' convoy comprised thirteen large merchant ships and the US-built tanker *Ohio*, which was loaded with 12,000 tons of fuel oil. Two battleships, HMS *Nelson* and *Rodney*, three aircraft carriers, HMS *Eagle, Indomitable* and *Victorious*, seven cruisers, and thirty-two destroyers escorted them. In addition, the aircraft carrier HMS *Furious* sailed at the same time carrying a further thirty-six Spitfires to be flown on to Malta, and nine submarines had been placed to intercept any foray by the Italian battle fleet. Malta's air forces had been strengthened in the days before the convoy sailed and comprised 100 Spitfires, 36 long-range Beaufighters, and 30 Beaufort torpedo-bombers, together with a number of reconnaissance aircraft. Vice-Admiral Sir Neville Syfret was in overall command of the convoy, and before the convoy departed, Churchill signalled to him: 'All good luck. I am so glad you have this great task to do.' The intention to sail such a large convoy could not be concealed from the enemy and, inevitably, Kesselring had also reinforced his air forces in Sicily and Sardinia. There were also at sea a considerable number of German and Italian U-boats and E-boats.

The convoy passed Algiers at noon on 11 August and Admiral Pound's first signal sent to Churchill in Moscow was sent at midnight that day under the designation, TULIP 94. It read as follows:

For Prime Minister from First Sea Lord
PEDESTAL according to plan except that EAGLE was sunk by U-boat south of Balearic Islands. To-morrow Wednesday is the critical day. Thirty-six SPITFIRES landed Malta from FURIOUS. Nothing else of naval interest except one Italian U. boat sunk.

The next signal, TULIP 109, was sent on the night of 12 August:

For Prime Minister from First Sea Lord
A. 1. PEDESTAL according to plan with following exceptions. INDOMITABLE damaged by air attack and reduced to 20 knots.
    2. Cruisers NIGERIA, KENYA and CAIRO mined or torpedoed. Condition not known.

    3. Destroyer FORESIGHT torpedoed but proceeding to Gibraltar in tow.

    4. Five ships of convoy sunk after dark tonight probably by E. boats.

    5. Two U. boats rammed and sunk by destroyers and a third almost certainly destroyed by air.

B. There may be a battle with enemy destroyers in the morning.

C. One enemy capital ship at sea but appears to have her eyes to East.

D. Not many casualties in EAGLE.

E. Covering force and Malta party parted company at 7 o'clock this evening

F. Our fighters must have done very well as enemy air concentration was very heavy.

G. Hope two empty ships from Malta got through.

This signal had only been marked 'Important', and Churchill, in thanking Pound for the news, asked that future signals be marked 'Most immediate'. Churchill then sent a message to Stalin telling him of the convoy's progress, and concluding, 'As we expected, this convoy to this vital outpost in the Mediterranean has had to fight its way through against very heavy opposition, and what will reach its destination is as yet unknown.' The next signal, TULIP 115, was sent at 1700 hours on 13 August:

Personal for PRIME MINISTER from First Sea Lord
PEDESTAL

A. At 1550 hours today, Thursday, the situation as follows as a result of combination of

    1. Heavy air attack at dusk last evening.

    2. U. boat attacks in vicinity of Cape BON.

    3. Continuous U. boat attack during the night.

B. Own Forces

    1. Cruisers MANCHESTER and CAIRO sunk.

    2. Cruiser KENYA fate uncertain.

    3. Destroyer FORESIGHT had to be sunk by own forces.

    4. NIGERIA believed to be clear of air attack to westward and proceeding GIBRALTAR.

    5. INDOMITABLE presumably with main force should be clear of dive bombing attack to the westward.

    6. FURIOUS arrived GIBRALTAR and loading Spitfires.

C. Convoy

    1. Admiral BURROUGH in destroyer ASHANTI and other destroyers has five merchant ships with him and should be 47 miles from MALTA.

2. Oiler OHIO damaged and in tow of destroyer making four knots is 80 miles from MALTA at 1500.

3. One merchant ship on fire but in tow of HUNT class destroyer but distance from MALTA uncertain.

D. Enemy Forces

   1. Cruisers turned back during the night.

E. Further signals will be sent later.

TULIP 120 followed in the early hours of 14 August:

Personal for Prime Minister from First Sea Lord.

A. 3 ships have arrived and between them carry 6000 tons of flour, 2000 tons aviation spirit and a considerable amount of ammunition besides other stores.

B. There is a possibility that the oiler and one other ship may get in but chances are not good.

C. NIGERIA proceeding at 12 knots towards GIBRALTAR and am hopeful she will get in.

D. KENYA situation still obscure.

E. INDOMITABLE was hit by 3 bombs and had 3 near misses, both lifts damaged and flying deck out of action. Engines undamaged and capable of 28½ knots. 6 Officers and 60 men killed and 55 wounded.

F. RODNEY damage to rudder from near miss.

G. All forces appear to have played their part well but the odds which were concentrated against them were too heavy.

H. TORCH appears all the more necessary.

To this signal Churchill replied on 14 August, writing: 'I am sure that all played their part to the utmost.' He went on to ask that he be sent a fuller account of the operation with details of losses suffered and of the supply position in Malta. Better news came later that day in TULIP 132.

Prime Minister from First Sea Lord

A. Reference Paras A. and B. of TULIP Number 120

   1. The other ship by determination and cunning has arrived making the total 4.

   2. Determined efforts under heavy attack are being made to tow the oiler in. She should be approximately 40 miles from MALTA at 1600 today.

B. Should the four ships complete unloading I estimate the situation should be

   1. Food position secure until 1st January on an improved seige [sic] ration basis.

2. Aviation spirit sometime between 15th November and 1st January depending on rate of Expenditure and allowing for submarines putting in as much as possible.

3. Fuel oil position will depend whether oiler gets in.

C. NIGERIA should arrive GIBRALTAR early 18th.

D. KENYA though torpedoed remained with the convoy and should arrive GIBRALTAR p.m. on 15th.

E. RODNEY and INDOMITABLE should have reached GIBRALTAR by now.

F. Survivors from MANCHESTER have reached TUNISIA so we had to announce her loss.

On his copy of this signal Churchill wrote: '1SL Many thanks for yr 132. Prolongation of life of Malta was worth the heavy cost.' Churchill's relief at receiving these signals prompted him to write to Stalin on 14 August. During their discussions one of the Prime Minister's most difficult tasks was to tell Stalin that there would be no landing in France that year, a statement that Stalin took badly. Consequently, Churchill was anxious to demonstrate that British forces were actively engaged with the enemy.

Dear Premier Stalin,

The following is the result of the Malta convoy battle. Only three merchant ships have reached Malta out of fourteen. Two more are being towed and may get in. The three that are there carry supplies for between two and three months. Thus, the fortress, which is of great consequence to the whole Mediterranean position, can hold out until after both the impending battle in the Western Desert of Egypt and TORCH have taken place.

2. For this we have paid a heavy price. The 'EAGLE' aircraft-carrier is sunk and the 'INDOMITABLE' aircraft-carrier severely damaged by 3 bombs and 3 near misses; two good cruisers are sunk, one damaged and the fate of another is uncertain; one destroyer is sunk together with nine or perhaps eleven fast merchant ships, of which we have not many left. 'RODNEY' was also damaged slightly by a near miss.

3. I am of opinion that the price was worth paying. The dangers of warships operating amid all this shore-based enemy aircraft have had another painful illustration. We sank three U-boats and must have inflicted heavy damage upon the attacking air force. The Italian cruisers and battleships did not venture to attack the remnants of the convoy when it got under the Malta aircraft umbrella. The enemy will no doubt proclaim this as a great victory at sea, and so it would be but for the strategic significance of Malta in view of future plans.

Yours sincerely,

Winston S. Churchill

Churchill left Moscow on 16 August and, after a brief stay at Tehran, arrived back in Cairo on 17 August where, among the many telegrams awaiting him, was a lengthy, six-part signal from the Admiralty giving the more detailed account of the 'Pedestal' convoy he had requested. Having read this, Churchill signalled to the First Lord and the First Sea Lord:

> Please convey my compliments to Admirals Syfret, Burrough, Lyster and all officers and men engaged in the magnificent crash through of supplies to Malta which cannot fail to have an important influence on the immediate future of the war in the Mediterranean.
>
> Two. Papers here report thirteen enemy aircraft shot down but this was only by the Malta force, and I have seen no mention of the 39 additional shot down by the carriers, which puts a very different complexion on the air fighting.[18]

Admiral Syfret replied to this on 20 August:

> On behalf Force F may I say how very much we appreciate your message and how encouraged we are to be told of the importance of what we achieved. We are all agreed that the work of the Merchant Navy in the operation was superb.

Churchill also read a telegram from Malta describing the arrival of the five ships of the convoy, the unloading of which was carried out at the rate of 5,000 tons a day by drafting in 3,000 troops, working in three shifts around the clock. The RAF, reinforced by the 36 additional Spitfires flown off HMS *Furious* on 11 August and a further 32 on 17 August, effectively screened the unloading operation. Eventually, approximately 35,000 tons of food and mixed stores, and 12,000 tons of fuels were unloaded from the five ships that had got through. Admiral Harwood passed on a copy of another signal from Admiral Leatham, the Vice-Admiral Malta, which gave further details of the eventual arrival of the *Brisbane Star*, 'whose Master showed fine determination and courage', and, later, of the *Ohio*. The tanker had been heavily damaged but was finally towed in to Valletta on the morning of 15 August, lashed between two destroyers. Her Master, Captain D. W. Mason, was awarded the George Cross for his outstanding courage and determination. This signal carries Churchill's large tick at the bottom. The determination to use every means to bring the *Ohio* into Malta stands in sharp contrast with the earlier decision in the June 'Harpoon' convoy to sink the tanker *Kentucky* when she, too, was disabled but still afloat.

The opportunity to hear the news from Malta at first hand came with the arrival of General Gort and his ADC, Lord Munster. Churchill later wrote

21. The tanker SS *Ohio* entering the Grand Harbour on 15 August 1942, carrying 12,000 tons of vital oil and petrol. She had been heavily bombed on her approach to Malta but was eventually towed in with her mid-decks awash.

that both men 'were very thin and looked rather haggard', but, he went on, 'we held long talks, and when we parted I had the Malta picture clearly in my mind'.[19] Lord Moran, Churchill's doctor who accompanied him to Moscow and Cairo, gives another account of these talks. 'The PM's relief is a joyful sight. The plight of the island – short of food and ammunition – has been distracting to him ... The PM dabbed his eyes with a handkerchief as he listened to Malta's story.'[20] After Churchill's return to London he went down to the House of Commons on 8 September to give an account of his visit to the Middle East and Moscow. He began by narrating the course of the 'Pedestal' convoy. 'Severe losses,' he told Members, 'were suffered both by the convoy and the escorting fleet ... But this price, although heavy, was not excessive for the result obtained, for Malta is not only as bright a gem as shines in the King's Crown, but its effective action against the enemy's communications with Libya and Egypt is essential to the whole strategic position in the Middle East.' He concluded by saying: 'The whole operation was carried out with the utmost discipline and determination, reflecting the highest credit on all officers and men concerned, both of the Royal Navy and the Mercantile Marine, and upon the skilful admirals in charge – Admiral Syfret, Admiral Burrough and Admiral Lyster.'[21]

The cost was indeed a high one. Between January and the end of August 1942, nineteen merchant ships were sunk on the Malta route. Only thirteen arrived and three of these were sunk after their arrival. The Royal Navy had also sustained heavy losses. But Churchill was in no doubt that, despite the loss of the supporting airfields in Cyrenaica and the virtual failure of the March and June convoys, a supreme effort must be made to relieve Malta in August. The documents quoted in this and earlier chapters make clear that the achievement of this objective in August, when the island's food stocks were close to exhaustion, owed much to his determination and driving force. The loss of Singapore in February, followed in June by the fall of Tobruk, seemed to him to show a fundamental lack of will power, an unwillingness to fight to the utmost. He had been unable to prevent the disasters at Singapore and Tobruk, but Malta was different. Here he could demand that the RAF be continually and strongly reinforced with Spitfires so as to wrest air control from the enemy, and then, despite, or even because of the failures in March and June, order a convoy on the largest possible scale to be fought through whatever the cost. The result was as much a moral as a naval victory. However, Malta's unique strategic value, as he reminded the House, was its ability to attack Rommel's stretched supply line, and to this aspect of Malta's war experience we must now return.

DESERT BATTLES AND MORE SUPPLIES FOR MALTA

We are thinking about you every day, and everything in human power shall be done.

Churchill to General Gort, 26 September 1942

When, after his discussions with Stalin in Moscow, Churchill returned to Cairo on 17 August, he at once became aware of intelligence information about Rommel's intentions. During the month of July a stalemate had been reached in the desert fighting and both commanders paused to rebuild reserves and deploy new units. Fortunately, it was during this period that the success of the British Intelligence organisation at Bletchley Park, GC&CS, in deciphering German Enigma signals, and the Italian C38m signals, which gave details of all convoys to North Africa, reached a new peak. As mentioned before, by July 1942 over 4,000 enemy signals were being deciphered each month with very little delay, and sophisticated systems had been developed to process and interpret this mine of information. By these means the Middle East C-in-Cs were able to follow, almost hour by hour, Rommel's progress in strengthening his forces for a renewed assault on the 8th Army's line at Alamein. Only the timing of this new attack remained in doubt, and this was removed when GC&CS sent to Cairo on 17 August what Professor Hinsley has described as 'perhaps the most important single item of information that the Enigma had yet contributed to the desert campaign'.[1] This was nothing less than Rommel's plan, signalled to Berlin only two days earlier, to launch his attack on 26 August. His plan rested on two vital conditions; firstly, that supplies already loaded in Italian ports arrive safely in North Africa, and, secondly, that he continue to receive a steady supply of ammunition and fuel. These conditions could be thwarted if Malta were able to resume the attack on Italian supply convoys which had been so successful in the closing months of 1941. This would reinforce the pressure already being applied by aircraft and submarines based in Egypt.

As soon as they learned of the rapid unloading of the five ships of the 'Pedestal' convoy, and with details of Rommel's plans in front of them, the

COS on 19 August reviewed Malta's offensive operations. They quickly agreed that 'for the next ten days or so supreme importance should be attached to these operations and that considerations of economy in petrol would not justify limiting these operations'.[2] The Governor and the Middle East C-in-Cs were instructed accordingly. This initial ten-day period was extended for a further ten days on 31 August, but the COS reassured the Governor, who was anxious about Malta's petrol reserves, as we shall see, that 'we will, however, economise utmost extent and select only really important shipping for attack'.[3] So detailed was British knowledge of enemy shipping plans that submarines and aircraft could be directed to attack ships carrying fuel, ammunition and other vital commodities while ignoring those carrying stores with which Rommel was already well supplied. Churchill saw a copy of the first instruction in Cairo before spending two days visiting Montgomery and the RAF commanders in the desert. He met many of the troops including a squadron of his old regiment, the 4th Queen's Own Hussars, and toured the area where Rommel's forthcoming attack was expected. Before leaving Cairo on the evening of 23 August, he sent the War Cabinet a cable describing in detail his visit to the desert. He concluded:

> To sum up, while I and others would prefer the September to the August battle, because of our growing strength, I am satisfied that we have lively, competent, resolute men in command, working together as an admirable team under leaders of the highest military quality. Everything has been done and is being done that is possible, and it is now my duty to return home, as I have no part to play in the battle, which must be left to those in whom we place our trust.[4]

Despite this statement to his colleagues in London, it appears that Churchill, with his characteristic wish to be close to the scene of action, had given some thought to staying in Egypt until Rommel had launched his attack. In the event, however, he was persuaded that his presence there would be a distraction to Alexander and Montgomery and it was, therefore, in London that he followed the course of events.

The author has examined in a previous study the complex factors involved in the battle of Alam Halfa and only a summary is presented here.[5] Rommel's initial attack date of 26 August was postponed to 30 August when, despite having fuel for only four and a half days' fighting, he attempted to dislodge the 8th Army from the Alam Halfa ridge where Churchill had stood only a week before. However, alerted by the interception of Rommel's plan, Montgomery had strongly reinforced this position with troops, guns and dug-in tanks, with the result that, under almost continuous air attack, Rommel's panzer divisions were brought to a standstill. On 6 September, intercepts told Montgomery that Rommel had decided 'to go over to the

22. Churchill on a visit to RAF squadrons in the Egyptian desert in August 1942.

defensive utilising the extensive British minefields'. In his subsequent report to the German High Command, Rommel wrote that his attack 'was broken off because the supplies of fuel and ammunition promised by *Comando Supremo* did not arrive'. His tank losses were not large, but he lacked the fuel to renew the battle. Rommel's supply shortages are explained by the fact that, during the period from 17 August to 6 September, twelve enemy supply ships on their way to North Africa were sunk. Malta-based forces sank six of these, including two tankers, and they also damaged and prevented the arrival of three more ships, of which another two were tankers. In the month of August as a whole, Rommel received only 51,600 tons of supplies compared with 91,500 in July. 25 per cent of the general cargo dispatched from Italy was lost and 41 per cent of the fuel. Rommel's defeat at Alam Halfa was succinctly summarised in the official RAF history in the following terms: 'The struggle had been won by good generalship, stout resistance on the ground, and overwhelming superiority in the air, in a situation created by relentless interruption of the enemy's supplies.'[6]

In his memoirs Churchill's doctor, Lord Moran, recalled that when, in 1953, he asked Churchill to pick out the most anxious months of the war, he replied, 'September and October, yes, 1942'.[7] This was echoed in the fourth volume of Churchill's own war memoirs, published in 1951, Chapter XXXI of which, describing this period, Churchill entitled 'Suspense and Strain'.[8] One contribution to Churchill's anxieties was the continuing, and worsening, supply position at Malta, to the consideration of which we must now return. The author is conscious that the following account of Malta's supply shortages, with interchanges of telegrams about calories of food and gallons of petrol, makes for rather dull reading. But it seemed essential to show that Churchill saw it as a part of his overall responsibility as Minister of Defence to acquaint himself with – and involve himself when he judged necessary – not just questions of high strategy, but the details of operations. He was often criticised at the time by his commanders (and even more so by some historians) for going into too much detail, but that was his manner and his conception of his duty.

The offensive effort demanded of Malta after 17 August inevitably made substantial inroads into the fuel stocks brought in by the surviving ships of the 'Pedestal' convoy. Particularly worrying was the consumption of aviation spirit, a problem which was to appear on the agenda of numerous COS meetings in September and October. Both the naval and air staffs presented memoranda on this subject in early September. The air staff noted that, even with the planned submarine supplies, petrol stocks would run out in early December. Since, they went on, matters could not be left until November 'in view of our other commitments at that time', they recommended that the Admiralty consider sending in a fast tanker in the October dark period.[9] A lengthier naval memorandum, presented by the VCNS, first examined the petrol problem and noted that the passage of supply ships from either east or west would be very difficult. A convoy from Gibraltar would conflict with the plans being made for Operation 'Torch' – the invasion of Morocco and Algeria – D-Day for which had been set for early November. A convoy from Alexandria would be exposed to the same enemy air and naval threats as had forced the withdrawal of the 'Vigorous' convoy in June and ruled out such a convoy in August. The VCNS explained that the minelayer HMS *Welshman* was being adapted to carry petrol in containers and might be ready to sail by mid-October. However, she could only carry one week's supply of petrol, and the risk of her loss was high. Two submarines could be expected to carry in 400 tons of petrol in the next two months. The Admiralty note asked that urgent consideration be given to the possibility of supplying petrol by air, arguing that 'it may well be that this is the only practicable method'. It recognised, nevertheless, that supplies by air, submarine or minelayer 'are only a palliative'.

As regards the much larger quantity of foodstuffs now urgently required at Malta, the VCNS declared that this would necessitate a major convoy. The prospects for such a convoy from the west would depend upon the progress of the 'Torch' campaign, and might be made more difficult if the German air force had by then seized bases in Tunisia. Easier conditions for an eastern convoy could only be expected if the 8th Army's planned offensive, set for mid-October, was successful enough to restore to the RAF the use of the Cyrenaican airfields from which a convoy could receive air cover. The relief of Malta, the VCNS concluded, would, therefore, depend on the progress of the two autumn campaigns. If neither had advanced very far by mid-November, relief of the island 'would require Fleet operations of considerable magnitude'.[10]

While these memoranda were being circulated, Churchill read copies of several cable exchanges between the Middle East C-in-Cs, the Governor and the COS. The C-in-Cs, upon the expiry of the second period of full-scale offensive operations from Malta, wanted this to continue. They wished to select the targets that Malta's forces should attack, but assured the Governor that they would keep a careful eye on the petrol situation. Having read this, the Prime Minister sent the following minute to General Brooke:

> Prime Minister's Personal Minute M. 355/2. 8 September 1942
> CIGS
>   These telegrams, and the Malta petrol situation, show the urgency of the operations of the 8th Army. We must not run Malta too hard if the others are going to take their time.
>   Pray let me know what you think of this.

Brooke told him in reply of the plans being made and merely noted that they had separately discussed the Prime Minister's reference to the 8th Army. There is no record of this discussion in Churchill's files, but in his diary for 8 September Brooke wrote:

> Not much more news from Middle East. Rommel is now practically back to where he started from. My next trouble will now be to stop Winston from fussing Alex and Monty and egging them to attack before they are ready. It is a regular disease that he suffers from, this frightful impatience to get an attack launched![11]

The COS discussed the two staff papers at their meeting on 9 September when Portal explained that, even with further restrictions on flying operations, aviation fuel would be exhausted by mid-November. Nevertheless, he rejected the naval proposal that fuel be flown in by bombers, pointing out this 'would practically entail the cessation of the night bombing of enemy bases and ports in North Africa'.[12] Despite this, the naval staff continued to press for a re-examination of supply by air. In a further note of 24 September they explained that a fast tanker was not available and that only submarine supplies could be expected before 'Torch' in November. They urged that 'Malta must be ordered to make drastic economies in aviation spirit'. In his diary, Brooke briefly noted that there were several heated exchanges between Pound and Portal. As General Gort anxiously reported in weekly telegrams the steady decline in petrol stocks, Portal agreed on 25 September that the weekly consumption rate be reduced from 200 tons to 150 tons. Five days later he presented another analysis of the problem of air supply. This showed that if as many as one half of the Middle East bombers were diverted to the aerial supply of Malta for a period of six weeks, this would only extend the date on which supplies would run out by three days.[13]

While Churchill's senior military advisers were debating, and arguing, about the best means to replenish Malta's aviation petrol stocks, they were abruptly made aware of a more alarming development. On 24 September, Churchill found at the top of his dispatch box a letter from the Colonial Secretary, Lord Cranborne. This letter began: 'I am distressed to let you have to know some very disturbing news which has just reached me regarding the food situation in Malta.' He reminded the Prime Minister that, after the arrival of the 'Pedestal' convoy, the Colonial Office had been led to expect that food supplies would last until the second week in December. He then went on to write:

Since then, I have had nothing to suggest that this estimate was inaccurate until today, when I had a visit from Mr. Rowntree, of the Ministry of Food, who has just come back from the island. He brought with him a report, a copy of which I attach. The gist of this report, as you will see, is (1) that the civil population are already on what amounts to starvation rations. The smallest number of calories on which life can be maintained is 1500, and they are already down to 1511 for all except adult males, who receive 1687, as against a minimum of about 3000 in this country. (2) Even this meagre ration can only be maintained till early in December, when all stocks will be completely exhausted. This means that the island will be faced with starvation unless a convoy can be got in during the dark period of November, which is, I understand, early in the month. I fully realise, for reasons into which I need not go, that this is going to be very difficult indeed.

Rowntree's attached report gave further details of the food situation. There had been some increase in rations since June, with an extra distribution of 3½ ounces of bread on five days each week. Those using the Victory Kitchens were receiving the calorie levels mentioned in Cranborne's letter, but there was much dissatisfaction about the quality of these meals. A War Office note in mid-September gave some details of the prevailing menus. On two days a week the meal would be macaroni and cheese, on another two days minestra, a vegetable minestrone, on the next two days a meal of meat and vegetables and on the remaining day an egg dish. The Victory Kitchens had been initially established to feed those who had lost their homes and their food stocks, but by June 1942 100,000 people were being provided with one meal a day, and six months later this figure had risen to 175,000. The report noted that 'the morale of the population is high [but] there are also signs that the public are beginning to be worried about the feeding of their children'.

Churchill cannot have been altogether surprised by this news. When he was still in Cairo in August, General Gort had given him a memorandum about the prevailing rations of vital commodities and, upon his return to London, he had asked Lord Woolton, the Minister of Food, to compare these figures with British food rationing. Woolton replied to Churchill on 5 September, telling him that comparisons with the UK were not easy to make because of the significant differences in diet, but he showed how much the Maltese rations had been reduced since December 1941. The consumption of the main item, flour, had fallen from 3,000 tons to 2,000 tons per month, and of edible oil, sugar, coffee and tea by more than a half. Woolton concluded by writing that although the average person in Malta was not suffering unduly, 'the heavy workers and the troops were not getting enough to eat'.

Having studied Cranborne's letter and the attached papers, Churchill directed Ismay to send copies of them to the COS with the following minute.

General Ismay for COS Committee.
Prime Minister's Personal Minute D. 161/2.   25 September 1942
   1. A summary of Mr. Rowntree's report on the gravity of the food position at Malta should be cabled at my direction to the Middle East C-in-Cs.
   2. Let me know what plans are made to slip individual ships through during the November dark period and 'TORCH' confusion.

The Prime Minister also signalled to Gort on 26 September, telling him: 'I have read Rowntree's report. We are thinking about you every day, and everything in human power shall be done. We hope to run some ships through in the flurry of 'TORCH'. All good wishes to you and Munster.' Gort sent his thanks for this signal on 30 September.

Cranborne had asked that Rowntree have the opportunity to explain the position in person to the COS. Consequently, on 28 September, Sir George Gater of the Colonial Office introduced Mr Rowntree, described as Deputy Director of the Communal Feeding Department at Malta, to the COS.[14] During a long discussion it emerged that the plan to slaughter all the island's livestock had not been fully implemented following opposition in the Council of Government. Rowntree also stressed that, although the theoretical date for the complete exhaustion of stocks was mid-December, assuming the arrival of 300 tons of dehydrated meat and milk powder, new supplies should arrive thirty days earlier, that is during the November dark period, to allow for unloading and distribution. In his diary entry about this discussion, General Brooke wrote: 'Long COS attended by Cater [sic] of Colonial Office and by Mr. Rowntree, catering adviser to the Governor of Malta. He had sad tales about food situation in Malta! Somewhat of an alarmist. I do not think he was examining the problem from a war point of view. Slaughtering cattle and horses has certainly not been taken fully into account in his calculations. In any case we must have a definite estimate of the situation from the Governor himself.'[15]

As a result of this discussion, the Colonial Office prepared a summary of the food situation and examined the effect on the exhaustion date of several additional measures. This concluded that, even with a renewed reduction in rations and the slaughter of all remaining livestock, supplies could only be eked out for a further two weeks. The report concluded: 'From the point of view of health the consequences [of these measures] would be serious and from the point of view of morale highly dangerous.'[16] This warning was echoed by the Governor, who signalled on 30 September. After stating that 'the Fortress should last mathematically until mid-December', he concluded:

> If we enter the first period of December without having received any substantial replenishments we shall find ourselves in a position of great difficulty. It would be impossible to conceal from the public the low state of stocks, as there are already indications that the people are apprehensive about the winter.[17]

The COS debated what action to take in three successive meetings in early October.[18] The outcome was a draft telegram to the C-in-Cs and the Governor, which Ismay submitted to the Prime Minister for his approval on 5 October. Churchill gave his consent on the following day, and directed that copies be sent to the War Cabinet and the Defence Committee. The approved signal first dismissed the possibility of resupply by air, and then set out plans for east and west convoys. At Alexandria, HMS *Manxman*, another of the Royal Navy's fast minelayers, would be loaded with food by the end of October with a view to making a high-speed dash to Malta, accompanied by several destroyers, if the 8th Army's advance allowed air cover to be provided. A further fourteen merchant ships would sail for Malta in November and December. At the western end of the Mediterranean, HMS *Welshman* would be loaded with either 300 tons of food or of petrol, the decision about this to be made around 20 October. Sixteen more freighters, and possibly an American tanker, would be ready to follow, the first four carrying 17,000 tons of food and 4,000 tons of aviation fuel. The signal also raised the possibility of sailing in several single ships in disguise, and then concluded:

4. It is not possible to make detailed plans in advance. All that can be done is to provide the ships and leave it to Admiral Cunningham [appointed as the 'Torch' naval commander] and Commander-in-Chief, Mediterranean, to pass them in from the West and East respectively, as they judge best.

5. It is clear that the first attempts to relieve Malta, i.e. 4 ships from either end plus minelayers and possibly destroyers in early November, depend largely on the success of our armies at either end. If these attempts fail, Malta must be prepared to hold out until the dark period in early December makes it possible to try again.

6. It is estimated here that the slaughter of all livestock other than draught animals would give approximately 1000 tons of carcase meat and postpone the exhaustion date of the population by about one week. The slaughter of draught animals would effect a further postponement of about one week. The decision as to the date and extent of the slaughter policy must rest with the Fortress Commander.

Some indication of the tense conditions in which these discussions were held can be seen in another entry in General Brooke's diary. On 2 October he wrote:

> Our COS meeting was again mainly taken up with discussing plans for the future feeding of Malta. The present supplies finish about the middle of October [sic]. Future supplies will depend on success of Middle East offensive and North African venture. If neither succeeds God knows how we shall keep Malta alive, and even so the timing of both these alternatives will inevitably run Malta very low before relief can come.[19]

While Churchill and the COS were engaged in finding a workable solution to this problem of resupplying Malta before stocks were exhausted, they were made aware of a further dangerous complication. On 10 September the Joint Intelligence Committee (JIC) had submitted a report entitled, 'Renewal of Air Attacks on Malta'.[20] The Committee knew from intercepted signals how alarmed the enemy had become about the loss of sea-borne supplies before and during the Alam Halfa battle at the end of August. They expected, therefore, that another attempt to neutralise Malta by air attack would be undertaken on the lines of the one carried out in July. However, since this would require the concentration of as many as 400 German aircraft from Russia and the eastern Mediterranean, supported by up to 200 Italian aircraft, the JIC did not think that a renewed air attack on Malta could be launched before the end of September.

When Churchill and the COS read this appreciation they were not to know that, three days later, Hitler gave directions for such an attack, but on 19 September an Enigma intercept gave details of the movement of German air force units from Crete, Russia and elsewhere to Sicily 'for a short-term attack on Malta'.[21] The assault began on 10 October but was called off by Kesselring on the 19th after failing to have any effect on Malta's attacks on Axis convoys to North Africa. Nevertheless, the fierce air fighting steadily reduced the number of AVM Park's serviceable Spitfires, and on 17 October Portal told his colleagues that 'a serious situation' had arisen.[22] As many as seventy-three Spitfires were awaiting repair, and, although steps had been taken to fly out spare parts, Park urgently needed another aircraft carrier delivery of Spitfires. Admiral Moore reported that the only available carrier was HMS *Furious*, but this had been committed to the preparations for 'Torch'. Moreover, the only immediately available Spitfires were also assigned to the air support of 'Torch'. Consequently, a second meeting was convened later that day with Churchill presiding and General Eisenhower, the 'Torch' Supreme Commander, in attendance.[23] Portal again explained that Malta's fighter defences 'would be reduced to a dangerously low level in the near future', and said that *Furious* could sail on 18 October and fly off her Spitfires on about the 26th. General Eisenhower raised no objection to the release of HMS *Furious* and the requested Spitfires 'as long as this did not mean any shortage of carriers for future operations'. He did, however, express some concern about any further diversion of Spitfires allocated to 'Torch'. HMS *Furious* was consequently loaded with twenty-nine Spitfires, and these safely arrived at Malta in Operation 'Train' on 29 October. By then, as noted above, the latest – and last – concentrated German air attack on the island had been called off. This was also the last of many successful, and indispensable, deliveries of fighters to Malta by the Royal Navy.

While the latest air battle was being fought out in Malta's skies, Admiral Pound told his fellow Chiefs on 20 October that a decision was now required about HMS *Welshman*'s passage to Malta. Should she be loaded with food or aviation spirit? The COS were not clear about the level of the remaining stocks of petrol, given the greater consumption during the current air attacks, and they cabled Malta for the latest figures. However, the point was made that 300 tons of food would amount to only about 1–2 days' supply of the island's needs, whereas 300 tons of petrol would provide a one-week extension of the petrol reserves. Provisionally, therefore, the COS thought that *Welshman* should carry fuel. However, they reversed this decision on the following day when Malta signalled that petrol reserves were significantly higher than the COS had thought.[24]

These decisions, unfortunately, provoked an angry signal from the Governor, as Churchill's papers reveal. On 22 October, Lord Gort cabled the COS to say that he was unable to carry out the instructions set out in their cable of the previous day about the use of petrol stocks. His signal began: 'Have not the advantage of knowing on what information your review is based unless perchance it was the outcome of A.877 of 20/10 Personal to CAS from AOC Med. [i.e. Park]'. He ended this cable by writing:

> It has always been my constant care to eke out our dwindling resources to the best advantage of Malta and the war effort in the Mediterranean, and unless specifically ordered to do so, I do not feel I can conscientiously discharge the instructions contained in OZ. 1621 [the COS cable of 21 October]. If I am failing to carry out the civil and military administration of this island in these critical times to the complete satisfaction of the Chiefs of Staff, I trust I may be informed as a matter of urgency in what direction they consider I should re-orientate my policy.

Only a former CIGS could have written such an angry signal to the COS. Disturbed by this, Churchill at once wrote on his copy of Gort's signal: 'Gen Ismay. I should like to discuss this with the COS before any reply is sent.' However, the COS had already replied to the Governor in a cable which, in an attempt to pacify him, concluded: 'We are quite content, however, to leave the matter to you.' When, on 23 October, Ismay reported all this to Churchill, he added: 'There is a background to Lord Gort's telegram which Lord Munster mentioned to me yesterday, and which I feel I ought to explain to you when convenient.' On this minute Churchill wrote 'Tell me'. A week later, Ismay sent a note to John Martin, Churchill's Private Secretary, which said: 'You will wish to know that I explained the position to the Prime Minister last night and therefore that this case has been disposed of.'

There being no record of what Ismay told the Prime Minister, we can only surmise about the matter. There seems little doubt, however, that an underlying antipathy between the Governor and the AOC, AVM Park, had caused this outburst. Gort had earlier complained that he was not being shown important Air Ministry signals to Park, and they frequently disagreed about the use of the severely limited petrol stocks. Protests by the Governor had led Portal to order the cessation of offensive fighter sweeps over Sicily, and later, as we have seen, to order that weekly consumption be reduced from 200 tons to 150 tons. Park's biographer, Vincent Orange, goes further by suggesting that Gort 'nourished a bitter resentment of the RAF for its failures, as he saw them, during the French campaign of 1940 and his relations with Park were, at best, tense'.[25] Gort also, in Orange's view, had a morbid fear of being taken prisoner and this led him to oppose all offensive air operations that consumed precious fuel. Park was a flamboyant, strongly opinionated airman who drew attention to himself by, for example, flying his own Hurricane, wearing white overalls, and in

Malta driving himself around in a bright red MG sports car. Not for the first or last time in the war, the behaviour and mores of the upstart junior service elicited only frowns from senior members of the older services. Tedder in Cairo gave him his full backing, but when later he proposed to put Park in command of the Tactical Air Force supporting the 8th Army, he recorded: 'I did consider him very carefully for the command of the TAF. What surprised me was the adverse reaction I got from different directions and levels when I put abroad the report that Park was relieving Coningham.' He went on: 'Park has for the moment lost some of his ability to coordinate with other people and services.'[26] It is important to add, however, that when, after ten days of fierce fighting over Malta, Kesselring conceded defeat, recognising that he had met a master in the art of aerial fighting, among the many messages of congratulation that Park received one of the warmest was from the Governor.

On a less controversial note, the Governor signalled to Churchill and the Colonial Secretary on 26 October to describe conditions in Malta after the end of the latest 'blitz'. He reported that, in the month to 20 October, Malta had suffered 61 bombing raids, which had resulted in the death of 64 civilians and serious injury to another 63. Nevertheless, despite this severe human cost, the Governor was able to add that 'from the outset of the new phase of attacks, it has been clear that the spirit of resistance has not fallen during the lull of the previous few months'. Two days later Churchill replied:

> Following Personal and Secret from Prime Minister to General Gort.
> Prime Minister's Personal Telegram T. 1385/2.
>   1. Your 517. All our main plans are working out steadily. The prospects of TORCH encountering only weak opposition have sensibly improved. The battle in Egypt has opened well.
>   2. The work you are doing in animating the magnificent resistance of the Island and its effective intervention on the enemy's line of communications commands general admiration.
>   3. Your name will be submitted to the King for promotion to the rank of Field Marshal in the New Year Honours List. Every good wish.

Gort replied on the following day. 'Thank you so much for your OZ 1688 of 28/10. I am most grateful for your encouraging and appreciative message and also for the indication in paragraph 3 which was wholly unexpected.' However, another letter from the Governor caused Churchill and Cranborne some perplexity. Gort had written to Cranborne on 18 October – in the middle of the air onslaught – setting out his early thoughts about the post-war reconstruction of Malta. Cranborne forwarded a copy of this letter to the Prime Minister with a note saying that he was not sure how to respond. On this note Churchill wrote: 'I don't wonder you are puzzled. For my part I am going to get on with the war.'

On the evening of 23 October, Churchill read a telegram from General Alexander. This simply said: 'Zip'. This was the code word they had agreed to signal the beginning of Montgomery's attack at El Alamein, Operation 'Lightfoot', when over 1,000 guns laid down the heaviest barrage so far seen in the desert war. The course of this hard-fought battle has attracted numerous accounts, and it was not until 4 November that Alexander was able to signal:

> After twelve days of heavy and violent fighting the Eighth Army has inflicted a severe defeat on the German and Italian forces under Rommel's command. The enemy's front has been broken, and British armoured formations in strength have passed through and are operating in the enemy's rear areas.

In reply Churchill sent his warmest congratulations, and told Alexander that, as soon as 20,000 prisoners had been taken, he would order the church bells throughout Britain to be rung for the first time in the war.[27]

The contribution that Malta's air and naval forces made to this notable victory may be briefly told.[28] The first benefit to General Montgomery was the absence from North Africa of many German and Italian aircraft that Kesselring had withdrawn in his last attempt to neutralise Malta. This allowed Montgomery to complete his final preparations under a comprehensive Allied air umbrella. Moreover, many of the Axis aircraft assigned to the attack on Malta did not return to the desert until several days after Operation 'Lightfoot' had begun. However, Malta's principal value was the continued attack on Rommel's supply lifeline across the Mediterranean, and it was noted earlier that Park's bomber aircraft continued to fly throughout the October blitz. In the month of September, Malta's forces sank six merchant ships, of which three were accounted for by 10th Flotilla submarines, two by aircraft, with one shared between them. In October a further ten ships were sunk, seven by submarines, one by aircraft, with two shared. As a result, although in September the Axis forces received a total of 77,500 tons of supplies, including 31,000 tons of fuel, these figures fell to 46,700 and 12,300, respectively, in October. The loss of fuel was particularly damaging since it limited Rommel's ability to manoeuvre his armoured divisions to meet Montgomery's varied thrusts. Rommel was later to write: 'In the period from 6th September to 23rd October the battle of supplies was waged with new violence. At the end of the period it had been finally lost by us and won by the British – by a wide margin.'[29] Although aircraft and submarines operating from Egypt also participated in these convoy attacks, the statistics make

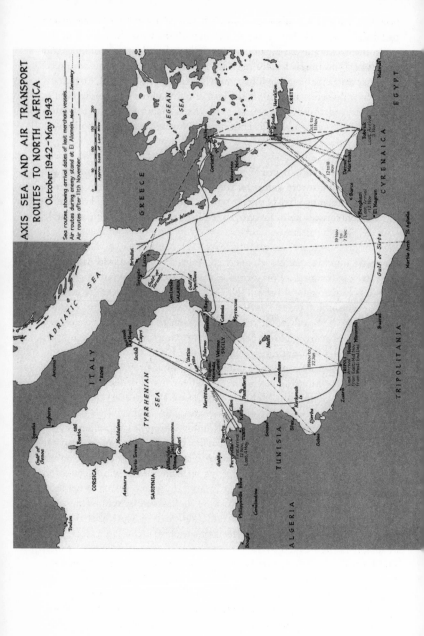

AXIS SEA AND AIR TRANSPORT ROUTES TO NORTH AFRICA
October 1942–May 1943

Sea routes, showing arrival dates of last merchant vessels. ———
Air routes during enemy stand at El Alamein. ·········
Air routes after 11th November. — · — ·

Approx. Scale of Land Miles
0   50   100   150   200

clear the value of Malta's contribution. Taking the five months from June to October as a whole, 24 of the 45 enemy merchant ships sunk in the central Mediterranean fell to Malta's forces, despite the critical shortages of fuel and food, which have been narrated in this and earlier chapters. Many other ships were damaged or delayed and thus unable to deliver their cargoes when needed. It should be emphasised that these results were achieved without the assistance of any surface warships at Malta. Rommel fully recognised all this when he wrote: 'Malta has the lives of many thousands of German and Italian soldiers on its conscience.'[30]

While this fierce fighting was taking place at El Alamein, Malta's stocks of food, essential supplies and petrol continued to fall, and the deadline for their exhaustion steadily approached. Nevertheless, the ships for east and west relief convoys were being assembled and loaded. The desert victory in early November held out the possibility that air protection could be provided for an eastern convoy, and a western convoy would be helped if the 'Torch' landings were quickly successful. Malta's survival depended, therefore, upon the success or failure of these two convoys, and to see how these events unfolded we must open a new chapter.

MALTA RELIEVED AND OPERATION 'BREASTPLATE'

We cannot divest ourselves of responsibility for the convoy from the east for Malta.

Churchill minute to Chiefs of Staff, 12 November 1942

In no month of the war were the advantages and disadvantages of the British naval and air base at Malta more clearly seen than in November 1942. The island's value as an offensive base had been amply demonstrated in the second half of 1941, and again in the summer and autumn months of 1942. During these periods Malta's pressure on the Axis supply route to North Africa made a major contribution to British victories in the desert war. When that pressure was removed by violent air attack, Rommel's counter-offensives prospered. The offsetting disadvantage of the retention of Malta was the need to keep supplied a large civilian population and a growing military establishment with civilian and military goods, which could only be delivered by sea through waters dominated by the enemy. This sea passage had not proved too costly in 1941 but it was otherwise in 1942. The relief convoys that had sailed in March, June and August had suffered severe loss, and on each occasion the island's ability to continue the fight had only been extended by a few months. Food rations had, consequently, been cut to levels that steadily undermined the health of the people and garrison, and could not, in October, be sustained for much longer. In November, however, the two land campaigns being launched to clear North Africa urgently needed all the help that Malta's offensive forces could provide, but, paradoxically, that help could only be given if those campaigns – or at least one of them – were successful enough to allow Malta to be resupplied. In the following pages we will follow the course of events in order to see how Churchill and his military advisers, American as well as British, attempted to balance Malta's needs with those of the commanders in North Africa.

As the last chapter has shown, the need to relieve Malta's increasingly desperate food position, and to defeat Kesselring's renewed air assault on the island, were the prime concerns of Churchill and the COS in October.

However, during that month, too, the demands of the 'Torch' campaign also began to claim their attention. Churchill felt a special responsibility for this campaign, not merely because it signalled America's first active participation in the European theatre, but also because, over the strenuous opposition of the US Chiefs of Staff, he had persuaded President Roosevelt that North Africa was the only area in which British and US forces could fight the Germans in 1942. After General Eisenhower had been appointed as overall commander, Anglo-American planning moved forward, an elaborate process which Eisenhower later described as 'the transatlantic essay contest'. It seemed to the planners that Hitler would respond to the threat to Rommel's rear by sending forces to Tunisia through the ports of Tunis and Bizerta, only 100 miles from Palermo in western Sicily. Malta's forces were ideally placed to attack this new enemy sea route, just as they had since 1940 preyed on the Axis convoys sailing to Tripoli and Benghazi. Accordingly, as early as 19 September, Admiral Pound had signalled to Admiral Harwood at Alexandria and Admiral Leatham at Valletta, warning them:

> It will be essential to prevent or delay enemy reinforcements reaching Tunisia before we do. To this end operations will be necessary from Malta on greatest possible scale … Light surface forces from TORCH may be sent to operate from Malta if air situation permits.[1]

After consulting AVM Park, Leatham replied that Malta could find room for as many as 285 aircraft, depending on the availability of petrol, and that there was enough naval fuel to support a small surface force for a period. Admiral Harwood reported from Alexandria that a convoy of four ships for Malta was being loaded, and that the cargo would include 5,000 tons of petrol. The 10th Submarine Flotilla at Malta, he added, would be reinforced, but he asked that he be given early warning of required operations against the Tunisian route so that the necessary plans could be made and submarines be diverted from the Tripoli route.

With this information in hand, Pound then raised the matter of Malta's role in 'Torch' at the COS meeting on 29 September, when 'Malta – Offensive Operations in Conjunction with Operation TORCH' appeared for the first time on the COS agenda.[2] Perhaps to Pound's surprise, General Brooke told him that 'the examination of offensive operations from Malta had been shelved when it had been decided to limit the extent of the initial landings'. This was a reference to an earlier debate, resolved again by a Presidential order, the result of which was that the easternmost landing would be made at Algiers, 400 miles from Tunis, rather than at Bône, 200 miles further east, which Eisenhower had initially urged. Nevertheless, Brooke agreed that the Joint Planning Staff should consider the matter and present their recommendations.

The JPS analysis was presented to the COS at their meeting on 8 October.[3] The paragraphs dealing with possible air action from Malta made it clear that 'intensification of offensive action after TORCH has begun must depend on the extent to which supplies have reached Malta in the early part of November'. Naval operations, too, were linked to the relief convoy, which, it was then hoped, might arrive about the 'Torch' D-Day, which had been set for 8 November. This was in turn dependent upon the progress of Montgomery's 'Lightfoot' offensive, but if this proved slower than expected, it might be possible to send a small naval surface force to Valletta at about D+1. Nevertheless, the most intriguing and controversial part of the JPC report was the analysis of a request from Eisenhower's staff that Malta provide a brigade force of infantry for a possible landing at Sousse, a small port sixty miles south of Tunis, at about the same time as the main landings to the west. This was then referred to as Operation 'Breastplate'. There were at the time fourteen infantry battalions in Malta – out of which, it was considered, three might be spared – with artillery and engineer support. However, the JPC observed, these troops were not fit for sustained operations due to the effects of their limited rations in recent months, and they had no experience of, or training for, combined operations. There were no specialised landing craft in Malta, the troops could carry with them only limited supplies, and could not be resupplied from Malta after they had left. Unless, therefore, the 'Torch' land forces made a very rapid advance towards Tunis, the Malta force, even if it could be put ashore, could easily be eliminated by German or Vichy French forces.

It is not difficult to imagine what General Brooke thought of this hare-brained scheme, although he recorded no comment in his diary. But he, too, had strongly recommended the 'Torch' landings, and the need to support Eisenhower persuaded the COS to send him a guarded reply on 8 October. They told him that a brigade group would be made ready at Malta, but that this force could not be landed until the advance from Algiers had made sufficient progress to enable the Malta force to be resupplied and protected from the west. The COS then signalled the Middle East C-in-Cs and the Governor: 'We have informed General Eisenhower that a brigade group from Malta may be available to assist him in these later stages, the decision as to its availability resting with us.' The C-in-Cs replied by warning that such a force could not be made available before D+35. At their meeting on 15 October the Chiefs reviewed all these matters with Eisenhower's three Service Commanders, Admiral Cunningham, General Anderson, and Air Marshal Welsh.[4] Although Brooke explained the difficulties facing the landing of a Malta infantry force, Anderson nevertheless said that, as long as the French forces acquiesced, he would like a force to occupy Sousse by D+5/6. Accordingly, the Middle East C-in-Cs were, on the following day, requested to draw up plans 'for a sortie from Malta in the early days of

Operation TORCH'. When the C-in-Cs replied by signalling that no such force could be available before twenty-nine days after the launch of 'Torch', Churchill, who had followed this discussion closely, minuted to the COS: 'This is a very pessimistic forecast. What do you say?' The Chiefs agreed that this was pessimistic and advised the Prime Minister that planning in London was still proceeding on a D+5 assumption. These discussions, it should be remembered, were overshadowed at that time by the renewed air attack on Malta. As we have seen in the previous chapter, Churchill presided over a COS meeting on 17 October at which Eisenhower agreed to release Spitfire reinforcements for the island. Attention then switched on 23 October to the Alamein offensive, the early days of which involved fierce fighting and only limited progress.

On 22 October, hopes about the success of 'Torch' were raised as a result of an unusual and hazardous special operation. That night the British submarine HMS *P.219* landed the US General Mark Clark fifty miles west of Algiers. There he met General Mast, the French commander of the 19th Corps. Mast told Clark that, with four days' notice of the intended landings, he could guarantee that his forces would only offer token resistance, and he also guaranteed free entry into Bône. Clark told his story to Churchill and Brooke at a lunch at 10 Downing Street on 26 October, and Brooke made a lengthy entry in his diary, part of which deserves quotation:

> [Clark] went ashore in canvas boat and upset by surf on landing. Met by Murphy [American Minister in North Africa], French Staff Officers and later by commanding French General. All contacts most favourable and every chance of [French General] Giraud coming over! Meeting interrupted by police. Clark and his companions hid in wine cellar when one of them, a British captain, started coughing fit! Clark asked him if chewing gum would help him and gave him bit out of his own mouth!! After a bit the captain asked for more. Clark said he hoped he hadn't swallowed it. The captain said, 'No, but the bit you gave me has not got much taste!' Clark replied, 'That is not surprising, as I have been chewing it for two hours'!!! The party then had a desperate time getting back again and were nearly drowned, the boats being swamped repeatedly. However, trip was a great success.[5]

This encouraging news prompted Churchill to minute the COS: 'How does the question of the intervention of the Malta force in TORCH now stand? Evidently the prospects of this operation are much improved by what we have heard about the mission of the American Eagle.'[6] Clark's report also led Eisenhower to ask the COS to reconsider the 'Breastplate' operation; moreover, he now asked that he be given executive authority to order such a landing at Sousse. The COS again sought the views of the Middle East C-in-Cs, and after further discussions General Brooke told Eisenhower that the Malta force would be held at his disposal from D+5. Nevertheless, he reiterated that this force would have no transport, and that the troops would not be fighting fit. In addition, he pointed out, the force or its equivalent might, in an emergency, be required to return to Malta. Brooke further clarified the COS position at their meeting on 30 October when he insisted that 'Breastplate' could not be undertaken against opposition, but 'only in circumstances amounting to an invitation by the French'.[7] Eisenhower accepted this condition. The Commanders in Cairo were, nevertheless, worried by these undertakings to Eisenhower, protesting in a long cable of 29 October that the early removal of a brigade of troops from Malta would endanger the unloading of the relief convoy. They urged that these troops should not leave before this had been completed. However, when Churchill read his copy of this signal he wrote on it for the COS: 'They do not know about Eagle's visit yet. Let everything be prepared. We alone can settle when and if to use it.' Churchill also brought Gort fully into the picture by sending him the following telegram:

Following Private from Prime Minister to Lord Gort. 30/10/42.
  1. 'TORCH' is moving forward so far with complete secrecy and good fortune, and the date will be punctually kept.
  2. For yourself alone, an American General of high rank visited 'TORCH' area and held long conference with friendly generals. We have every reason to hope, and indeed believe, that very little opposition will be encountered and that powerful aid will be forthcoming. Thus events may move more rapidly – perhaps far more rapidly – than we had planned. Decisive reactions may be looked for in France. Nothing sinister has yet cropped up from Spain. We have no evidence that the enemy have any idea of what is coming and certainly not of its imminence or scale. Bear all this in mind when thinking about BREASTPLATE.[8]

While these awkward decisions about Operation 'Breastplate' were being debated, final arrangements for the Malta relief convoys were being made. On 29 October, the Middle East C-in-Cs were told that the eastern convoy, designated 'Stoneage', should be made ready to sail by 8 November. They were also instructed: 'If sailed, the convoy must be a first charge on the Air Forces and the requirements for operations ashore are to give way to its requirements.' As regards the western convoy, a difficulty arose at the end of October in finding the six slow ships required for the follow-up convoy. Sir Cyril Hurcomb, from the Ministry of War Transport, attended a COS meeting on 2 November to explain that only four slow ships could be made available, and even these would need to be withdrawn from the North Atlantic. Admiral Pound emphasised that the western convoys were essential since it was by no means certain that the eastern convoy would get through before Malta's supplies were exhausted. General Brooke argued that at least four slow ships must be found, and the COS agreed to refer the problem to the Prime Minister.[9] Churchill replied on the following day: 'Proceed as you propose. I have spoken to Lord Leathers [Minister of War Transport]. The four ships will cost 32,000 tons of imports.'

These preparations having been made, all eyes were drawn to the progress of the Alamein battle. In the last days of October anxiety had increased when there was a pause in the fighting while Montgomery regrouped his forces for a final assault. General Brooke noted in his diary on 29 October his difficulty in persuading an impatient Prime Minister that all was going to plan, although he later admitted that he, too, had some doubts about the outcome.[10] However, as we noted in the previous chapter, all anxieties were dispelled by Alexander's signal on 4 November that Rommel's forces were in full retreat. The loaded ships of the eastern convoy for Malta, with their naval escort, now waited for news that the 8th Army's advance had secured airfields from which the RAF could provide essential air cover.

A serious setback then arose, which, in the circumstances, was almost inevitable. The Anglo-American landings in French Morocco and Algeria had encountered some opposition but this was ended on 10 November when Admiral Darlan, the Vichy French Minister of Marine who happened to be visiting Algiers, ordered a ceasefire. What caused alarm, however, was the swiftly accumulating evidence that German and Italian reinforcements were being rushed into Tunisia, initially by air and, soon after, in increasing amounts by sea. In the early planning stage of 'Torch', the British Joint Intelligence Committee (JIC) had expressed the view that such reinforcements would be limited and slow to arrive, an estimate that Professor Hinsley later described as 'an under-estimate in every respect'.[11] In his view, a significant element in this misjudgement was a failure, on the part of trained, rational British Intelligence officers, to believe that Hitler might act 'irrationally' in opening another active front when German forces were under considerable strain in Russia and Egypt.

But Hitler in 1942 was driven by different strategic concepts. As soon as he heard of the landings in the early hours of 8 November, he immediately ordered Kesselring to send major air and ground forces to Tunisia, and the first aircraft arrived on the next day. Churchill and the COS soon had a full and accurate picture of this swift German reaction. Reports from French sources in Tunisia, supplemented by air reconnaissance photographs from Malta, showed the deployment of the air and ground forces flowing into Tunisia. In addition, GC&CS at Bletchley Park had been warned to expect a large volume of Enigma signals after 8 November and had made arrangements to process this information as quickly as possible. This process was hastened by the fact that the great majority of these signals were in the German air force series of ciphers or in the Italian C38m. Both these series had been most easily broken in the past. As a result, Churchill's daily buff dispatch boxes will have been filled with intercepted signals detailing the rapid Axis build-up in Tunisia. But it was not only with regard to the size and rapidity of this reinforcement that the Allies were wrong-footed. Contrary to their expectation that only second-line units could be made available, intercepted signals soon disclosed the presence of experienced formations. On 23 November, for example, it was revealed that the commander and HQ staff of the 10th Panzer Division had arrived in Tunis. Five days later the first components of this division, supported by the first of the new heavy 'Tiger' tanks, had been unloaded, and at once went into action. In the air, the strength of *Fliegerkorps II*, based in Sicily and Sardinia, rose from 283 aircraft in October to 445 in mid-November, including some FW 190 fighters that outclassed any aircraft in the Allied air forces. Equally important, the number of German transport aircraft available to Kesselring increased in the same period from 205 to 673, an achievement that Hinsley described as 'impressive, indeed astonishing'.[12]

As the early intelligence reports came in, which made clear the German intention to occupy Tunisia, the COS, on 11 November, discussed what assistance Malta might be able to give.[13] Since Montgomery's advance into Cyrenaica was by now gathering momentum, the Chiefs hoped that the vital airfields near Derna on the north-west bulge of Cyrenaica might be captured within a few days. They therefore signalled to the Middle East C-in-Cs, as follows:

> It is important that Malta take maximum air action against German forces in Tunisia at once. Extent to which they can afford to use up their fuel depends on date of arrival of convoy from your end. Please give us earliest date to which it would be safe for Malta to work.

The C-in-C's reply came in later that day. After noting their intention to sail the convoy on 15 November, they went on: 'It is not possible to give safe date for Malta to work on as Italian fleet may intervene, but we hope convoy will arrive 19th.' On his copy of this telegram Churchill circled the word 'may' and then wrote at the bottom: '1SL. What is being done to guard against this? In view of rapid advance into Libya we ought not unduly sacrifice too many merchant ships.' The COS had the Cairo reply before them at their meeting on 12 November. They were confident that the convoy would not sail before supporting airfields had been secured. But with regard to the air support to be given to the 'Torch' landings, they took the view, after hearing from Portal about the level of the remaining petrol stocks at Malta, that they should leave it to the Governor to decide on the level of Malta's air activity.

Churchill disagreed with this decision and later that day sent the COS a detailed minute, which merits quotation in full:

PM Personal Minute D.196/2

Chiefs of Staff Committee   ACTION THIS DAY

We cannot divest ourselves of responsibility for the convoy from the east for Malta. If it is to sail on the 15th, what arrangements are made to protect it against surface attack by the Italian fleet? Is it to approach Malta in darkness or in daylight? What protection would it have against bombers from Crete, and generally until it gets under the Malta Air umbrella? This is no time to throw away four fast heavily-laden ships. Will the airfield at Derna be working by the time the convoy gets there? If it is not, we ought to wait a few more days till it is. The prospects in Cyrenaica are now so good that there is no need for forlorn, desperate ventures. Admiral Harwood should submit his scheme, showing exactly his daylight and darkness passage, and how he plans to get through.

2. It is of course of the utmost importance that Lord Gort should intervene by air in Tunisia. But I do not think we ought simply to leave the responsibility of using up his petrol to him. What view do the Chiefs of Staff take about the amount he should keep in hand?

3. It would seem that everything should be calculated from the date when the Derna airfield is effectively occupied.[14]

The COS discussed this minute on the following day and authorised Lord Gort to use some of the petrol being held in reserve for December operations. However, they took a more cautious view when, at the same meeting, they read a paper from the Ministry of War Transport requesting a reduction in the amount of shipping allocated to Malta convoys. The paper detailed the plans already agreed to deliver to Malta 170,000 tons of supplies, enough to last twelve months or at least six months if only 50 per cent got through. The COS, conscious of their many past anxieties about Malta, and the fact that the island's supplies would be exhausted within a few weeks, firmly rejected this request. The minutes recorded:

The Committee was emphatic that we were not yet in a position to relax any of the proposed measures for provisioning Malta. It was not a matter on which we could afford to take any chances. A degree of what might appear to be over-insurance was essential, and advantage must be taken of the longer winter hours of darkness to stock up Malta to an extent which would ensure that the anxieties and dangers of the last six months would not be repeated.

Churchill's copy of this minute is not in his Malta files, but it seems highly likely that it was marked with his large tick.

In previous chapters we have noted several attempts by the Admiralty to send single merchant ships to Malta, disguised as French or Spanish vessels. They tried again in November. From the east, the *Empire Patrol* sailed with 1,500 tons of mixed fuels, but was forced by engine defects to put into Famagusta in Cyprus for repairs. Since by that time the ship had been spotted by German air reconnaissance this attempt was then abandoned. Two smaller ships, the *Ardeola* and the *Tadorna*, both carrying foodstuffs, entered the Mediterranean via Gibraltar with the 'Torch' convoys. However, both were fired on by French coastal batteries off Bizerta and forced into port, where they were interned. Offsetting these failures was the arrival in early November of two large submarines with aviation petrol, and on 12 November of HMS *Manxman* from Alexandria. In Churchill's Malta papers is a brief note from John Martin, one of Churchill's Private Secretaries: 'PM. *Manxman* has arrived at Malta with 300 tons of food.' Her sister ship, HMS *Welshman*, arrived from Gibraltar on 18 November with a similar cargo of food, as the COS had agreed in October.[15] Meanwhile, Churchill and the COS received the news on the evening of 16 November that the four merchant ships of the 'Stoneage' convoy, with an escort of five cruisers and seventeen destroyers, had entered the Mediterranean and set course for Malta.

While further news of the convoy's progress was awaited in London, two other matters related to Malta claimed attention, both presenting the COS with a dilemma. At a COS meeting on 17 November, Admiral Pound read out a signal from Admiral Harwood seeking guidance about the future employment of his light forces. Pound's answer was that 'he thought it right to lay down that the duty of escorting convoys to Malta must have priority over any operations against enemy sea communications'. The Committee also reviewed a further telegram from Lord Gort warning that aviation petrol stocks would be exhausted within two weeks, but 'they agreed that the present policy was the right one'.[16] More disturbing was a telegram received the previous day from General Eisenhower, who had arrived in Algiers on 13 November. Eisenhower requested

> executive authority for ordering 'Breastplate' to be placed in the hands of the Allied Commander-in-Chief now in order that the full use might be made of this detachment, in co-ordination with the Eastern Task Force, to assist in the establishment of our forces in Tunisia.

The Prime Minister ordered that this telegram be referred to a meeting of the Defence Committee, which convened at 10.00 p.m. that evening. Brooke at once pointed out that the date suggested for this operation clashed with expected arrival of the 'Stoneage' convoy. If the Malta brigade were sent to Tunisia it would not be available to assist with the unloading of the convoy, a task which needed to be completed as quickly as possible because of the air threat. Moreover, the brigade would lack air cover in Tunisia, since all Malta's fighters would be committed to provide an air umbrella over the Grand Harbour. Churchill again intervened:

> The arrival and safe unloading of this convoy would be a big event for Malta whereas 'Breastplate' could not hope to do more than divert a few aircraft and the attention of the enemy for a short while from the Allied advance on Tunis. Due regard should be paid to the importance which was attached to the timely arrival of supplies and aviation petrol in Malta; Operation 'Breastplate' might prove to be too big a price to pay for a relatively small diversion of [German] air forces.

Without further discussion the Committee agreed that the help that 'Breastplate' could give to the Allied forces in Algeria was not 'commensurate with the risks', and, therefore, that no troops should be sent from Malta until the convoy had been safely unloaded. General Eisenhower was advised accordingly.[17]

There was then some confusion. Eisenhower understood that he would be given authority to order 'Breastplate' as soon as the 'Stoneage' relief convoy had arrived at Malta, and it took another meeting of the COS and another telegram to correct this misinterpretation. It was explained to Eisenhower that there were, in the Chiefs' view, four essential prior conditions to the launching of Operation 'Breastplate'. These were that the Malta convoy should have been safely unloaded; that the port of Sousse be free of enemy troops; that the troops would receive a friendly reception; and that air cover be provided. On his copy of this signal Churchill first wrote: 'We should tell him it is off', but he then deleted this when he read a later telegram to Lord Gort reassuring him that 'Breastplate' remained under COS control.

Eisenhower nevertheless persisted. On 19 November, he accepted that 'Breastplate', as originally envisaged, should be cancelled, but he then advised the COS that General Anderson, Commander of the 1st Army, planned to advance on Bizerta and Tunis on 22 November. 'It would be a great help,' Eisenhower continued, 'if you could land even one battalion group at or in vicinity of Sousse on the day of Anderson's advance ... If you carry out this operation a small body of paratroops will be dropped [at] Sousse prior to arrival of ships to indicate friendly reception or otherwise.' He also promised air cover, and asked if this revised plan was acceptable in principle. Although the records do not reveal the reaction of the COS to this latest proposal, it is safe to assume that it was with considerable exasperation that the Chiefs once more sought the Governor's views. It was scarcely surprising that Lord Gort, in reply, rejected a scheme that must have seemed to him even more hazardous than the earlier plan. He did not feel that the landing at Sousse of one battalion 'will do much to further the initial phases of the attack by General Anderson', and 'would not cause the enemy serious concern or encourage whole-hearted support of the French in this area'.

This left the COS caught between their obvious dislike – to put it no more strongly – of Eisenhower's latest request, and their broader wish to support the Allied commander in this first Anglo-American campaign. They therefore sought the Prime Minister's decision. On 20 November, they sent him a draft telegram to Eisenhower which indicated that 'if, in spite of hearing our views, he still wants this small diversion, he should have discretion to arrange it direct with the Governor'. On the file copy of this telegram is the notation: 'PM approved attached telegram by phone from Chequers.' It must have occasioned much relief in London and Valletta when, on 22 November, Eisenhower signalled: 'All idea of assistance from Malta by modified Breastplate will be abandoned.' The last word on this muddled and ill-considered venture came in a minute that Churchill addressed to General Brooke on 5 December after it had become clear that the Germans were mounting a strong resistance to the Allied advance towards Bizerta and Tunis.

> It seems to me in view of what has happened that Lord Gort was right not to do the SOUSSE operation … What sort of position would we have been in now if he had acted as was suggested by Eisenhower?[18]

There is no record of Brooke's reply.

The tangled history of the 'Breastplate' operation has been recounted here at some length although, since it was never undertaken, it attracted only a footnote in the official history. It nevertheless demonstrates in the context of this study how closely Churchill followed these protracted discussions. Although he initially favoured the plan as part of his overall support for Eisenhower, his views changed when he became aware that not only would the proposed force make little or no impact on the military situation in Tunisia, but also that Malta's escape from the threat of looming starvation might be jeopardised by the withdrawal of these troops.

On 17 November, attention in London was firmly fixed on the four-ship 'Stoneage' convoy, which was now at sea. It is curious that this convoy, just as vital as the August 'Pedestal' convoy, since the island had only two or three weeks' of supplies left, has received only passing notice in many accounts of the Mediterranean war. Part of the reason, no doubt, is that the later convoy arrived safely, with only one seriously damaged warship, whereas 'Pedestal' suffered severe loss in conditions, which were highly dramatic and were given, then and later, wide publicity. Nevertheless, the 'Stoneage' convoy faced the same hazards as 'Pedestal' and the earlier eastern convoy in June. As we have seen, Kesselring had strongly reinforced the German air forces in Sicily, while the Italian navy still possessed the battleships that had compelled the abandonment of the eastern convoy, Operation 'Vigorous' in June. To meet these capital ships Admiral Harwood could only deploy 6-inch and 5.25-inch cruisers and destroyers. It was widely recognised that these Axis advantages could only be countered if adequate air protection could be given from airfields in Cyrenaica, and this in turn depended on the progress of the 8th Army's advance.

On 17/18 November, the convoy kept close to the African shore under the cover of RAF fighter squadrons whose bases moved forward closely behind the advance units of the 8th Army. On the evening of the 18th, the convoy was subjected to several torpedo-bomber attacks. None of the merchant ships was hit but the cruiser HMS *Arethusa* was severely damaged and had 155 members of her crew killed and many others wounded. During the night of 18/19 November, the convoy steered north-west for Malta and by dawn on the 19th was under the cover of Malta's long-range fighters. The Italian navy made no attempt to intercept the convoy, hampered, it seems, by lack of information about its progress. It may also have been deterred by the threat posed by the increased number of torpedo-bombers and submarines based at Malta. Moreover, the German and Italian torpedo boats, which had sunk five ships of the 'Pedestal' convoy, were unable to operate in the rougher November open seas as the convoy approached Malta from the south-east. Nevertheless, the failure of the Italian cruisers and battleships even to attempt an interception of this critical convoy must be considered a major missed opportunity. The ships all received a vociferous welcome as they berthed in the Grand Harbour at about 3.00 a.m. on 20 November and unloading began at once.

Churchill was kept in touch with these events by the Admiralty, and there is in his papers a memorandum from Leslie Rowan, one of his Private Secretaries, on 19 November advising him: 'The Duty Captain Admiralty informed me that if all the Malta convoy gets in safely food supplies will be secured till the end of January and petrol for an additional five months.' His military advisers also watched closely. On 19 November, General Brooke noted in his diary: 'COS mainly concerned with support Malta could be expected to give operations directed against Tunis. All dependent on convoy to Malta arriving safely and being unloaded.' On the following day he wrote: 'Malta convoy of 4 ships arrived safely, thank God. This puts the island safe again for a bit.' However, the consequences of the unavoidable delay in resupplying Malta caused him to add: 'Attacks against Tunis and Bizerta not going as fast as I should like, and reinforcements of Germans and Italians arriving fairly freely.'[19] The minutes of the COS meeting, held that morning, record Portal as saying:

> With the safe arrival of the supply ships, attention of the Middle East should be drawn to the need for the air forces at Malta to assist to the utmost in the battle for Tunisia by preventing enemy reinforcements reaching there and by assisting land operations.[20]

Despite this recognition of the need for urgent air operations from Malta against the enemy's Tunisian supply route, the COS held to their earlier resolution that further convoys must be sailed to the island to remove any possibility that yet another crisis might arise in three months' time. Consequently, when, on 24 November, Sir Cyril Hurcomb from the Ministry of War Transport asked the COS once again for the release of some of the twenty-three ships loaded with supplies for Malta, he was told that none could for the present be released from this commitment. The Chiefs were unanimous that if these twenty-three ships could be got through, the Ministry would be 'free of this embarrassing commitment for some time to come'.[21] Preparations, therefore, continued for the next eastern convoy, Operation 'Portcullis', comprising four fast merchant ships and another American tanker. These ships, carrying a total of 29,000 tons of mixed cargo, arrived without loss on the morning of 5 December. Later that morning, Churchill read a copy of a telegram from Admiral Harwood at Alexandria reporting the convoy's arrival, but also requesting that it be given no publicity lest it attract enemy attention to Operation 'Quadrangle'. Puzzled, Churchill wrote on this message, 'When and what is Quadrangle?', to which Admiral Pound replied that this was the code name for the plan to dispatch a further six slow ships during the December dark period.

Before we end this chapter and return to Malta's part in the final campaign to clear the enemy from North Africa, it will be appropriate to describe one other matter that arose during this period, and which is documented in Churchill's Malta files. This demonstrates another aspect of Churchill's concern for the people of Malta. This was the question of payment for war damage, which, by the autumn of 1942, had reached a level that reminded General Brooke, when he briefly visited the island in August 1942, of the devastation in Flanders in the First World War.[22] In Chapter V we noted that Churchill in January 1941 pressed the Chancellor of the Exchequer to include Malta in legislation that was about to be introduced to cover war damage in Britain. However, he was persuaded then, when the war situation was highly uncertain, to approve a more general statement that the British Government would meet the cost of repairing war damage in Malta that could not reasonably be met locally.

There matters rested until August 1942 when, during his visit to the Middle East, he had a long conversation with Lord Gort in Cairo about Malta. He asked the Governor to give him a note about these discussions and upon his return to London he sent a copy of Gort's note with the following minute to Lord Cranborne, the Colonial Secretary, on 27 August:

> I asked Lord Gort to give me some notes on the points he raised in conversation and I shall be glad to know what action you feel able to take on these suggestions, all of which seem modest and desirable.[23]

Some of Gort's suggestions related to post-war town planning, the need to expand education facilities, and propaganda, subjects on which he sought expert help from Britain. But his first point read:

> 1. War Damage Bill
> Malta only able to pay up about £770,000 and present re-building estimate about £6,000,000 (excluding clearing debris and ground).
> Colonial Office have been asked to ascertain whether HM Government will give a guarantee now to defray the extra cost when peace comes.

Churchill first discussed this with Cranborne on 2 September and the Colonial Secretary then promised a written reply after consulting his officials. This report, when it came, disappointed Churchill. Cranborne began by writing: 'I was myself strongly inclined to take the view you took that the Governor's request should be conceded, in view of the very special position of Malta, the extent to which it has been exposed to enemy attack and the services which it has rendered to the Empire by its resistance.' He then continued, however, by pointing out several difficulties. These centred largely on the problem that, if the Government gave a guarantee to Malta, other war-torn colonies, such as Malaya, would see this as a precedent to support their own claims. The Government's future liabilities might then become impossibly large. Cranborne then irritated the Prime Minister by sending a copy of this response to the Chancellor of the Exchequer, Kingsley Wood. Churchill replied as follows:

> I have a very clear opinion that the case of Malta is unique and that, on account of its superb exertions and shattering damage, the Imperial Government should assume responsibility for building it up.
>
> I do not know why you wanted to get the Chancellor of the Exchequer inclined against the proposal by sending him a copy of your minute before you had discussed it with me.

Cranborne defended himself by arguing that if he had not sent the copy to the Chancellor he would have been accused of 'trying to fix things up with you behind his back'. The Chancellor, predictably, argued against a guarantee, and suggested instead 'a general undertaking of specially generous assistance'. Cranborne and Wood, under the weight of the Prime Minister's disapproval, then worked out a proposal, which Kingsley Wood put before the Prime Minister in a minute dated 5 October. 'Our proposal,' the Chancellor wrote, 'is that Parliament should be invited immediately to vote a sum of £10,000,000 for the restoration of war damage and the rebuilding of Malta.' He went on to write that, if this initial sum proved inadequate, the British Government would promise to provide any additional funds that could not be found from Malta's own resources. Churchill signified his consent to this plan by his initial, and on 10 November Kingsley Wood put this to the House of Commons for their approval. In the event, the amounts provided steadily rose to a total of £30,000,000.

Upon receipt of this news in Malta, the Governor sent Lord Cranborne a telegram on 11 November quoting a resolution that had been passed in the Council of Government. This read:

> The Council of Government tender their heartfelt thanks to His Majesty's Government for the generous free gift of £10,000,000 to enable us to restore barbaric damage inflicted on these islands by our enemies.
>
> This material appreciation of the trials we have undergone, coupled with assurance that further assistance will be provided if necessary, demonstrates to the people of Malta in the most forcible manner that our well-being is receiving the constant attention of His Majesty's Government.
>
> The victorious advance of the Eighth Army and the Forces of the United States of America will remove us before long from position of complete isolation in the forefront of battle and we trust and pray that Malta may be privileged to be the spearhead of the first thrust into Axis home territory.
>
> We take pride in reassuring the Motherland that with God's help the Union Jack and Maltese flag will still be flying proudly over the ruins of our historic monument when final victory is achieved.

Nine days later the 'Stoneage' convoy entered the Grand Harbour, lifting the anxiety about food supplies that had weighed so heavily since early October. Delivering a speech at a Lord Mayor's Luncheon at the Mansion House in London on 10 November, the Prime Minister struck a cautiously optimistic note. After describing the victory at Alamein and the successful 'Torch' landings, he told his audience: 'Now this is not the end. It is not even the beginning of the end. But it is, perhaps, the end of the beginning.'[24] With the safe arrival of the 'Stoneage' convoy on 20 November, the Governor and the people of Malta may have begun to share Churchill's rising optimism.

MALTA'S PART IN NORTH AFRICAN VICTORY

The first duty of the Navy for the next ten days is to stop the reinforcements to Tunisia.

Churchill minute to Admiral Pound, 6 December 1942

In the preceding chapter, attention was focussed on the measures taken by the COS and the Middle East C-in-Cs, prompted at times by a minute from the Prime Minister, to ensure the safe arrival and unloading of the 'Stoneage' convoy. Moreover, we have seen that Churchill and his military advisers were determined that further convoys should be sailed to Malta so that the desperate food shortages that had arisen in July and October should not happen again. Hence the Prime Minister's continuing interest in these subsequent convoys until, in early 1943, he was assured that Malta was safe.

Nevertheless, the delayed arrival of the 'Stoneage' relief ships on 20 November had unfortunate consequences. For, as we have also noted, Hitler responded to the news of the 'Torch' landings on 8 November by ordering an immediate and substantial transfer of German and Italian army and air force units to Tunisia. Kesselring and his staff carried out these orders with speed and skill, and the Allied commanders in London and North Africa could only watch, through intercepted Enigma signals, while this Axis build-up gathered momentum. It was particularly frustrating that Malta's air and naval forces, ideally placed to attack this new supply route, were prevented from doing so by the shortage of fuel and the need to protect the approaching relief convoy. It was only after the arrival of the convoy on 20 November that the need for action in Tunisia became imperative. This required a major reorganisation of Malta's air forces, and the move to Valletta of a naval surface force. Although both proceeded concurrently, we will look, firstly, at the RAF redeployment, before turning to the Admiralty's orders.

Portal had already, on the day the convoy arrived in the Grand Harbour, reminded his fellow Chiefs of 'the need for the Air Forces at Malta to assist to the utmost in the battle for Tunisia', and two days later they telegraphed the Middle East C-in-Cs as follows:

1. It is evident that that if the First and Eighth Armies are to achieve speedy and decisive victory the object of prime importance at the present time must be the stoppage of sea-borne supplies to Tunisia and Tripolitania.

2. It is also clear that air power can only make its full contribution to this object in the immediate future if Malta with its limited airfield capacity is exploited to the utmost extent as an offensive base from which shipping at sea and ports of disembarkation can be attacked.

3. We suggest that first priority at Malta should be given to Torpedo Bombers particularly those able to operate by night and request you to consider the immediate move of your two Albacore squadrons and a Beaufort squadron to Malta

4. We should like to hear from you as soon as possible how you propose to use the full capacity of the Malta airfields to achieve the object stated in paragraph 1.

At the foot of his copy of this signal, Churchill simply wrote 'Good'.[1]

The C-in-Cs in reply said that more Albacore torpedo-bombers would be sent to Malta, the first six of which would leave at once. They warned, however, that Beaufort torpedo-bombers could not safely operate against the Axis convoys to Tunisia by day since they would face superior German fighter aircraft. The Beauforts were subsequently sent away to make room for more Wellington bombers, the number of which soon rose to thirty-six, the maximum Malta could accommodate. After these re-dispositions, AVM Park commanded a force which comprised (a) Spitfires and Beaufighters for local air defence and ground attacks on enemy bases in Sicily; (b) several squadrons of Albacores, Swordfish and Wellington torpedo-bombers for night attacks on shipping, and mine laying; (c) thirty-six Wellington medium bombers for night attacks on targets in Tunisia, Tripolitania and Italy; and (d) a variety of aircraft, including at the end of December a squadron of Mosquitos, for photo-reconnaissance. On 8 December, Churchill, in order to meet an urgent request from General Eisenhower, gave his approval for two Wellington squadrons to be released from Bomber Command for service in Algeria. During November, both Park and Tedder flew to Algeria to co-ordinate air operations, but it was not until February 1943 that Tedder was given overall command of all North African and Middle East air forces.

In the planning for 'Torch' it had been decided that naval operations in the Mediterranean should be split between two commands. As a result, Admiral Harwood, C-in-C Mediterranean, based at Alexandria, controlled all naval operations to the east of a line between Cape Bon in Tunisia to the western tip of Sicily. To the west, Admiral Cunningham, recalled from a staff appointment in Washington, became Eisenhower's naval commander with the title 'Allied Naval Commander, Expeditionary Force' (NCXF). At the time of the 'Torch' landings, the only naval units at Malta were the U-class submarines of the 10th Flotilla under the command of Captain Simpson, reinforced by other boats from Gibraltar and Alexandria. His initial task was to prevent any interference with the 'Torch' convoys by the Italian fleet, and it was only after this threat failed to materialise that Captain Simpson was ordered to redeploy his boats to attack the new supply route to Tunisia.[2]

At a Defence Committee meeting held on 23 November, the minutes recorded: 'The Prime Minister enquired what the Admiralty proposed to do to interrupt with surface ships based on Malta the Axis convoys to Tunis and Bizerta.'[3] There had not been any Royal Navy surface warships based at Malta since the last units of Force K had been withdrawn in March as the early 1942 blitz on Malta intensified. Prior to that, however, the destructive power of a force of cruisers and destroyers, guided to their targets by C38m intercepts and ASV Wellingtons, had been demonstrated on several occasions. Churchill had pressed hard for the earlier deployments and it was understandable that he should now urge the establishment of another such force.

On this occasion, however, Admiral Pound had anticipated the Prime Minister. On the previous day he had sent signals to Admirals Cunningham and Harwood asking to be informed of their plans to attack the enemy's supply routes to Tripoli and Tunisia. Moreover, in his signal to Harwood he specifically asked him to consider sending to Malta, in advance of the next Malta convoy, Operation 'Portcullis', a force of two cruisers and four destroyers. While awaiting their replies he was able to tell the Prime Minister at the Defence Committee meeting:

> The placing of surface ships at Malta was closely bound up with the running of the next convoy to Malta from the Eastern Mediterranean. The Admiralty had suggested to Admiral Harwood that he might send ahead of the convoy half of the force which would otherwise escort it, so that operations from Malta might begin earlier.

The Admirals' replies came in on the following day.[4] Cunningham signalled: 'It is my intention to base a light force at Bône as soon as efficient fighter protection for the port by day can be provided. It is hoped that this may be within the next few days.' Harwood, for his part, reported that the 'Portcullis' convoy was expected to sail on 1 December with a large naval escort, but he added that he could send ahead an advance force of two cruisers and four destroyers on 25 November. This force would be able to protect the convoy as it approached Malta and would then remain there. The Admiralty accepted this proposal and this new Force K arrived at Valletta on 27 November. Three days later, Force Q was constituted at Bône with a further three cruisers and two destroyers. The results of this naval reinforcement were quickly demonstrated. On the night of 1/2 December, Force Q, guided by an ASV Wellington from Malta, sank a convoy of four merchant ships and one of the escorting Italian destroyers sixty miles north-east of Bizerta. On the following night Force K sank another ship off the west coast of Tunisia.

The Axis response to these losses was immediate and effective – night sailings to Tunisia were suspended, and the convoys crossed the 100 miles between Sicily and Tunisia by day under a strong German fighter umbrella. Faced with this change of tactics, Cunningham at once warned the Admiralty of the need to compel the enemy, by heavy air attack, to resume night crossings. 'Otherwise,' he continued, 'he will do so by day unhampered unless we are prepared to throw away Cruisers and Destroyers in what will undoubtedly be a vain attempt to stop him.'[5] Churchill found copies of all these signals in his daily dispatch boxes and on 6 December sent the following minute to Admiral Pound:

Prime Minister to First Sea Lord   6 December 1942

Apparently, from the attached telegram, Admiral Harwood is going to use *Orion* and seven destroyers to convoy back empty merchant ships from Malta to Alexandria, after which the escort will return to Malta. But this is the week of all others when the Malta surface force must strike upon the communications of the Axis forces in Tunis. A week or ten days later will be too late. Infinite harm will be done and the whole battle compromised.

2. This also is the time for Admiral Cunningham to use his cruisers and destroyers, even at heavy risk, against enemy convoys. These vessels could never play so useful a part as in stopping the reinforcements of the enemy during the battle. The first duty of the Navy for the next ten days is to stop the reinforcements to Tunisia. This duty should be discharged even at a heavy cost.[6]

General Eisenhower had also been pressing for heavier air and sea attacks on the Tunisian convoys, and the whole problem was discussed again by the COS on 7 December.[7] In his diary for that day, General Brooke wrote:

Situation in North Africa none too good. Eisenhower far too busy with political matters connected with Dakar and Boisson. Not paying enough attention to the Germans, who are making far too much progress and will now take a great deal of dislodging out of Tunis and Bizerta.[8]

Two days later, Admiral Pound replied to the Prime Minister's minute. He passed on Cunningham's reservations about daylight attacks by Force Q on the heavily escorted convoys, adding that if such attacks were attempted, 'it is hardly to be expected that Force Q will arrive at Bône without serious loss or damage'. He concluded by warning Churchill that 'two convoys might be stopped at cost of whole of Force Q. There are no ships for another.'⁹ At the foot of this minute Churchill wrote: '1SL. Thank you for your full explanation of the difficulties. I trust they may be overcome.'

Despite these strenuous efforts to increase the interruption of the Axis convoys to Tunisia, the balance of advantage lay with the enemy during the last two months of 1942. In November the Italian navy landed 34,000 tons of supplies at Tunis and Bizerta without any loss. In December a further 60,000 tons arrived, although 29 per cent of the goods shipped were lost. In the same month 63,000 tons of supplies were safely unloaded in Tripoli, after losses of 26 per cent. During November Malta's air and naval forces sank nine merchant ships, aggregating 27,000 tons, and in December more than doubled these figures to twenty ships of 63,000 tons. In a minute of 5 January 1943 addressed to the COS and General Eisenhower, Churchill judged that the enemy were losing about one third of their supplies at sea.¹⁰ Admiral Pound thought at the time that this claim was somewhat exaggerated, but post-war figures reveal that the Prime Minister's estimate was close to the truth. Nonetheless, the steady flow of men and material to Tunisia, across the relatively short sea crossing to well-equipped ports, enabled the German General Nehring in early December to throw back a weak Allied thrust for Tunis. Torrential rain then brought ground operations to a standstill. As Churchill later wrote: 'There now came a definite check and setback in North Africa.'¹¹

While his commanders sought answers to these dangers and difficulties, Churchill found time to congratulate Lord Gort upon his promotion to Field Marshal, signalling on 3 January 1943: 'Heartiest congratulations on peak promotion. Delighted to hear it. Pray you are now on top and frowns of Fortune all passed.'¹² However, in a rare breakdown in staff work, Churchill had not been told that General Gort had just returned to London for urgent medical attention. He did not return to Malta until March, and Admiral Leatham, the Vice-Admiral Malta, was appointed as Acting-Governor.

Churchill and the COS now made preparations for a conference at Casablanca, at which the President and the Prime Minister, accompanied by their military advisers, and joined by the local commanders, concerted Allied plans for 1943 and beyond. The original intention was that Stalin should also attend, but when he declined to leave Russia, Roosevelt and Churchill decided to meet without him. Churchill flew to North Africa on 12 January and Roosevelt arrived two days later. The principal decision with a bearing on Malta was their agreement to continue the Allied offensive in the Mediterranean theatre, after the clearance of Tunisia, by invading Sicily. For Operation 'Husky', Malta would clearly be an advance base. After the conference ended, Churchill persuaded President Roosevelt to spend another two days with him at Marrakech where, together, they watched the sunset on the snow-covered Atlas Mountains. After Roosevelt left on 25 January, Churchill stayed a further two days there and painted the only canvas he attempted during the war; he later presented this to the President.[13]

Before returning to London, Churchill flew to Turkey in an attempt to persuade the Turkish government to enter the war against Germany. Having failed in this mission he flew back, via Cyprus, to Tripoli where he took the salute at a massed parade through the streets of the city. It was there that tentative plans were made for him to make a short visit to Malta, a story that he later recounted in his memoirs. Montgomery had made initial arrangements for him to fly to the island in a light aircraft with a fighter escort, but later persuaded Churchill that this would be too dangerous. The Prime Minister reluctantly bowed to this advice. He subsequently wrote: 'I am sorry for this, as I should have liked to have a memory of Malta while it was still in its struggle.'[14] On 8 February, Churchill flew back to London, and three days later gave the House a wide-ranging, two-hour review of the war situation. Shortly after that he was laid low by an attack of pneumonia and Lord Moran insisted that he give up, for a while, his strenuous daily work routine. It was only towards the end of the month that he resumed his full duties as Minister of Defence.

Throughout these months, Churchill had kept an eye on the continuing

23. Churchill at the Casablanca Conference in January 1943. At this conference, plans were agreed for the clearance of Tunisia and the Allied invasion of Sicily. With Churchill (from left to right) are: Anthony Eden, General Brooke, Air Marshal Tedder, Admiral Cunningham, General Alexander, General Marshall, General Eisenhower, and General Montgomery.

resupply of Malta. Just before leaving for Casablanca he read a report of 12 January about the arrival at Valletta of a further four freighters and a tanker, and at once asked, 'What cargo?' He was told that the ships carried 25,000 tons of general stores and enough food to last until the middle of June. Upon his return to London, news on 11 February of another six merchant ships prompted a further enquiry: 'General Ismay. What does this kit them up to?' Colonel Jacob replied that the island was now stocked up to late July and Churchill then wrote another minute on the subject: 'I presume it is intended to press on with the Malta convoys till the island is chock full. Let me know the future programme.' He was then sent copies of various signals that had been sent while he was in Africa. These gave details of the convoys planned until the end of March, after which, 'it is intended to keep up a steady flow so that the island will always be stocked up for at least six months ahead'. This reply, bearing Churchill's initial and date, '22/2', is the last enclosure in the lengthy 'Convoys' file in Churchill's Malta papers, which began in July 1941.[15] It provides abundant evidence of Churchill's concern for the sustenance of Malta throughout the worst period of the war in the Mediterranean. It also stands as a silent tribute to all those who manned the merchant ships and their escorts, many of whom lost their lives on the Malta convoys.

In his speech on 11 February, the Prime Minister told the House of new command arrangements in the North African theatre. As Rommel retreated into southern Tunisia, General Alexander was appointed as Deputy C-in-C to General Eisenhower, while Tedder became overall commander of all the air forces in the area. Admiral Cunningham took over responsibility for the whole of the Mediterranean. The COS decided, however, that Malta, for the present, should remain under the control of the Middle East C-in-Cs. The other Malta-related matter that came before the COS from February onwards was the role that the island should play in the invasion of Sicily. Admiral Pound presented a detailed note on the naval aspect of this on 14 February, which emphasised the need to repair the damaged dock facilities around the Grand Harbour.[16] The COS endorsed this report and signalled the Middle East C-in-Cs on 18 February:

1. We have been considering the part that Malta will be called upon to play in forthcoming operations and the importance of the Island as an advance base.

2. The Middle East Command will ensure that all preparations are made in the Island in accordance with the requirements of General Eisenhower's plan, and that work begins as soon as possible.

3. There will undoubtedly be competing claims by the three services for labour and resources such as fuel storage. The food situation should now permit of additional labour being drafted into Malta from the Middle East. Use of Tripoli as an advance base may help to overcome

the difficulty of fuel supply once operations have started.
4. General Eisenhower is asked to keep you particularly informed of the part that Malta will be required to play in the HUSKY plan.[17]

Specific instructions were then sent from Cairo to the Acting-Governor, Admiral Leatham.

By the end of February General Gort had completed his convalescence in London, and on 3 March he attended a meeting of the COS.[18] There he was brought up to date with the planning for 'Husky' and the preparations that had been ordered at Malta. He did not meet Churchill before he left England to return to Malta, but the Prime Minister sent him a message, which read, 'All good luck. All best wishes for good fortune.' In reply, Gort wrote: 'We look forward to the day when we can welcome you to Malta.'[19]

The defeat of the Axis forces in Tunisia took longer than Churchill and the COS had initially hoped, but the reinforcements that Hitler had ordered to the area had the advantage for the Allies of increasing the size of the surrendered forces when the end finally came on 12 May 1943. The story of these last months lies outside the scope of this study, but it should be emphasised that much of the damage done to the Axis convoys to Tunisia was the result of air and naval operations from Malta. Briefly, between January and May 1943, Malta's forces sank 57 ships, with an aggregate tonnage of 190,000 tons, equal to 45 per cent of the Axis shipping losses on the route described by the Italian navy as the *rotta del morte*. It was while Churchill was in Washington again on 13 May that he received a telegram from General Alexander stating:

Sir. It is my duty to report that the Tunisian campaign is over. All enemy resistance has ceased. We are masters of the North African shores.[20]

D-Day for the invasion of Sicily was set for 10 July, and in the weeks prior to that there was an unprecedented concentration of naval and air forces at Malta. Hundreds of landing craft and support ships of all sizes were moored in the island's harbours and creeks, and as many as thirty-five squadrons of fighters and bombers were flown in to the airfields. A new airfield to accommodate three US fighter squadrons was completed within seventeen days. One of the three invasion forces was to sail from Malta, and in the early days of July troops poured in from North Africa. These included the return of three battalions of the garrison, which had been sent to Egypt in March for specialised training. These formed the 231st Brigade, and they took the Maltese Cross as their brigade sign.[21] They were among the first troops to land in south-east Sicily. In the final few days, Generals Eisenhower, Montgomery and Alexander, and Admiral Cunningham established temporary headquarters in and around Valletta and Floriana. H-Hour for the landings was set at 2.45 a.m. on 10 July, and the assault proceeded despite last-minute anxieties about the deteriorating weather in the Sicilian Narrows. Churchill was at Chequers, where he stayed up all night playing cards with his daughter-in-law, Pamela. When first news came of the success of the landings he at once sent telegrams to Stalin and the Dominion Prime Ministers. Two days later, as the beachhead was consolidated, he cabled Eisenhower: 'It is a tremendous feat to leap on shore with nearly 200,000 men.'[22]

In the following weeks, events moved quickly. The capture of Sicily was signalled to Churchill on 17 August, when he was attending the Quebec Conference. Three weeks later, on 8 September, Mussolini was deposed and arrested. This date has a particular significance for the people of Malta, since it is celebrated as the day in 1565 when the Turks abandoned their attempt to conquer the island. On 8 September, too, the people of the harbour community of Senglea, 80 per cent of whose buildings lay in ruins, welcomed back, with great celebration, the statue of Our Lady, which had been kept for safe-keeping in Birkirkara. If anything further were needed to demonstrate to the people and garrison of Malta how much had changed since the grim days of 1942 it would have been the sight of the surrendered Italian fleet anchored in Maltese waters. For on 11 September, Admiral Cunningham was able to signal to the Admiralty: 'Be pleased to inform their Lordships that the Italian Battle Fleet lies at anchor under the guns of the fortress of Malta.' It was on the decks of HMS *Nelson* on 29 September that General Eisenhower, his Service Commanders, and Lord Gort watched while Marshal Badoglio signed the instrument of Italy's unconditional surrender.

With these formalities Malta's active part in the Mediterranean war may be said to have ended, and Churchill's special Malta files, upon which this narrative has so heavily drawn, come to a close. He had, as we have seen in these pages, followed the course of the fighting around and over Malta with constant care. As soon as Mussolini began the bombing of the island in June 1940, Churchill resolved that everything possible be done to defend and supply Malta. He saw this as a clear duty to people under British protection. But Churchill was also convinced that the island could, if properly equipped, play a significant part in the widening Mediterranean war. In the event, how much Malta's forces actually achieved might have surprised even him. Many of the advantages that the Allies derived from the possession of Malta have been discounted, if not wholly ignored. For example, for the RAF in 1940–1, Malta was a vital staging post for air reinforcements to the Middle East. It was also the only place from which reconnaissance aircraft could keep watch on enemy ports and the main units of the Italian fleet. Taranto was also a victory for Malta's reconnaissance aircraft. RAF bombers, operating from Luqa, dropped thousands of tons of high explosive on targets in Italy, Sicily and North Africa, while Fleet Air Arm Swordfish and Albacores laid hundreds of mines in and around enemy harbours. The island's fighters and AA gunners shot down at least 1,000 German and Italian aircraft, and damaged many others, aircraft that would otherwise have reinforced Rommel in the desert. But, above all, aided by breakthroughs in the decryption of enemy signals and the development of ASV radar, Malta's submarines, surface ships, bombers and torpedo-bombers inflicted great damage on Rommel's vulnerable supply system. If just one statistic may be taken as a measure of Malta's contribution to the war against fascism it is that, between June 1940 and May 1943, her forces sank 210 enemy merchant ships with an aggregate tonnage of 852,000 tons. This is 58 per cent of the ships sunk in supplying the Axis forces in North Africa.[23] And for each ship sunk another was damaged or delayed and therefore unable to deliver its cargo. In an earlier study, the author has estimated that the overall contribution of Malta's forces may have shortened the Mediterranean war by as much as one year. How much of this was due to Churchill's stubborn tenacity and refusal to accept defeat the reader is invited to judge from these pages.

But the human cost was a grievous one. Several thousand Maltese civilians, together with many others serving with the armed forces, lost their lives, or suffered injury, and these were deeply felt in a small, closely-related, traditional community. The losses in the periods of very heavy bombing might have been considerably higher but for the early evacuation of the harbour communities and the provision of underground shelters. Churchill had, on various occasions, sometimes in Secret Sessions of the House of Commons, paid tribute to the courage and endurance of the Maltese civilian population, and it seems fitting to end this story by quoting the Foreword that he wrote to *The Epic of Malta*.[24] This widely distributed volume of photographs of war-torn Malta, with an introductory essay by Captain Lewis Ritchie, appears to have been published in early 1943, and all the sale proceeds were donated to the Malta Relief Fund. Churchill's Foreword is not dated, but was probably written towards the end of 1942 when Malta was still very much in the front line of the Mediterranean war. He wrote as follows:

10, Downing Street
Whitehall

Malta is a little island with a great history. The record of the Maltese people throughout that long history is a record of constancy and fortitude. It is with those qualities, matchlessly displayed, that they are now confronting the dark power of the Axis. But it is not given to them, any more than it is to other peoples, to maintain resolute defence without suffering or to escape loss in achieving victory.

This book, therefore, is prepared with the aim of serving a double purpose; to contribute in some measure to the alleviation of their suffering and to portray to distant eyes the scene upon which their heroism is enacted.

Winston Churchill

EPILOGUE

By the autumn months of 1943, the tide of war had begun to recede from Malta's shores, and the people of the island started to rebuild, physically and emotionally, their much-battered homes and lives. But the end of the war was not yet in sight. In a speech delivered at the Mansion House on 30 June 1943, when he received the Freedom of the City of London, Churchill warned his audience: 'It is very probable there will be heavy fighting in the Mediterranean and elsewhere before the leaves of autumn fall.'[1] Seven days later, the British government gave a significant undertaking to the people of Malta. We have already noted in an earlier chapter the decision to make a major contribution to the repair of the island's extensive war damage, but the rebuilding of Malta's political and constitutional life was also judged essential, both in London and Malta.

On 7 July 1943, therefore, the Secretary of State for the Colonies, Lord Cranborne, rose in the House of Commons to make an announcement. He first paid tribute to the 'steadfastness and fortitude' of the civilian population and the garrison, and to their 'service of incalculable value to the Allied cause'. He then reminded the House that between 1921 and 1933 the island had enjoyed full legislative and administrative responsibility in the conduct of internal affairs. He then continued:

> It is the policy of His Majesty's Government that Responsible Government in the same sphere should again be granted to Malta after the war. It will not be possible while war continues for His Majesty's Government to undertake a detailed examination of the various constitutional, financial and administrative questions which must be resolved before Responsible Government can be introduced ...
>
> But it is the intention of His Majesty's Government, as soon as hostilities are brought to an end, that these matters should be pursued without delay and that steps should be taken to consult responsible opinion in Malta with a view to giving expression as far as possible to the wishes of the Maltese people regarding the form which the new Constitution might take.[2]

While the war continued, Churchill's attention inevitably followed the fighting forces, but, on several occasions in the following years, Malta again occupied his thoughts. In an earlier volume the author has written at greater length about these occasions and only a summary is presented here.[3] In November 1943, Churchill at last had the opportunity to visit Malta. He then made a three-day visit to the island on his way to the Tehran Conference with Stalin and President Roosevelt. He had last visited Malta in 1927, and he was now determined to see for himself how the people were coping with the immense damage caused during three years of unrelenting attack. Despite a heavy, feverish cold, he insisted on touring the dockyard area and Valletta, where he greeted a large crowd from the balcony of the Grand Master's Palace in which he had stayed during his first visit to Malta in 1907. Before leaving for Alexandria he cabled to his wife: 'Had great welcome from workmen in Malta Dockyard.'

His final visit to Malta came in late January 1945 when he and President Roosevelt met there, before proceeding together to the Yalta Conference in the Crimea. Once again his activities were curtailed by a heavy cold, but he attended a dinner hosted by the Governor at San Anton Palace and received from the Malta Chamber of Commerce a model of a medieval Maltese cannon.

When the war against Germany finally came to an end in May 1945, among the many thousands of telegrams of congratulation Churchill received was the following from the men of the Malta Dockyard:

24. Churchill inspecting in November 1943 the Malta Dockyard, where he received an enthusiastic welcome. He is accompanied by Rear-Admiral Mackenzie.

25. Churchill inspecting the ruins of Valletta during his November 1943 visit. General Brooke, who was with him, said that the devastation reminded him of the Western Front during the First World War.

26. Churchill with US President Franklin Roosevelt and Soviet leader Josef Stalin at the Tehran Conference on 30 November 1943 when they celebrated Churchill's sixty-ninth birthday. On the right is Churchill's indispensable Russian interpreter, Major Birse.

27. Churchill talking to President Roosevelt on board USS *Quincy*, moored in the Grand Harbour, in January 1945. With them are their respective daughters: Sarah Churchill, in WAAF uniform, and Anna Boettiger. They were on their way to the Yalta Conference in the Crimea.

On Thursday 24th May at a fully authorised Victory March through the yard in the dinner hour a motion was passed by acclamation from between four and five thousand workmen begins: 'We desire that a telegram be forwarded to the Prime Minister, Mr. Winston Churchill, who has visited this dockyard and is well acquainted with our circumstances, conveying our congratulations for the Great Victory in Europe and Malta Dockyard pledge of unshaken loyalty to our Beloved King and the British Cause.'[4]

In July 1945, Churchill's Conservative Party was defeated in the General Election, and it therefore fell to the Labour government of Clement Attlee to honour the wartime pledges that had been made to the Maltese people. The financial support for reconstruction, voted in 1942, steadily increased. Equally important, Malta received in 1947 the new Constitution that Churchill's government had, in July 1943, undertaken to establish. Churchill once again became Prime Minister in 1951, but during the following three years no problems of major significance affecting Malta demanded his attention.

After his resignation in April 1955 brought to a close over fifty years of public service, he did not visit Malta again. At a personal level, however, his links with Malta remained fresh in his mind. In the corner of his study at Chartwell he hung the fine silver plaque given him in July 1946 by Edward Ceravolo, a Maltese citizen. This displays the coat of arms of Grand Master Jean de la Valette who led the Knights of St John and the people of Malta in the Great Siege of 1565.[5] On his eightieth birthday he received a warm greeting, on behalf of the people of Malta, from the Prime Minister, Borg Olivier, and it fell to the latter's successor, Dom Mintoff, to send another telegram of congratulation when Churchill retired in April 1955. He was particularly delighted with the eightieth birthday gift of the bust by Vincent Apap, the arrangements for which have been described in the

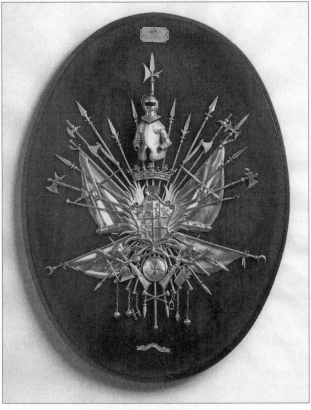

28. What Churchill called his 'Malta Shield'. Made in Malta by Antonio Attard, it was presented to Churchill in July 1946 in recognition of his efforts to defend Malta. The array of weapons surrounding the coat of arms of Grand Master Valette commemorates the Great Siege of Malta of 1565. The shield hangs today in Churchill's study at Chartwell.

29. The bust of Churchill, sculpted by Vincent Apap, which stands in the Upper Barrakka Gardens in Valletta. It was presented to Churchill in August 1955, and the inscription reads: 'To the Rt. Honourable Sir Winston Spencer Churchill KG. The people of Malta and Gozo MCMLV'.

30. The battlemented waterfront of Valletta in the present day. Churchill's bust stands under the arcade of the Barrakka Gardens at the top of the photograph.

preface to this volume. The presentation by Justice Montanaro-Gauci in London in August 1955 would have brought back many memories of his long association with Malta. This bronze bust, which now stands quietly in the sunlit gardens of Valletta, is surely, therefore, a fitting tribute to the unflinching determination he displayed in protecting and sustaining the people of Malta during those dark, but ultimately victorious, years.

Churchill's death in January 1965 brought to an end a life of great achievement, which was marked by many tributes. We may end this volume by quoting the simple words that Earl Attlee, his wartime Deputy Prime Minister, addressed to the House of Lords on the day after Churchill's death:

My Lords, we have lost the greatest Englishman of our times – I think, the greatest citizen of the world of our time.

NOTES

Preface

1. The documents quoted here are among the Churchill Papers at the Churchill Archives Centre, Cambridge, under the references CHUR 2/ 341, 425 and 558B.
2. This presentation volume is now held at the Churchill Archives Centre in Cambridge.

Introduction

1. For a detailed account of Churchill's pre-war visits to Malta see D. Austin, *Churchill and Malta: A Special Relationship* (Spellmount, Stroud, 2006).
2. Reprinted in Winston Churchill, *The Second World War: Volume II, Their Finest Hour* (Cassell & Co., London, 1949), p. 17.
3. Those seeking a comprehensive account of Churchill's working methods are strongly recommended to read *Action This Day: Working with Churchill* (Macmillan, London, 1968). This volume, edited by Sir John Wheeler-Bennett, contains the recollections of six people who worked most closely with Churchill during and after the war.
4. A more detailed description of this system is given in Sir Martin Gilbert, *Winston S. Churchill*, Vol. VI, *Finest Hour 1939–1941* (Heinemann, London, 1983), pp. 891–4.
5. Churchill, *Second World War*, Vol. II, p. 17.
6. General Lord Ismay, *The Memoirs of The Lord Ismay* (Heinemann, London, 1960), p. 164.
7. Charles Eade, (ed.), *The End of the Beginning: The Third Volume of Winston Churchill's War Speeches* (Cassell & Co., London, 1943), p. 220.
8. Lord Moran, *Churchill: The Struggle for Survival, 1940–1965* (Constable, London, 1965), p. 46.

Chapter I
At the Admiralty, September 1939 – May 1940

1. Churchill, *Second World War: Volume I, The Gathering Storm* (Cassell, London, 1948), pp. 320–1.

2. National Archives (NA), PREM 1/345, Churchill Memorandum to Chamberlain, 27 March 1939.

3. M. Muggeridge, (ed.), *Ciano's Diary 1939–1943* (Heinemann, London, 1947), p. 10.

4. Churchill, *Second World War*, Vol. I, p. 334.

5. NA CAB 99/1, Supreme War Council Meeting, 12 September 1939.

6. NA CAB 66/1, Churchill Memorandum to War Cabinet, 17 September 1939.

7. NA ADM 205/2, Admiralty Meeting, 18 September 1939.

8. D. Austin, *Malta and British Strategic Policy 1925–1943* (Frank Cass, London, 2004) pp. 49–90.

9. Churchill, *Second World War*, Vol. I, pp. 580–1.

10. NA CAB 66/2, Churchill Memorandum, 'Possible "Détente" With Italy in the Mediterranean', 18 October 1939.

11. M. Gilbert, *The Churchill War Papers, Vol. I, At the Admiralty, September 1939 to May 1940* (Heinemann, London, 1993), Churchill broadcast, 12 November 1939, p. 359.

12. Churchill, *Second World War*, Vol. I, p. 593.

13. Churchill, *Second World War*, Vol. II, p. 338.

14. NA CAB 21/765, Churchill minute to Wood, 14 November 1939.

15. NA CAB 66/3, Churchill Memorandum to War Cabinet, 21 November 1939.

16. NA CAB 80/6, COS Memorandum, 'Review of Military Policy in the Middle East', 5 December 1939.

17. NA CAB 65/2, War Cabinet (39) 107th Meeting, 7 December 1939.

18. NA CAB 79/3, COS (40) 15th Meeting, 25 January 1940.

19. NA CAB 83/3, MCC (40) 9th Meeting, 8 February 1940.

20. Churchill, *Second World War*, Vol. I, pp. 599, 600.

21. *Documents on German Foreign Policy 1918–1945* (HMSO, London 1956), Series D, Vol. IX, no. 17, 17 [sic] March 1940.

22. Gilbert, *At the Admiralty*, p. 913, Churchill minute to Fraser, 24 March 1940.

23. NA CAB 82/2, DCOS (40) 15th Meeting, 3 April 1940.

24. Quoted in D. Cannadine (ed.), *The Speeches of Winston Churchill* (Penguin, London, 1990), p. 117; Chapter V of Vol. I of Churchill's *Second World War* is entitled 'The Locust Years 1931–1935'.

25. NA CAB 99/3, Supreme War Council Meeting, 9 April 1940.

26. Gilbert, *At the Admiralty*, p. 1147, Churchill minute to Pound, 27 April 1940.

27. NA CAB 66/7, COS Memorandum, 'Measures to Deter Italy from Entering the War Against the Allies', 28 April 1940.

28. NA CAB 65/6, War Cabinet (40) 108th Meeting, 30 April 1940.

29. Gilbert, *At the Admiralty*, p. 1187, Churchill minute to Pound, 3 May 1940.

30. W. H. Thompson, *I Was Churchill's Shadow* (Christopher Johnson, London, 1951), p. 37.

31. Churchill, *Second World War*, Vol. I, pp. 526–7.

Chapter II
The Threat from Italy

1. Churchill, *Second World War*, Vol. II, p. 86.

2. Muggeridge (ed.), *Ciano's Diary*, p. 251.

3. Churchill, *Second World War*, Vol. II, pp. 107–8, where both letters are quoted in full.

4. NA CAB 80/11, 'Allied Military Action in the Event of War with Italy', 13 May 1940.
5. See S. Dobbie, *Faith and Fortitude: The Life and Work of General Sir William Dobbie* (privately printed, Gillingham, Kent, 1979). From October 1940, Sybil Dobbie acted as her father's personal secretary.
6. NA CAB 69/1, Defence Committee (40) 3rd Meeting, 16 May 1940.
7. Churchill, *Second World War*, Vol. II, pp. 42–3.
8. NA CAB 66/7, WP (40) 168, 'British Strategy in a Certain Eventuality', 25 May 1940.
9. NA CAB 69/1, Defence Committee (40) 8th Meeting, 25 May 1940.
10. Details of Italian preparations for war, and British assessments of these, are considered in Austin, *Malta and British Strategic Policy*, pp. 76–84.
11. F. H. Hinsley et al., *British Intelligence in the Second World War*, Vol. I, (HMSO, London, 1979), pp. 199–205.
12. NA CAB 80/11, JIC Memorandum, 'The Italian Situation', 24 May 1940.
13. The minutes of these War Cabinet meetings between 26 and 28 May 1940 are in NA CAB 65/13.
14. Quoted in I. Kershaw, *Fateful Choices: Ten Decisions that Changed the World, 1940–1941* (Penguin, London, 2008), p. 35.
15. D. Dilks (ed.), *The Diaries of Sir Alexander Cadogan 1938–1945* (Cassell, London, 1971), p. 290.
16. Churchill, *Second World War*, Vol. II, p. 73.
17. This paper is reprinted in full in Churchill, *Second World War*, Vol. II, pp. 78–9.
18. NA CAB 66/7, Foreign Secretary Memorandum, 'Suggested Approach to Signor Mussolini', 26 May 1940.
19. Quoted in Gilbert, *Churchill War Papers, Vol. II, Never Surrender*, p. 170.
20. J. Colville, *The Fringes of Power: Downing Street Diaries 1939–1955* (Hodder & Stoughton, London, 1985), pp. 140–1.
21. Dilks (ed.), *Cadogan Diaries*, p. 291.
22. Churchill, *Second World War*, Vol. II, p. 87.
23. Ibid., p. 88.
24. Ibid., pp. 109–110.
25. Ibid., p. 111.
26. R. Jenkins, *Churchill* (Macmillan, London, 2001), p. 599.
27. Ibid., p. 602.
28. Kershaw, *Fateful Choices*, pp. 47–8.

Chapter III
Italy Declares War

1. NA CAB 80/12, Prime Minister's minute, COS (40) 404, 'Policy in the Mediterranean', 28 May 1940.
2. Churchill, *Second World War*, Vol. II, p. 102.
3. NA CAB 79/4, COS (40) 157th Meeting, 29 May 1940.
4. NA CAB 80/12, JPC Memorandum, COS (40) 421 (JP), 'Policy in the Mediterranean', 30 May 1940.
5. Reprinted in M. Simpson (ed.), *The Cunningham Papers*, Vol. I, (Ashgate for the Navy Records Society, Aldershot, 1999), p. 47.
6. NA ADM 186/800, Cunningham to Pound, 6 June 1940.
7. Admiral Viscount Cunningham, *A Sailor's Odyssey* (Hutchinson, London, 1951), p. 188.

8. J. Colville, *Footprints in Time* (Collins, London, 1976), p. 188.

9. NA CAB 82/5, DCOS (40) 24th Meeting, 29 May 1940.

10. NA CAB 80/12, JIC Memorandum, COS (40) 407 (JIC), 'Possible Military Courses Open to Italy', 29 May 1940.

11. See Austin, *Churchill and Malta*, p. 81; *Malta and British Strategic Policy*, pp. 76–82.

12. Muggeridge, *Ciano's Diary*, p. 257.

13. This is all set out in detail in Hinsley, *British Intelligence*, Vol. I, pp. 198–205.

14. The minutes of this meeting are reprinted in Gilbert, *Never Surrender*, pp. 207–19.

15. General Sir Edward Spears, *Assignment to Catastrophe* (Reprint Society, London, 1956), p. 303.

16. Churchill, *Second World War*, Vol. II, p. 100.

17. Gilbert, *Never Surrender*, p. 220.

18. Ibid., p. 220.

19. Muggeridge, *Ciano's Diary*, pp. 263–4.

20. Colville, *The Fringes of Power*, p. 152.

21. Quoted in Churchill, *Second World War*, Vol. II, p. 116.

22. Churchill, *Second World War*, Vol. II, p. 192.

23. Ibid., pp. 194–5.

24. Ibid., p. 390.

25. Reprinted in Simpson, *Cunningham Papers*, Vol. I, p. 74.

26. NA CAB 79/5, Admiralty Memorandum, 'Policy in the Eastern Mediterranean', annexed to Minutes of COS (40) 183rd Meeting, 17 June 1940.

27. NA CAB 79/5, COS (40) 183rd Meeting, 17 June 1940.

28. Reprinted in Churchill, *Second World War*, Vol. II, p. 563.

29. Reprinted in Simpson, *Cunningham Papers*, Vol. I, p. 76.

30. Ibid., pp. 76–7.

31. NA CAB 80/13, JPC Memorandum, COS (40) 469 (JP), 'Military Implications of the Withdrawal of the Eastern Mediterranean Fleet', 17 June 1940.

32. NA CAB 79/5, COS (40) 185th Meeting, 18 June 1940.

33. NA CAB 80/14, COS (40) 512 (JP), 'Military Policy in Egypt and the Middle East', 2 July 1940.

34. Quoted in Dobbie, *Faith and Fortitude*, p. 222.

35. Quoted in Gilbert, *Never Surrender*, p. 402.

Chapter IV
Malta Rearmed

1. Churchill, *Second World War*, Vol. II, pp. 370, 374.

2. Ibid., pp. 293–6.

3. These three documents are annexed to the minutes of COS (40) 214th Meeting, 9 July 1940, in NA CAB 79/5. Churchill will have seen them when reading these minutes.

4. Reprinted in Churchill, *Second World War*, Vol. II, p. 568. This is the first paper placed in a new series of Malta-related files. The first file was later designated PREM 3/266/10A, and it is a general file covering the whole period from July 1940 until October 1943. Other files containing papers related to more specific matters were opened as the war progressed.

5. The minutes and memoranda of the COS Meetings are in NA CAB 79 and 80, respectively. The Defence Committee (Operations) minutes and memoranda are in NA CAB 69 and 80.

6. NA PREM 3/266 10A, fols. 961–3.

7. Reprinted in Churchill, *Second World War*, Vol. II, p. 392.

8. Ibid., pp. 392–3.

9. Simpson, *Cunningham Papers*, Vol. I, Cunningham to Pound, 13 July 1940, pp. 110–111.

10. The two signals are reprinted in NA ADM 186/800, Vol. I, pp. 105–7.

11. Gilbert, *Never Surrender*, Churchill speech to the House of Commons, 5 September 1940, p. 778.

12. Reprinted in Churchill, *Second World War*, Vol. II, p. 375.

13. The minutes and memoranda of the 'Ministerial Committee on Military Policy in the Middle East' are held in NA CAB 95/2.

14. NA PREM 3/266/10A, fols. 954–5.

15. NA CAB 80/17, COS Memorandum (40) 670, 'Malta: AA Defences', 27 August 1940.

16. NA ADM 186/800, Cunningham to Admiralty, 22 August 1940, p. 112.

17. Reprinted in Churchill, *Second World War*, Vol. II, pp, 417–8.

18. NA CAB 69/1, Defence Committee (Operations) (40) 31st Meeting, 24 September 1940.

19. Reprinted in Churchill, *Second World War*, Vol. II, p. 442.

20. Ibid., p. 443.

21. For details of the Italian position see Austin, *Churchill and Malta*, p. 84; *Malta and British Strategic Policy*, pp. 105–6.

22. Simpson, *Cunningham Papers*, Vol. I, Cunningham to Pound, 3 August 1940, p.123–4.

23. Reprinted in Churchill, *Second World War*, Vol. II, pp. 443–6.

24. Simpson, *Cunningham Papers*, Vol. I, 'Report on Operation MB8, 6–14 November 1940', p. 175.

25. Ibid., 'Fleet Air Arm Operations against Taranto on 11 November 1940', p. 178.

26. Gilbert, *Never Surrender*, Churchill to Alexander and Pound, 23 November 1940, p. 1129.

27. Ibid., Churchill to Ismay, 1 December 1940, p. 1167.

28. NA PREM 3/266/10A, Churchill to Ismay, 1 December 1940, fol. 898.

29. Ibid., Jacob to Churchill, 3 December 1940, fol. 897.

30. Churchill, *Second World War*, Vol. II, p. 529.

31. NA CAB 79/6, COS (40) 278th Meeting, 23 August 1940.

32. NA PREM 3/266/10A, Ismay to Churchill, 17 September 1940, fol. 947.

33. NA CAB 65/9, War Cabinet (40) 254th Meeting, 19 September 1940.

34. NA PREM 3/266/10A, Governor to Colonial Office, 24/25 September 1940, fols. 935–40.

35. NA CAB 80/21, Churchill to Portal, 3 November 1940.

Chapter V
The First German Air Attack, January – June 1941

1. NA CAB 80/56, Churchill to COS, 21 January 1941.

2. For the strategies adopted by both sides see Austin, *Malta and British Strategic Policy*, pp. 107–110.

3. Reprinted in Churchill, *Second World War*, Vol. III, p. 52.

4. NA PREM 3/266/10A, fol. 885, Governor to Colonial Office, 19 January 1941. Unless otherwise indicated, the documents referred to in this chapter are to be found in NA PREM 3/266/10A, AIR 8/499, 500, 504, and AIR 23/5706.

5. Reprinted in Churchill, *Second World War*, Vol. III, p. 54.

6. Gilbert, *Churchill War Papers*, Vol. III, *The Ever-Widening War*, p. 198.

7. Churchill, *Second World War*, Vol. III, p. 54.

8. NA CAB 69/2, Defence Committee (Operations) (41) 6th Meeting, 20 January 1941.

9. NA CAB 80/56, Churchill to COS, 21 January 1941.

10. For German invasion planning see Austin, *Churchill and Malta*, pp. 94–5; *Malta and British Strategic Policy*, p. 117.

11. NA WO 106/3065, CIGS to Governor, 22 January 1941.

12. NA CAB 79/9, Governor to Dill, 5 February 1941, annexed to Minutes of (41) 43rd COS Meeting, 6 February 1941.

13. Reprinted in Churchill, *Second World War*, Vol. III, p. 55.

14. See Austin, *Malta and British Strategic Policy*, p.116.

15. NA ADM 205/10, Churchill minute to COS, 9 March 1941.

16. These matters and many of the relevant documents are described in detail in Churchill, *Second World War*, Vol. III, pp. 83–134.

17. NA CAB 69/2 Defence Committee (Operations) (41) 10th Meeting, 27 March 1941.

18. See also R. Woodman, *Malta Convoys 1940–1943* (John Murray, London, 2000), pp. 165–7.

19. Full details of the AA and coastal gun defences of Malta are to be found in D. Rollo, *The Guns and Gunners of Malta* (Mondial Publishers, Malta, 1999).

20. The author has vivid childhood memories of the ear-splitting roar which accompanied the simultaneous firing of a battery of thirty-two 3-inch rockets.

21. Reprinted in Churchill, *Second World War*, Vol. III, p. 185.

22. NA CAB 69/2, Defence Committee (Operations) (41) 13th Meeting, 13 April 1941.

23. This is reprinted in full in Churchill, *Second World War*, Vol. III, p. 187.

24. NA ADM 199/1932, Churchill to COS, 30 April 1941.

25. Air Marshal Sir Hugh Lloyd, *Briefed to Attack: Malta's Part in African Victory* (Hodder & Stoughton, London, 1949), p. 13.

26. For details see Austin, *Churchill and Malta: A Special Relationship*, Chapters I–VI.

27. Churchill's papers on this matter are in NA PREM 3/266/7, fols. 594–607.

28. NA WO 106/3066, Governor to Colonial Office, 10 May 1941.

29. For more detailed analysis see Austin, *Malta and British Strategic Policy*, pp. 86–8.

Chapter VI
Building Malta's Offensive Capability

1. Churchill, *Second World War*, Vol. III, pp. 39–40.

2. NA PREM 3/266/10A, fols. 895–6, Portal to Churchill, 2 January 1941. Unless otherwise indicated, other references in this chapter are to documents in this file, or in AIR 8/499–504.

3. Reprinted in Churchill, *Second World War*, Vol. III, p. 8.

4. For details of the loss of aircraft in this period see C. Shores, B. Cull, and N. Malizia, *Malta: The Hurricane Years, 1940–41* (Grub Street, London, 1987), pp. 150 ff.

5. These signals of 28 January and 1 February 1941 are in NA WO 106/3065.

6. NA CAB 65/21, War Cabinet (41) 13th Meeting, 5 February 1941.

7. Reprinted in Churchill, *Second World War*, Vol. III, p. 58.

8. Ibid., p. 173.

9. Ibid., pp. 174–5, 179.

10. NA CAB 79/9, COS (41) 122nd Meeting, 4 April 1941.

11. NA CAB 79/55, COS (41) 10th 'O' Meeting, 4 April 1941.
12. NA DEFE 3/686, Signal OL 26, 2 April 1941.
13. F. Hinsley, *British Intelligence*, Vol. I, pp. 392–4, and Appendix 13.
14. NA ADM 223/76, Signal F294, 7 April 1941.
15. NA CAB COS (41) 127th Meeting, 7 April 1941.
16. NA ADM 223/76, Cunningham to Pound, 8 April 1941.
17. See Rear-Admiral G. W. G. Simpson, *Periscope View* (Macmillan, London, 1972).
18. NA PREM 3/274/1, Cunningham to Pound, 10 April 1941.
19. This is reprinted in full in Churchill, *Second World War*, Vol. III, pp. 186–8.
20. This attack is fully described in K. Poolman, *Night Strike from Malta: 830 Squadron RN & Rommel's Convoys* (Janes Publishing Company, London, 1980), pp. 56–9.
21. A full account of this action, with detailed charts, is contained in *The Royal Navy and the Mediterranean*, Vol. II (Whitehall History Publishing, London, 2002.) pp. 90–2. This is a reproduction of a confidential 1957 publication of the Admiralty Historical Section, now filed at the National Archives as ADM 186/801.
22. This interchange and the related signals are in NA PREM 274/1.
23. NA CAB 79/9, COS (41) 132nd Meeting, 12 April 1941.
24. Reprinted in Simpson, *Cunningham Papers*, Vol. I, Cunningham to Pound, 26 April 1941, p. 359.
25. Ibid., Cunningham to Pound, 25 April, 1941, p. 355.
26. Churchill's detailed account of this operation is set out in Churchill, *Second World War*, Vol. III, pp. 212–6.
27. Reprinted in Simpson, *Cunningham Papers*, Vol. I, Cunningham to Admiralty, 22 April 1941, p. 353.
28. Reprinted in Gilbert, *The Ever-Widening War*, Vol. III, pp. 545–6.
29. Reprinted in Simpson, *Cunningham Papers*, Vol. I, Cunningham to Churchill, 29 April 1941, pp. 361–3.
30. Admiral Viscount Cunningham, *A Sailor's Odyssey* (Hutchinson, London, 1951), pp. 349–51.
31. Simpson, *Cunningham Papers*, Vol. I, Churchill to Cunningham, 1 May 1941, pp. 395–6.
32. Ibid., Cunningham to Pound, 3 May 1941, p. 399.
33. Reprinted in Churchill, *Second World War*, Vol. III, p. 677.
34. Simpson, *Cunningham Papers*, Vol. I, Cunningham to Admiralty, 2 May 1941, p. 396.
35. Ibid., Cunningham to Pound, 18 May 1941, p. 406.
36. For an analysis of the Axis supply problem see Austin, *Malta and British Strategy*, pp. 104–6, 130–1.

Chapter VII
Reinforcements and Attack, Summer 1941

1. Reprinted in Churchill, *Second World War*, Vol. III, Churchill to Dobbie, 6 June 1941, p. 687.
2. Hinsley, *British Intelligence*, Vol. I, p. 429.
3. NA CAB 80/57, COS Memorandum (41) 92 (O), 31 May 1941.
4. For further detail and references see Austin, *Malta and British Strategy*, p. 117.
5. NA CAB 79/12, COS (41) 216th Meeting, 18 June 1941.
6. NA CAB 80/28, COS Memorandum (41) 348, 'Malta: AA Defences', 3 June 1941.
7. NA CAB 69/2, Defence Committee (Operations) (41) 44th Meeting, 25 June 1941.

8. Reprinted in Churchill, *Second World War*, Vol. III, p. 721.
9. Lloyd, *Briefed to Attack,* p. 13.
10. NA AIR 8/500, Lloyd to Portal, 20 June 1941.
11. NA CAB 79/55, COS (41) 22nd 'O' Meeting, 27 July 1941.
12. NA AIR 8/500, Ludlow-Hewitt to Portal, 21 July 1941.
13. NA CAB 79/13, COS (41) 281st Meeting, 8 August 1941; Churchill, *Second World War*, Vol. III, p. 433.
14. Colville, *The Fringes of Power*, p. 403.
15. NA CAB 80/58, COS Memorandum (41) 113 (O), 'Defence of Egypt', 21 June 1941.
16. NA CAB 69/2, Defence Committee (Operations) (41) 53rd Meeting, 1 August 1941.
17. Reprinted in Gilbert, *The Ever-Widening War*, p. 1025.
18. Ibid., pp. 1028–9.
19. Ibid., p.1030.
20. Ibid., p.1029.
21. NA PREM 3/274/1, Churchill to COS, 30 June 1941.
22. Hinsley, *British Intelligence*, Vol. II, pp. 283–5.
23. Ibid., pp. 644–6.
24. NA AIR 8/500, Freeman to Tedder, 27 August 1941.
25. Ibid., Portal to Tedder, 1 October 1941.
26. Hinsley, *British Intelligence*, Vol. II, p. 285.
27. NA CAB 79/55, COS (41) 29th 'O' Meeting, 28 August 1941.
28. NA PREM 3/266/10A, COS to Governor, 4 October 1941.

Chapter VIII
Force K Joins the Attack, Autumn 1941

1. Reprinted in Gilbert, Vol. III, *The Ever-Widening War*, p. 1081.
2. NA PREM 3/274/1, Churchill to Ismay, 20 August, and Ismay to Churchill, 22 August 1941.
3. For further analysis see Austin, *Malta and British Strategic Policy,* pp. 137–9.
4. Churchill himself quoted this minute in his *Second World War*, Vol. III, pp. 434–5.
5. Gilbert, Vol. III, *The Ever-Widening War*, Churchill to Randolph Churchill, 30 October 1941, pp. 1391–2.
6. Harold Macmillan, *The Blast of War: 1939–1945* (Macmillan, London, 1967), p. 424.
7. David French, *Raising Churchill's Army: The British Army and the War against Germany 1919–1945* (Oxford University Press, Oxford, 2000), pp. 283–4.
8. Colville, *The Fringes of Power*, p. 428.
9. This signal and the following papers are held in NA PREM 3/274/1.
10. Ibid., Pound to Churchill, 24 August 1941.
11. NA CAB 79/55, COS (41) 27th 'O' Meeting, 25 August 1941.
12. Churchill, *Second World War*, Vol. I, p. 321.
13. Robin Brodhurst, *Churchill's Anchor: Admiral of the Fleet Sir Dudley Pound* (Leo Cooper, Barnsley, 2000), p. 38.
14. Simpson, *Cunningham Papers*, Vol. I, Pound to Cunningham, 3 September 1941, p. 506.
15. Both minutes are quoted in Hinsley, *British Intelligence*, Vol. II, pp. 644–5.
16. Gilbert, Vol. III, *The Ever-Widening War*, Churchill to Pound and reply, 24 August 1941, p. 1095.

17. Ibid., Churchill to Pound, 3 September 1941, p. 1150.
18. NA PREM 3/274/1, Churchill to Pound, 14 September 1941.
19. Simpson, *Cunningham Papers*, Vol. I, Cunningham to Pound, 18 September 1941. p. 508.
20. NA PREM 3/274/1, Churchill to Pound, 5 October 1941.
21. Ibid., Pound to Churchill, 8 October 1941.
22. Simpson, *Cunningham Papers*, Vol. I, Pound to Cunningham, 11 October, p. 514. Cunningham's reply is on p. 520.
23. Churchill, *Second World War*, Vol. III, p. 492. Emphasis added.
24. Ibid., Churchill to President Roosevelt, 20 October 1941, pp. 482–6.
25. For details see Hinsley, *British Intelligence,* Vol. II, p. 294.
26. Reprinted in Churchill, *Second World War*, Vol. III, p. 492.
27. Ibid., Churchill to Cunningham, and the latter's reply, 23–24 November 1941, p. 508.
28. Hinsley, *British Intelligence*, Vol. II, p. 321.
29. Churchill, *Second World War*, Vol. III, Churchill to Captain Agnew, 27 November 1941, p. 751.
30. Both signals are reprinted in Gilbert, Vol. III, *The Ever-Widening War*, p. 1531.
31. Churchill, *Second World War*, Vol. III, p. 752.
32. For further analysis see Austin, *Churchill and Malta*, pp. 112–3; *Malta and British Strategic Policy*, pp. 137–9.
33. Churchill, *Second World War*, Vol. III, p. 513.

Chapter IX
The Second German Air Attack, January – April 1942

1. NA CAB 79/17, JIC (42) 4, 'An Axis Attack on Malta', 3 January 1942, annexed to the minutes of COS (42) 4th Meeting, 5 January 1942.
2. For further detail see P. Vella, *Malta: Blitzed But Not Beaten* (Progress Press, Valletta, 1985), pp. 87–90, and Appendix I, which reproduces the Deportation Order and the names of those deported. The Governor's correspondence on this subject is in NA CO 968/42/6, and CO 968/65/1.
3. NA CAB 79/17, COS (42) 4th and 12th Meetings, 5 and 12 January 1942.
4. NA PREM 3/266/2, Dobbie to Brooke, 13 January 1942. This new file in Churchill's PREM 3/266 Malta series is entitled '1941 July – 1943 February. Convoys.' Many of the signals, memoranda and minutes quoted in this chapter are contained in this lengthy file and in the 3/266/10A file.
5. Churchill's account of these events is in *Second World War*, Vol. IV, pp. 30–31.
6. NA CAB 80/34, COS Memorandum (42) 130, 'Supplies to Malta', 22 February 1942.
7. NA CAB 79/18, COS (42) 62nd Meeting, 24 February 1942.
8. NA CAB 79/18, JIC Memorandum (42) 61, 'Scale of Attack on Malta', annexed.
9. Reprinted in Churchill, *Second World War*, Vol. IV, p. 261.
10. Ibid., Vol. IV, p. 81.
11. NA CAB 79/18, COS to Middle East C-in-Cs, 27 February 1942.
12. NA CAB 105/9, Telegram No. 43, Middle East C-in-Cs to COS, 4 March 1942.
13. NA CAB 80/61, COS Memorandum (42) 55 (O), Annex III.
14. Lord Moran, *The Struggle for Survival*, p. 46.
15. Field Marshal Lord Alanbrooke, *War Diaries 1939–1945*, edited by A. Danchev and D. Todman (Weidenfeld & Nicolson, London, 2001), p. 235.
16. NA CAB 69/4, Defence Committee (Operations) Memorandum (42) 48, 'Tank Enquiry', 2 June 1942.

17. NA CAB 69/4, Defence Committee (Operations) (42) 7th Meeting, 2 March 1942.

18. J. Connell, *Auchinleck* (Cassell, London, 1959), p. 461.

19. NA CAB 105/17, Telegram No. 7, COS to Middle East C-in-Cs, 3 March 1942.

20. NA CAB 105/9, Middle East Telegrams Nos. 43 and 51, 4 and 5 March 1942.

21. Simpson, *Cunningham Papers*, Vol. I, Cunningham to Pound, 15 March 1942, p. 584.

22. Alanbrooke, *War Diaries*, p. 239.

23. Reprinted in Churchill, *Second World War*, Vol. IV, pp. 262–3.

24. Ibid., pp. 263–4.

25. NA CAB 69/4, Defence Committee (Operations) Memorandum (42) 31, Annex II, 26 March 1942.

26. NA CAB 69/4, Defence Committee (Operations) (42) 9th Meeting, 26 March 1942.

27. NA CAB 69/4, COS Memorandum (42) 36, Annex I, Middle East C-in-Cs to COS, 5 April 1942.

28. Reprinted in Churchill, *Second World War*, Vol. IV, p. 267.

29. NA AIR 8/504, Portal to Freeman, 6 February 1942.

30. Churchill, *Second World War*, Vol. IV, p. 268.

31. NA CAB 79/20, COS (42) 104th Meeting, 2 April 1942, with attached JIC (42) 106 (O), 31 March 1942.

Chapter X
The George Cross and a New Governor

1. The most vivid account of this climax of Malta's 1942 blitz, enhanced by numerous illustrations, is to be found in P. Vella, *Malta: Blitzed But Not Beaten* (Progress Press, Valletta, 1985).

2. These and most of the signals cited in the first part of this chapter are to be found in the National Archives under the reference PREM 3/266/2.

3. This minute is reprinted in Churchill, *Second World War*, Vol. IV, p. 269.

4. NA CAB 79/20, COS (42) 106th Meeting, 4 April 1942.

5. Ibid., COS (42) 109th Meeting, 7 April 1942; the War Office report is in CAB 80/62, CIGS Memorandum (42) 91 (O), 'Malta Supply Situation', 6 April 1942.

6. NA CAB 79/20, COS (42) 121st Meeting, 16 April 1942.

7. NA CAB 69/4, Governor to COS, 20 April 1942, annexed to Defence Committee Memorandum (42) 41, 'Malta', 21 April 1942.

8. Quoted in Vella, *Malta: Blitzed*, p. 110.

9. Churchill Archives Centre, Cambridge, Amery Papers, AMEL 2/1/34, Amery to Sir Alexander Hardinge, 10 April 1942.

10. This quotation and a detailed account of this period are in C. Shores, B. Cull, N. Malizia, *Malta: The Spitfire Year* (Grub Street, London, 1991), pp. 195–226. See also the personal account of Laddie Lucas, who commanded 249 Squadron during these months, in L. Lucas, *Malta: The Thorn in Rommel's Side* (Stanley Paul, London, 1992).

11. These reports are collected in NA PREM 3/267/1–2.

12. NA CAB 69/4, Defence Committee (Operations) (42) 12th Meeting, 22 April 1942. The various papers are annexed to the minutes.

13. Most of Churchill's papers relating to the relief of General Dobbie and the appointment of General Gort to succeed him as Governor are held in NA PREM 3/266/1. However, some other relevant documents are held at the Churchill Archives Centre, mainly under the reference CHAR 20/74.

14. Her own account of these years is in S. Dobbie, *Grace Under Malta* (Lindsay-Drummond, London, 1943); see also Dobbie, *Faith and Fortitude*.

15. NA CAB 79/18, COS (42) 67th and 70th Meetings, 28 February and 3 March 1942.

16. NA CAB 105/9, Signal No. 42, COS to Dobbie, 3 March 1942.

17. Alanbrooke, *War Diaries*, p. 251.

18. This and the other papers considered by the Committee are annexed to the minutes of this meeting in NA CAB 69/4.

19. NA WO 106/3068, Governor to War Office, 29 April 1942.

20. Eade (ed.), *Churchill War Speeches, Vol. III, The End of the Beginning*, p. 106.

21. J. Wheeler-Bennett, *King George VI: His Life and Reign* (Macmillan, London, 1958), p. 573.

22. Lord Tedder, *With Prejudice: The War Memoirs of Marshal of the Royal Air Force Lord Tedder* (Cassell, London, 1966), p. 264.

23. It is reprinted in C. Eade (ed.), *Secret Session Speeches by the Right Hon. Winston S. Churchill* (Cassell, London, 1946), pp. 46–75.

Chapter XI
Spitfires and the Growing Food Crisis, April – June 1942

1. This is reprinted in Churchill, *Second World War,* Vol. IV, p. 274.

2. Unless otherwise indicated, the documents referred to in this chapter are held at the National Archives under the reference PREM 3/266/1–2, or at the Churchill Archives Centre under the reference CHAR 20.

3. Sir John Colville, Churchill's Private Secretary during much of the war, later wrote a fine biography of Lord Gort, under the title *Man of Valour: The Life of Field-Marshal The Viscount Gort, VC* (Collins, London, 1972).

4. Churchill, *Second World War*, Vol. IV, p. 275.

5. This was circulated to the War Cabinet as WP (42) 195, now filed in NA CAB 66/24.

6. Alanbrooke, *War Diaries*, p. 255.

7. Reprinted in Churchill, *Second World War*, Vol. IV, p. 275.

8. NA CAB 66/24, WP (42) 196, Middle East Defence Committee to Minister of Defence and Chiefs of Staff, 9 May 1942.

9. Alanbrooke, *War Diaries*, p. 256.

10. Major-General Sir John Kennedy, *The Business of War: The War Narrative of Major-General Sir John Kennedy* (Hutchinson, London, 1957), p. 226.

11. NA CAB 65/30, War Cabinet (42) 60th Meeting, 10 May 1942.

12. Reprinted in Churchill, *Second World War*, Vol. IV, pp. 275–6.

13. See Austin, *Churchill and Malta*, for an account of the pre-war visits.

14. Lord Moran, *The Struggle for Survival*, p. 47; Nigel Nicolson (ed.), *Harold Nicolson: Diaries and Letters 1939–1945* (Collins, London, 1967), p. 230.

15. Lord Ismay, *Memoirs*, p. 273.

16. See Lloyd, *Briefed to Attack*, pp. 182–5.

17. For details see Hinsley, *British Intelligence*, Vol. II, p. 345.

18. For more detail of the planning of this operation see Austin, *Churchill and Malta*, p. 123; *Malta and British Strategic Policy*, pp. 153–4.

19. NA CAB 79/20, COS (42) 136th Meeting, 1 May 1942.

20. NA CAB 79/20, JP (42) 482, 'Supplies for Malta', 7 May 1942, annexed to Minutes of COS (42) 145th Meeting, 9 May 1942.

21. NA CAB 80/62, COS (42) 131(O), 'Supplies for Malta', 9 May 1942.

22. Reprinted in Churchill, *Second World War*, Vol. IV, p. 323.

23. Lloyd, *Briefed to Attack*, p. 214.

24. NA AIR 24/908, RAF Malta, June Convoy Report, para. 53.
25. NA CAB 79/56, COS (42) 52nd (O) Meeting, 15 June 1942.

Chapter XII
The 'Pedestal' Convoy, August 1942

1. Churchill, *Second World War*, Vol. IV, p. 343.
2. Ismay, *Memoirs*, p. 254.
3. Alanbrooke, *War Diaries*, p. 275.
4. Churchill, *Second World War*, Vol. IV, p. 377.
5. NA PREM 3/266/2, fols. 289–91, Churchill to Attlee and Eden, 17 June 1942.
6. NA CAB 79/56, COS (42) 56th and 57th (O) Meetings, 23 June 1942.
7. NA CAB 79/21, COS (42) 190th Meeting, 26 June 1942.
8. CAC CHAR 20/78, Prime Minister's Personal Telegram T. 1035/2, 25 July 1942.
9. Lloyd, *Briefed To Attack*, p. 13.
10. Ministry of Defence, Air Historical Branch unpublished narrative 'Malta', quoted in Lucas, *The Thorn in Rommel's Side*, p. 190.
11. This letter and several related documents are filed in NA PREM 3/266/5.
12. NA CAB 79/21, COS (42) 194th Meeting, 1 July 1942.
13. NA CAB 79/22, COS (42) 222nd Meeting, 30 July 1942.
14. Alanbrooke, *War Diaries*, p. 288.
15. Ibid., p. 288.
16. Churchill Archives Centre, CHUR 2/149B, fol. 230.
17. Churchill's account is in his *Second World War*, Vol. IV, pp. 453–5. See also Major-General Playfair, *The Mediterranean and Middle East*, Vol. III (HMSO, London, 1960), pp. 316–323; Woodman, *Malta Convoys*, pp. 369–454.
18. Reprinted in Churchill, *Second World War*, Vol. IV, p. 455.
19. Ibid., p. 455.
20. Moran, *Struggle for Survival*, p. 69.
21. Eade (ed.), *Churchill War Speeches: Vol. III, The End of the Beginning*, pp. 164–5.

Chapter XIII
Desert Battles and More Supplies for Malta

1. Hinsley, *British Intelligence*, Vol. II, p. 408.
2. NA CAB 79/57, COS (42) 94th 'O' Meeting, 19 August 1942.
3. NA CAB 105/10, Middle East War Telegram No. 140, 29 August 1942.
4. Reprinted in Churchill, *Second World War*, Vol. IV, p. 467.
5. Austin, *Malta and British Strategic Policy*, pp. 161–70.
6. D. Richards and H. St. G. Saunders, *Royal Air Force 1939–1945, Vol. II, The Fight Avails* (HMSO, London, 1954), p. 231.
7. Moran, *The Struggle for Survival*, p. 71.
8. Churchill, *Second World War*, Vol. IV, pp. 493–504.
9. NA CAB 80/37, Air Staff Memorandum COS (42) 392, 1 September 1942.
10. NA CAB 80/64, Admiralty Memorandum COS (42) 262 (O), 7 September 1942.
11. Alanbrooke, *War Diaries*, p. 319.
12. NA CAB 79/57, COS (42) 116th 'O' Meeting, 9 September 1942.
13. NA CAB 80/64, Air Staff Memorandum COS (42) 289 (O), 20 September 1942.
14. NA CAB 79/57, COS (42) 130th 'O' Meeting, 28 September 1942.

15. Alanbrooke, *War Diaries*, p. 325.

16. NA CAB 80/64, Colonial Office Memorandum, COS (42) 287 (O), 30 September 1942.

17. NA PREM 3/266/2, Governor to COS, 30 September 1942. Most of the other signals quoted in this chapter may be found in this file.

18. NA CAB 79/57, COS (42) 135th, 136th and 137th 'O' Meetings, 2, 3, and 5 October 1942.

19. Alanbrooke, *War Diaries*, p. 326.

20. NA CAB 79/73, JIC (42) 349, annexed to Minutes of COS (42) 261st Meeting, 11 September 1942.

21. Hinsley, *British Intelligence*, Vol. II, p. 231.

22. NA CAB 79/57, COS (42) 150th 'O' Meeting, 17 October 1942.

23. NA CAB 79/58, COS (42) 151st 'O' Meeting, 17 October 1942.

24. NA CAB 79/58 COS (42) 154th and 155th 'O' Meetings, 20, 21 October 1942.

25. Vincent Orange, *Sir Keith Park* (Methuen, London, 1984), pp. 162–76.

26. Ibid., p. 185.

27. These signals and Churchill's account of the battle are set out, with four maps, in Churchill, *Second World War*, Vol. IV, pp. 526–41.

28. For a longer account see Austin, *Malta and British Strategic Policy*, pp. 167–70.

29. B. H. Liddell Hart (ed.), *The Rommel Papers* (Collins, London, 1953), p. 287.

30. Ibid., p. 286.

Chapter XIV
Malta Relieved and Operation 'Breastplate'

1. NA CAB 121/632, Pound to Harwood and Leatham, 19 September 1942. Many of the signals and papers quoted in this chapter are collected in this file, which is entitled, 'F/Malta/2. Offensive Operations. September 1942 – July 1943'.

2. NA CAB 79/57, COS (42) 131st 'O' Meeting, 29 September 1942.

3. NA CAB 79/23, JP (42) 862, annexed to Minutes of COS (42) 283rd Meeting, 8 October 1942.

4. NA CAB 79/57, COS (42) 148th 'O' Meeting, 15 October 1942.

5. Alanbrooke, *War Diaries*, p. 334.

6. NA CAB 121/632, Churchill to COS, 27 October 1942.

7. NA CAB 79/58, COS (42) 166th 'O' Meeting, 30 October 1942.

8. CAC CHAR 20/81/129, Churchill to Lord Gort, 30 October 1942.

9. NA CAB 79/58, COS (42) 168th 'O' Meeting, 2 November 1942.

10. Alanbrooke, *War Diaries*, pp. 335–6.

11. Hinsley, *British Intelligence*, Vol. II, p. 466. Hinsley explores the reasons for this in pp. 466–75.

12. Ibid., p. 488. Further details of the Axis reinforcements are given in Playfair, *Mediterranean and Middle East*, Vol. IV, pp. 170–3.

13. NA CAB 79/58, COS (42) 178th 'O' Meeting, 11 November 1942.

14. Reprinted in Churchill, *Second World War*, Vol. IV, pp. 805–6.

15. Playfair, *Mediterranean and Middle East*, Vol. IV, p. 196.

16. NA CAB 79/24, COS (42) 318th Meeting, 17 November 1942.

17. NA CAB 69/4, Defence Committee (Operations) (42) 17th Meeting, 16 November 1942.

18. NA CAB 121/632, Churchill minute M.586/2 to Brooke, 5 December 1942.

19. Alanbrooke, *War Diaries*, p. 342.

20. NA CAB 79/24, COS (42) 322nd Meeting, 20 November 1942.

21. Ibid., COS (42) 326th Meeting, 24 November 1942.
22. Alanbrooke, *War Diaries*, p. 288.
23. Churchill's papers about this matter are to be found in a separate file, entitled 'War Damage and British Government's Gift', under the reference, NA PREM 3/266/7.
24. Eade (ed.), *Churchill War Speeches*, Vol. III, p. 214.

Chapter XV
Malta's Part in North African Victory

1. NA PREM 3/266/10A, COS to Middle East C-in-Cs, 22 November 1942.
2. Admiral Simpson, *Periscope View*, pp. 268–9.
3. NA CAB 69/4, Defence Committee (Operations) (42) 18th Meeting, 23 November 1942.
4. These signals between Pound, Cunningham and Harwood are collected in NA CAB 121/632.
5. NA CAB 121/500, Cunningham to Pound, 5 December 1942.
6. Reprinted in Churchill, *Second World War*, Vol. IV, p. 808.
7. NA CAB 79/24, COS (42) 337th Meeting, 7 December 1942.
8. Alanbrooke, *War Diaries*, p. 346.
9. NA ADM 205/27, Pound to Churchill, 9 December 1942.
10. NA CAB 80/67, COS Memorandum (43) 2 (O), 'Enemy Strength in Tunisia', 5 January 1943.
11. Churchill, *Second World War*, Vol. IV, p. 592.
12. Quoted in Colville, *Man of Valour*, p. 254.
13. See Churchill, *Second World War*, Vol. IV, pp. 621–2.
14. Ibid., p. 646.
15. These are the last enclosures in NA PREM 3/266/2.
16. NA CAB 80/67, COS Memorandum (43) 59 (O), 'Naval Repair Facilities at Malta', 14 February 1943.
17. NA CAB 121/632, COS to Middle East C-in-Cs, 18 February 1943.
18. NA CAB 79/59, COS (43) 33rd (O) Meeting, 3 March 1943.
19. Copies of both messages are in CAC, CHAR 20/96B, fols. 104–5.
20. Quoted in Churchill, *Second World War*, Vol. IV, p. 698.
21. For a first-hand account of this unit see Major R. T. Gilchrist, *Malta Strikes Back: The Story of 231 Infantry Brigade* (Gale & Polden, Aldershot, *c.* 1945).
22. Quoted in Gilbert, *Churchill*, Vol. VII, p. 441.
23. For a fuller analysis of Malta's contribution to the Mediterranean war, see Austin, *Malta and British Strategy*, pp. 186–90.
24. *The Epic of Malta* (Odhams Press, London, no date, *c.* early 1943).

Epilogue

1. Eade (ed.), *Churchill War Speeches, Vol. IV, Onwards to Victory*, p. 132.
2. Quoted in J. J. Cremona, *The Maltese Constitution and Constitutional History Since 1813* (Publishers Enterprises Group, Valletta, Malta, 1994), pp. 168–9.
3. Austin, *Churchill and Malta*, pp. 154–73.
4. CAC, CHAR 20/229A, pp. 56–7.
5. Details of this gift are set out in Austin, *Churchill and Malta*, pp. vi–vii; see also Austin, 'Churchill's "Maltese Shield"', in *Treasures of Malta*, Vol. XV, No. 2, pp. 72–6.

BIBLIOGRAPHY

I. Records at the National Archives, Kew

The principal records consulted in this study are included in the series of Malta-related files among the Prime Minister's papers. The cover titles of these PREM files are:

3/266/1   April – December 1942. Appointment of Lord Gort as Governor and C-in-C.
3/266/2   July 1941 – February 1943. Convoys.
3/266/3   May – June 1941. Defence of Malta and Gozo.
3/266/4   March – May 1942. Flying in of Spitfires from USS *Wasp* and HMS *Eagle*.
3/266/5   July – August 1942. Bombing Attacks and supply situation.
3/266/7   January 1941 – November 1942. War damage and British government's gift.
3/266/8   November 1942. Air reconnaissances.
3/266/10A July 1940 – October 1943. Various.

Records of the following series of official British government papers have also been consulted: Admiralty (ADM); Air Ministry (AIR); War Cabinet (CAB 65, 66); Defence Committee (Operations) (CAB 69); Chiefs of Staff Committee (CAB 79, 80); Prime Minister's Operational Papers (PREM); Colonial Office (CO); War Office (WO).

II. Churchill Archives Centre

The Churchill Papers, a very large collection of Sir Winston Churchill's private papers, are now lodged in the Churchill Archive Centre (CAC) at Churchill College, Cambridge. Several documents are cited in this study with the prefix CHAR or CHUR.

III. Published Documents

Cannadine, D. (ed.), *The Speeches of Winston Churchill* (Penguin, London, 1990)
Documents on German Foreign Policy: Series D Vol. IX, March 18– June 22, 1940 (HMSO, London, 1956)
Eade, C. (ed.), *War Speeches by the Right Hon. Winston S. Churchill, Vols. II–VI* (Cassell, London, 1942–6)
Gilbert, M., *The Churchill War Papers, Vol. I, At The Admiralty, September 1939– May 1940; Vol. II, Never Surrender, May 1940–December 1940; Vol. III, The*

Ever-Widening War, 1941 (Heinemann, London, 1994–2000)

Simpson, M., *The Cunningham Papers, Vol. I, The Mediterranean Fleet, 1939–1942* (Ashgate for The Navy Records Society, Aldershot, 1999)

IV. Books (list of principal works consulted)

Alexander, J., *Mabel Strickland* (Progress Press, Valletta, 1996)

Attard, J., *The Battle of Malta* (Hamlyn Paperbacks, London, 1982)

Attard, J., *Britain and Malta: The Story of an Era* (Publishers Enterprise Group, Valletta, 1988)

Austin, D., *Churchill and Malta: A Special Relationship* (Spellmount, Stroud, 2007)

Austin, D., *Malta and British Strategic Policy 1925–1943* (Frank Cass, London, 2004)

Barnett, C., *Engage The Enemy More Closely: The Royal Navy in the Second World War* (Penguin, London, 2000)

Best, G., *Churchill: A Study in Greatness* (Hambledon & London, London, 2001)

Blake, R. and Louis, W. (eds.), *Churchill* (Oxford University Press, Oxford, 1993)

Blouet, B., *The Story of Malta* (Progress Press, Malta, 2004)

Bragadin, Commander M'A., *The Italian Navy in World War II* (United States Naval Institute, Annapolis, 1957)

Brodhurst, R., *Churchill's Anchor: Admiral of the Fleet Sir Dudley Pound* (Leo Cooper, Barnsley, 2000)

Casey, Lord, *Personal Experience 1939–1946* (Constable, London, 1962)

Churchill, R., *Winston S. Churchill, Vols. I–II*; and associated *Companion Volumes* (Heinemann, London, 1966–7)

Churchill, Sir W., *The Second World War*, 6 vols. (Cassell, London, 1948–54)

Churchill, Sir W., (Foreword) *The Epic of Malta* (Odhams Press, London, *c.* October 1942)

Colville, J., *Man of Valour: The Life of Field-Marshal The Viscount Gort, V.C.* (Collins, London, 1972)

Colville, J., *Footprints in Time* (Collins, London, 1976)

Colville, J., *The Fringes of Power: Downing Street Diaries 1939–1955* (Hodder & Stoughton, London, 1985)

Connell, J., *Auchinleck* (Cassell, London, 1959)

Cremona, J., *The Maltese Constitution and Constitutional History since 1813* (Publishers Enterprise Group, Valletta, 1994)

Cunningham, Admiral Viscount, *A Sailor's Odyssey* (Hutchinson, London, 1951)

Danchev, A. and Todman, D. (eds.), *War Diaries 1939–1945: Field Marshal Lord Alanbrooke* (Weidenfeld & Nicolson, London, 2001)

Dobbie, S., *Faith and Fortitude: The Life and Work of General Sir William Dobbie* (privately printed, Gillingham, Kent, 1979)

Dobbie, S., *Grace Under Malta* (Lindsay-Drummond, London, 1943)

Eden, A., *The Eden Memoirs: The Reckoning* (Cassell, London, 1965)

French, D., *Raising Churchill's Army* (Oxford University Press, Oxford, 2000)

Gilbert, M., *Winston S. Churchill: Vols. III–VIII*; and associated *Companion Volumes* (Heinemann, London, 1971–1988)

Gilbert, M., *Churchill: A Life* (Heinemann, London, 1991)

Gilchrist, Major R. T., *Malta Strikes Back: The Story of 231 Infantry Brigade* (Gale & Polden, Aldershot, *c.* 1945)

Hastings, M., *Finest Years: Churchill as Warlord 1940–45* (Harper Press, London, 2009)

Hinsley, F. et al., *British Intelligence in the Second World War*, 5 vols. (HMSO, London, 1979–90)

Hollis, General Sir L., *One Marine's Tale* (Andre Deutsch, London, 1956)

Ismay, Lord, *The Memoirs of General The Lord Ismay* (Heinemann, London, 1960)

Jacob, General Sir I. *Churchill By His Contemporaries: An 'Observer' Appreciation* (Hodder & Stoughton, London, 1965)

Jenkins, R., *Churchill* (Macmillan, London, 2001)

Kennedy, General Sir J., *The Business of War* (Hutchinson, London, 1957)

Kershaw, I., *Fateful Choices: Ten Decisions that Changed the World, 1940–1941* (Penguin, London, 2007)

Knox, M., *Mussolini Unleashed: Politics and Strategy in Fascist Italy's Last War* (Cambridge University Press, Cambridge, 1988)

Knox, M., *Hitler's Italian Allies* (Cambridge University Press, Cambridge, 2000)

Liddell Hart, B., *The Rommel Papers* (Collins, London, 1955)

Lloyd, Air Marshal Sir H., *Briefed to Attack: Malta's Part in African Victory* (Hodder & Stoughton, London, 1949)

Lukacs, J., *Five Days in London, May 1940* (Yale University Press, New Haven, 1999)

Lucas, L., *Malta: The Thorn in Rommel's Side* (Stanley Paul, London, 1992)

Macintyre, D., *The Battle for the Mediterranean* (Batsford, London, 1964)

Macmillan, H., *The Blast of War: 1939–1945* (Macmillan, London, 1967)

Martin, Sir J., *Downing Street: The War Years* (Bloomsbury, London, 1991)

Ministry of Information, *The Air Battle of Malta: The Official Account of the RAF in Malta, June 1940 to November 1942* (HMSO, London, 1944)

Moran, Lord, *Winston Churchill: The Struggle for Survival, 1940–1965* (Constable, London, 1966)

Muggeridge, M. (ed.), *Ciano's Diary 1939–1943* (Heinemann, London, 1947)

Nicolson, N. (ed.), *Harold Nicolson: Diaries and Letters 1939–45* (Collins, London, 1967)

Orange, V., *Sir Keith Park* (Methuen, London, 1984)

Perowne, S., *The Siege Within the Walls: Malta 1940–1943* (Hodder & Stoughton, London, 1970)

Playfair, General I. et al., *The Mediterranean and Middle East*, 6 vols. (HMSO, London, 1954–73)

Poolman, K., *Night Strike from Malta* (Jane's Publishing, London, 1980)

Richardson, C., *From Churchill's Secret Circle to the BBC: The Biography of Lieutenant-General Sir Ian Jacob* (Brassey's, London, 1991)

Roberts, A., *'The Holy Fox': A Biography of Lord Halifax* (Weidenfeld & Nicolson, London, 1991)

Roberts, A., *Masters and Commanders* (Penguin, London, 2008)

Rogers, A. (ed.), *185: The Malta Squadron* (Spellmount, Staplehurst, Kent, 2005)

Rollo, D., *The Guns and Gunners of Malta* (Mondial Publishers, Malta, 1999)

Roskill, S., *The War at Sea*, 3 vols. (HMSO, London, 1954–1961)

Roskill, S., *The Navy at War 1939–1945* (Collins, London, 1960)

Roskill, S., *Churchill and the Admirals* (Collins, London, 1977)

Saunders, H. St. G., *Royal Air Force 1939–1945, Vol. III* (HMSO, London, 1954)

Shores, C., Cull, B., with Malizia, N., *Malta: The Hurricane Years 1940–41* (Grub Street, London, 1987)

Shores, C., Cull, B., with Malizia, N., *Malta: The Spitfire Year 1942* (Grub Street, London, 1991)

Simpson, Rear-Admiral G., *Periscope View* (Macmillan, London, 1972)

Spears, General Sir E., *Assignment to Catastrophe* (Reprint Society, London, 1956)

Spooner, T., *Supreme Gallantry: Malta's Role in the Allied Victory 1939–1945* (John Murray, London, 1996)

Tedder, Lord, *With Prejudice* (Cassell, London, 1966)

The Royal Navy and the Mediterranean: Vol. II, November 1940-December 1941 (Whitehall History Publishing, London, 2002)

Thompson, W. H., *I Was Churchill's Shadow* (Christopher Johnson, London, 1951)

Times of Malta

Trevor-Roper, H. (ed.), *Hitler's War Directives 1939–1945* (Pan Books, London, 1966)

Vella, P., *Malta: Blitzed But Not Beaten* (Progress Press, Valletta, 1985)

Wheeler-Bennett, Sir J. (ed.), *Action This Day: Working with Churchill: Memoirs by Lord Normanbrook, John Colville, Sir John Martin, Sir Ian Jacob, Lord Bridges, Sir Leslie Rowan* (Macmillan, London, 1968)

Wheeler-Bennett, Sir J., *King George VI: His Life and Reign* (Macmillan, London, 1958)

Wingate, J., *The Fighting Tenth: The Tenth Submarine Flotilla and the Siege of Malta* (Leo Cooper, London, 1991)

Woodman, R., *Malta Convoys: 1940–1943* (John Murray, London, 2000)

INDEX